UNDERSTANDING CHINA AND INDIA

UNDERSTANDING CHINA AND INDIA

Security Implications for the United States and the World

Rollie Lal

Foreword by Karl D. Jackson

Introduction by Walter Andersen

PRAEGER SECURITY INTERNATIONAL
Westport, Connecticut · London

Library of Congress Cataloging-in-Publication Data

Lal, Rollie.
 Understanding China and India : security implications for the United States and the
  world / Rollie Lal ; foreword by Karl D. Jackson ; introduction by Walter Andersen.
   p. cm.
 Includes bibliographical references and index.
 ISBN 0–275–98968–2 (alk. paper)
 1. China—Military policy. 2. India—Military policy. 3. National security—China.
  4. National security—India. 5. China—Relations—India. 6. India—Relations—China.
  7. World politics—21st century. I. Title.
 UA835.L36 2006
 355'.033551—dc22   2006003363

British Library Cataloguing in Publication Data is available.

Library of Congress Catalog Card Number: 2006003363
ISBN: 0–275–98968–2

First published in 2006

Praeger Security International, 88 Post Road West, Westport, CT 06881
An imprint of Greenwood Publishing Group, Inc.
www.praeger.com

Printed in the United States of America

The paper used in this book complies with the
Permanent Paper Standard issued by the National
Information Standards Organization (Z39.48–1984).

10 9 8 7 6 5 4 3 2 1

For my mother, Manju Lal, and my father, Rajendra B. Lal

Thank you for all your sacrifices and encouragement

Contents

Foreword

For several thousands of years scholars and journalists, statesmen, and military strategists have wondered why states do what they do. Some of these have focused on the short-term, others on the long-term. Modern sophisticated states invest substantial intelligence resources in determining the capabilities of other nations on the assumption that capabilities will predict behaviors in the international arena. In addition, foreign-policy establishments, academics, and journalists constantly monitor the twists and turns of state policies, assuming that today's policy statements will foreshadow tomorrow's behaviors. In spite of investing ardor and intellect, predictions of state behavior often fail. Passing epiphenomena are often mistaken for the underlying motivations of national leaders and their surrounding elites, just as particular policy descriptions may be mistaken for definitions of long-term national interests. An experienced politician, Neville Chamberlain, mistook Hitler's policies at Munich, not understanding that Hitler's conception of German national interest entailed dominating the European continent. Hitler, in turn, looked at Great Britain's behaviors at Munich and her military resources and concluded, "Our enemies are small worms. I saw them in Munich," not understanding that the same Neville Chamberlain preferred world war to accepting German domination of the European continent. Similar miscalculations were made in Korea in 1950. Joseph Stalin and Kim Il Sung took the United States at its word when high-level officials in Washington indicated that South Korea was not within the American defense perimeter in the Far East, only to be surprised when President Truman and his advisors rapidly reversed course once the North Korean invasion of the South had begun. Finally, the American involvement in Vietnam fundamentally misjudged the depth and intensity of the drive of North Vietnam and its southern allies for national reunification, no matter what the cost in blood and economic well-being.

What makes foreign policy making so difficult is the precise calculation of the long-term motives. Anyone who has ever been involved in a workplace or a family knows how difficult it is to unmask the underlying motivations, even of those we know well and can intensely observe. Motivations are the ultimate black box of human behavior. Motives are an intellectual construct that we divine imperfectly from a combination of capabilities and stated intentions. We have all experienced the unreliability of asking friends as well as rivals about their long-term intentions, and hence we spend a great deal of time "reading between the lines."

Nation-state behavior is even more difficult to fathom because it involves a combination of leaders, foreign-policy elites, and mass public opinion. Depending on the nature of the political system, particular leaders may exercise inordinate influence over the behaviors of whole nations. Both the personalities of leaders and the type of political system in which they are operating must be calculated. Furthermore, public opinion also plays a significant role. Even in established dictatorships, public opinion remains a factor as leaders calculate, often by hunch alone, what "the people" will enthusiastically support.

No single book or methodology will ever conclusively unravel why nations do what they do. Rollie Lal's book represents an innovative attempt to move beyond surface policies and the calculation of raw capabilities to describe the national interests of two emerging regional powers, China and India. While policies come and go, long-term national motives remain the premier predictors of long-term nation-state behavior. She could have conducted her research by simply asking her respondents directly about the long-term national interests of China and India. This methodology does not work terribly well in families or in the workplace or within foreign-policy elites. Dr. Lal instead asked elite samples in both countries about why each nation was pursuing economic reform and military modernization. Strikingly she finds that these two large emerging nations are pursuing approximately the same policies (economic reform and military modernization) but that the explanations offered by the two elites reveal sharply distinct visions of the national interests of China and India. Present-day policy directions are the same, but the underlying and long-term motivations are different. While both nations are motivated by sovereignty, the Chinese respondents focus on territorial concerns, such as Taiwan and Tibet and the fragility of a one-party system in the event of either loss of territory or failure of national economic performance. Those interviewed in India cite quite different motives for economic reform and are so confident of Indian territorial identity that the Kashmir problem is not mentioned by any Indian respondent. In contrast, to those interviewed in China, Indian respondents also showed little concern over long-term institutional stability. Indians apparently assume their democratic institutions have become permanent. If a government fails, it will simply be replaced by another coalition government, without delegitimizing the political system. While both countries have become nuclear weapons states, China's motives are bound up with the maintenance of its territorial integrity while Indian motives involve raising its general status in the world order rather than specific military contingencies.

The success or failure of the international system in the twenty-first century will be judged by its capacity to integrate India and China peacefully into a system that has been largely dominated by Europeans and Americans. When Germany and Japan emerged as major powers in the twentieth century, two world wars were required to sort out differing perceptions of national interest. Unless we understand how the elites of India and China perceive their national interests, devising wise policies toward them will remain as uncertain as it is uninformed. Much remains to be done along the lines set out by Dr. Lal. Any case study is but a snapshot at a single point in time. Furthermore, it remains difficult to determine the exact representativeness of any elite sample. In addition, elite opinion is not the same as public opinion. These caveats notwithstanding, Lal's work contributes an important model for understanding the emerging national interests of India and China.

Karl D. Jackson
Director, Asian Studies
The Paul H. Nitze School of Advanced International Studies
Johns Hopkins University
Washington, D.C.
July 7, 2005

Acknowledgments

I owe a debt of gratitude to many individuals and organizations for this research. The research for this book was supported by a three-year grant from The Paul and Daisy Soros Fellowships for New Americans. I thank them for this invaluable support. The program is not responsible for the views expressed.

I am grateful to the members of my dissertation committee, Professors Karl Jackson, Michael Lampton, Walter Andersen, Ilya Prizel, and Francis Fukuyama for their support and comments. In particular, I thank my advisor and friend, Karl Jackson, for his encouragement from the beginning of this process and his kindness in reading and rereading the drafts of the chapters. His cheerful support truly made this research enjoyable.

Others at the Johns Hopkins School of Advanced International Studies also provided advice for this project. Dean Paul Wolfowitz and Professors Eliot Cohen and Ramon Borges-Mendez offered useful insights early in the process. Professor David Brown helped make possible my first research visit to China. I also benefited immensely from the comments and support of my colleagues, particularly Bee Apirat, Chen-Yuan Tung, Irene Wu, Barbara Kotschwar, and David-Michel. Working together with Bee every day made writing feel like a day in the sun.

I am indebted to many people in China, India, and Japan for making this research possible. Professor Han Hua of Peking University hosted my first research visit to Beijing. Fudan University kindly hosted my research in Shanghai. Cao Jin also provided great kindness and friendship in Beijing. The Institute of American Studies of the Chinese Academy of Social Sciences provided valuable assistance in my second research visit to China. My friend Chen Yali generously gave introductions to many Chinese scholars and officials. I am also extremely grateful to Colonel Susan Puska at the U.S. Embassy in Beijing and Akira Fujino of the *Yomiuri Shimbun* for their kindness and advice, as well as Colonel Tomoyuki Sekitani, Michael H. Finegan, and Joseph Young. Yoshiko Tanaka offered yet more introductions, and her invaluable friendship. In India, I was hosted by the Indian Council of Social Science Research. I also owe a debt of gratitude to Supergod and Dadiji for housing me in New Delhi, to Admiral and Mrs. Vasan in New Delhi for their friendship and generosity in providing numerous introductions to Indian officials and policy makers, to Geeta Pasi at the U.S. Embassy in New Delhi for her kindness, and to M. V. Rappai at the Institute of China Studies for his friendship and comments. Of course, I also thank my assistant Sarah Harting for her time and patience in preparing the manuscript.

I thank my sisters, Chetna and Smita, for their comments and patience in reading various chapters and listening to my travails, my nephew Armaan for creating much needed laughter, and my parents for their constant encouragement. I am also sincerely thankful to all of my friends, who make my life so wonderful.

Introduction

Rollie Lal has contributed to the field of bureaucratic politics in a unique way. She explores the processes shaping "national interest" and, by extension, analyzes how views of national interest influence security and foreign policy. This is a subject not much addressed in the discussions of bureaucratic politics, which is surprising considering the importance of attitudes held by bureaucrats/politicians and the political class in general on a critical issue such as the national interest in foreign policy.

Ms. Lal employed extensive fieldwork, including interviews of senior policy makers and scholars in India and China, to discern the process of the formulation of views on "national interests" among senior officials and scholars in the two countries. She discovered a remarkable similarity of views on the key elements of national interest among elites in these two large developing Asian countries. Her sample of the political class in each country identified factors of "globalization," "national identity," "sovereignty," and "political structure" as key elements of national interest. However, these elites differed widely on the hierarchy of factors that informs the larger concept of national interest. They also differ on how these various elements advance national interest. While globalization is viewed by both sets of elites as a key factor, they differ widely on explanations of how the presumed faster economic growth that results from globalization contributes to the national interest. Those in the Indian sample said that the major contribution of globalization to national interest is the enhancement of India's international prestige and influence. This enhancement presumably makes India a more consequential actor on the world stage. Ms. Lal's Chinese respondents, on the other hand, saw the resultant faster economic growth as important in promoting national unity. Indian respondents were much less concerned about "unity" than were Ms. Lal's Chinese interlocutors, perhaps because the six decades of democracy have demonstrated to Indians that the political system can withstand the multiplicity of challenges to it. The authoritarian system in China apparently has not created a similar confidence in the strength of the political system among the country's political class.

Ms. Lal has contributed to the literature of bureaucratic politics by adding to it an analysis of how the concept of national interest is formulated among political elites in two large Asian countries and how it influences decision making. This literature rests on such seminal works as Graham

Allison's *The Essence of Decision: Explaining the Cuban Missile Crisis* (1971) and Morton Halperin's *Bureaucratic Politics and Foreign Policy* (1972). This literature postulates that bureaucrats/politicians coordinate complexity by an intricate network of bargaining. To use Allison's epigram, where you stand depends significantly on where you sit in this bureaucratic complex. Of course, one's "stands" are also influenced by culture, history, and a country's political context—which all influence views on national interest. This bureaucratic politics literature is at odds with what is taken to be Max Weber's view that bureaucrats faithfully and efficiently follow rules because they have in some way internalized them. Ms. Lal, in line with the bureaucratic politics literature of Graham and Halperin, downplays explanations of state behavior that assumes that the state—in this case China and India—are unified and rational actors. State actions rather are the product of a complex bargaining/negotiating process among sets of officials.

From this perspective, states should not be viewed as a person who knows and pursues a national interest. Decision making by bureaucrats/politicians is influenced by a combination of variables, such as their values as well as the opportunities their position makes available to pursue power, status, jurisdiction, and resources. Policy emerges from bargaining among knowledgeable and experienced professionals with sets of diverse values and interests. It is also influenced by prominent scholars who, in India and China, often have close ties with the government and thus in turn exert influence on bureaucrats. The rules of bureaucratic engagement differ within the parts of government and also between states because of the differing cultural and power contexts in which they are embedded. This coordination of bureaucratic complexity can veer in the direction of the imperative, as in the case of an authoritarian China, or more in the direction of the deliberative, as in a democratic India. But what is analytically interesting in my view is that policy emerges from the complex web of negotiations among officials who bring to the exercise notions of national interest. We will do a better job predicting policy if we can discern the definitions key policy makers give to national interest and how these views influence—and are influenced by—the complex bargaining process that takes place in any decision-making system. Ms. Lal, rightly in my view, focuses on individual actors, the key policy and scholarly elites who shape the decision-making process and who preeminently define the national interest within their bureaucratic niches.

Walter Andersen
Associate Director, South Asia Studies
The Paul H. Nitze School of Advanced International Studies
Johns Hopkins University
Washington, D.C.

CHAPTER **1**

National Interests in China and India

As a concept, "national interest" is widely debated yet vaguely understood. In the West, it is seen primarily as a foreign-policy issue and is often equated with national security.[1] This analysis is then used to explain the behavior of other countries, neglecting to notice that developing countries or various regions may formulate their national interests in diverse ways and in response to different needs.

Countries often follow similar policies to attain competitive economic or military capabilities. In the period leading up to the First World War, Britain and Germany each constructed dreadnoughts. During the Cold War, the Soviet Union and the United States each built massive arsenals of nuclear tipped ballistic missiles. The pursuit of similar capabilities has often masked different intentions. The most difficult analytic challenge in state-to-state relations is to deduce the intentions that serve as the basis for similar policies and capabilities. Intentions become clear only when capabilities are merged with perceived national interests.

China and India both have defined economic reform and defense modernization as policies necessary for pursuing their national interests. Both countries face the internally divisive forces of ethnic unrest, economic disparities, and separatism. In addition, both countries must confront the external challenges caused by the globalization of technology and the international economy. Despite the similar threats facing China and India, their national interests are not ranked the same, and the similarities in capabilities sought do not reflect similar goals. Why have these large, rapidly developing countries arrived at different national interests?

A combination of factors could be expected to affect the formation of the national interest, such as the forces of globalization[2] and economics, geopolitical realities, and national identity.[3] Domestic political institutions also have an effect on which factors are dominant and how decisions are filtered and processed. As a result, globalization could be the main determining factor in one country, whereas national identity may be more critical in the other.

This research aims to broaden the understanding of how national interests are formulated, using China and India as case studies. The study investigates each country's national interests by asking why China and India have adopted similar policy paths of how to pursue their national interests in the cases of their economic reform and defense modernization programs. Interviews were conducted in two stages and include data from interviews of Chinese and Indian policy and scholarly elites taken in 2004 and 2005 and 40 interviews of elites conducted in each country during 2001. Thirty additional interviews were conducted prior to this in Beijing and Shanghai to determine what political and scholarly circles perceived as the most important goals of the economic reforms and defense modernization programs. From these responses, it is clear that globalization, national identity, sovereignty, and political structure all have influence in China and India, but in different degrees and combinations. This book outlines the relationship among these factors, presents a hierarchy of national interests for each country, and subsequently provides some conclusions on national-interest formation and the foreign policies of these countries.

National Interests

National interest is a term that connotes many ideas to political theorists and policy makers. Often encompassed within national interest are power, wealth, morality, and nationalism. Inferred is the fact that a nation-state is the actor, and the definition of what or who comprises the nation becomes a critical question in determining the meaning of national interest. It follows that the authorities holding the title of the nation can determine which interests to pursue on behalf of the nation. Whether a normative national interest exists for each country independent of the will of the people or if the national interest is a factual and objective entity, composed of the sum of individual and group interests in the nation, is a decision that is imposed by the state. Although national interest as a term usually refers to foreign policy, it contains a domestic component that should not be ignored.

Existing capabilities alone cannot provide a reliable analysis of national objectives. The future is not like the past; if it were, a capability analysis would be redundant. Situations and beliefs are dynamic, not enduring, facets of a nation. Thus, a substantial analysis of national interests should incorporate some element of national perceptions and other dynamic factors in the domestic and international environment.

National interest has meant different things to different leaders and scholars, but in all instances it has involved whole states and an implied moral imperative for all members of a national group to support this most basic of national goals. What is absent among historians, formal theorists of international relations, and empiricists is a description of the process by which different elites in a variety of countries come to define their national interests.

This research undertakes to fill some of these gaps in the theory of national interests by analyzing how national interests are formulated in China and India. The most effective method for studying national-interest formation is to analyze two or more countries that are pursuing similar national policy guidelines and seek their perspectives of national goals. By asking their elites why these policies are being followed, one can elicit perceptions of the national interest. This holds present policy goals (defense modernization and economic reforms) constant while allowing an investigation of the underlying imperatives of the policies. Elite perceptions of both foreign and domestic factors are analyzed to elucidate the primary national interests of China and India. Analyzing the reasons given for pursuing the national interest, i.e., defense modernization and economic reform programs, will indicate what these national interests are for each country. The relationship between national identity, globalization, and sovereignty and the formation of national interest is analyzed. Finally, the influence of political institutions on national interests is examined, revealing that political institutions have effects on the hierarchy of existing national interests.

India

In India, respondents felt that globalization was the major force pushing India toward both economic reforms and defense modernization. Without adapting to the new globalized world order, India would be left behind economically, politically, and militarily. Indian respondents were most concerned about the ability for globalization to erode state sovereignty, particularly in the arena of economic and political decision making on topics such as trade, environmental issues, intellectual property rights, labor standards, and security decisions. To face the threats to state sovereignty on these areas, they felt that the most effective policy path was to increase state power through economic reforms and defense modernization.

With respect to the economic reforms, respondents thought the economic system had been proven a failure both by India's own dismal performance in the decades after independence, as well as by the failure of the Soviet Union and the other Communist states as seen in their collapses. The remarkable success of the Asian tigers added to this reassessment, showing that even after the Asian financial crisis, these countries had been able to sustain a better standard of living than India. The only viable option left for India was to accept international trade and the liberalizing forces of globalization, as well as the accompanying requisite economic and structural reforms in order to achieve development and competitiveness. India's economic successes after the initial movements toward liberalization and privatization during the early 1990s reinforced these ideas and proved that there could be no turning back in economic policy. By pursuing economic reforms, India could achieve its goals of economic competitiveness and strength.

The prevailing thought on security issues was linked very closely with these economic ideas. Respondents viewed national security as integrally related with economic security, and so a strong defense held a twofold purpose. The main purpose of a traditional strong land-based conventional capability was still to defend against territorial incursions and insurgencies. However, the purpose of an expanded navy, missile capability, and nuclear deterrent was as a tool to maintain sovereignty of decision making rather than capabilities for conventional defense. In this capacity, it was the combined strength of the state economy and military that formed an independent factor referred to as the comprehensive national strength, or national power. Respondents determined that sovereignty of decision making on economic issues was particularly critical and that comprehensive national strength could affect leverage in international negotiations. India's economic leverage in international economic institutions such as the World Trade Organization (WTO), in bilateral trade agreements with a variety of countries, in international environmental regulations, labor regulations, intellectual property rights, technology transfers, and in international organizations such as the United Nations were stressed. If India could not maintain a credible military deterrence, then its position and leverage in these types of negotiations would be irreparably damaged. As a result, it would be forced into disadvantageous agreements that could hinder growth, making India's long-term economic goals unattainable.

The primary example given of a country that was unable to deter external pressure was Iraq. Conversely, respondents viewed countries such as China and North Korea as formidable because of their superior military or nuclear capabilities. If India were to avoid being strong-armed, and maintain its independence of decision making, then it would have to maintain a nuclear deterrent. The possession of high-technology weaponry by other countries and the effectiveness of high technology in modern-war fighting led India to concede that defense modernization was mandated by the globalization of technology. Also, respondents believed a blue-water navy was critical for defending India's economic and trade interests in the sea-lanes. Again, it was the globalization of India's interests into these areas and the globalization of high technology to other countries that necessitated an expansion of India's military capabilities.

China

Although the Chinese respondents agreed that the Soviet case and the Asian tigers proved the failure of socialist economics, the perceptions of why economic reforms were needed in the Chinese case were markedly different from those of the Indians. The main goal of economic reforms was to promote economic growth in China and thereby maintain state unity and the political stability of the Communist Party. However, respondents emphasized that the forces of globalization made both economic reforms and defense modernization a necessity in order for China to keep up with international standards on everything from consumer goods to military equipment.

Chinese respondents felt a continuation of the economic reforms was needed primarily to subdue social unrest in the underdeveloped areas. The main concerns were that a continuation of the wide disparities of income both within regions and between regions would create discontent, which would soon translate into erosion of the legitimacy of the Communist Party. Because the Communist Party is perceived as the only body that has been able to unify China since 1949, this would lead to further problems in maintaining the unity of the state. Respondents viewed bolstering the power base of the Chinese Communist Party (CCP) while pursuing the economic reforms program as critical for maintaining state unity.

In addition, instituting economic reforms was part of a larger program that included political reforms. Without political reforms, particularly legal reforms and a reduction of corruption, economic reforms could not be continued. However, it was the economic reforms that allowed political reforms to be brought to the table. With the opening to the world, expectations had risen and new actors had arrived on the political scene. Having said this, the respondents maintained that rapid or radical political reform would lead to possible collapse, such as seen in the former Soviet Union. They believed that overall, the process of economic reform was extremely fragile. A slowdown of the pace of economic reform could lead to loss of legitimacy from disparities of income, but faster reform without appropriate political reform could lead to the same result. The only avenue available was to continue economic reforms while attempting moderate political reforms to maintain stability. But again, the purpose of the economic and political reforms was primarily for maintaining state unity, with the ultimate goal of preserving the legitimacy of the Party.

In the pursuit of the defense modernization program, the Chinese respondents agreed with the Indians on the importance of protecting the sovereignty of decision making. Having influence on economic and political rule making in the future would prove important for protecting and continuing China's economic growth. Increasing comprehensive national strength was critical for protecting state sovereignty. However, Chinese respondents defined sovereignty far more in terms of territorial integrity. Whereas for the Indians sovereignty of decision making in the political and economic arenas was a priority, for China state sovereignty was critical for maintaining territorial unity. The Chinese respondents stated that defending territorial rights on Taiwan was the primary goal of the defense modernization program, with Tibet and Xinjiang auxiliary concerns. In addition to the internal threat of secession by these regions, respondents expressed apprehension that the United States or other external actors might intervene in a contingency involving Taiwan. Chinese respondents also cited the Iraq conflict as a powerful example of why strong defense capabilities are critical. They stated that the Chinese defensive capability must be powerful enough to deter aggression from both internal and external threats in order to maintain territorial integrity. In this context, the respondents emphasized that the forces of globalization combined with the need for territorial consolidation meant that a better, high-technology military was necessary in order to protect the national interest from internal and external threats.

National Identity

So why is sovereignty, on balance, territorial for the Chinese but political for the Indians? This discussion leads to the differing perceptions of national identity in both countries. For Indian respondents, the territory itself that defined India was not critical. Historically, India was a collection of many kingdoms and peoples that were consistently perceived as "Hindustan" from the outside and were formally unified under the British Empire.[4] The general territory encompassing India changed little over thousands of years due to natural geographic boundaries, but the political leadership was continuously in flux. With independence, former kingdoms and regions were given a voice in a federated system of parliamentary democracy, allowing an area with tremendous diversity to be unified under a single democratic political system. Indian respondents did not express concern for the stability or legitimacy of the state in the event that the government failed to perform well either economically or militarily. Rather, the state could withstand such stresses due to

popular legitimacy of its institutions and norms. In case of poor performance, the political party in power would lose popularity, leading to a new
political leadership under the same parliamentary system. Thus, the democratic structures provided a unifying force for the otherwise ethnically,
economically, and linguistically divided country. The relatively strong
definition of a political national identity has allowed India to focus its
attention on external issues such as integration into the international
system rather than on maintaining national unity as its prime national
interest.

Chinese respondents believed that the historical territory under various
Chinese imperial rulers formed China, and the culture is Han or Confucian. However, they said that this admittedly popular rather than legal
definition did not include several areas such as Tibet or Xinjiang. In addition, respondents defined the territory of China as all those regions that
had been added to China over the centuries via conquest. Since China's
Communist Revolution, the areas historically considered part of China
were consolidated by the Communist Party and given commonality
through their existence as part of the People's Republic of China and the
Communist Revolution. Nonetheless, respondents did not view the political structure, the Communist Party of China, as a strong unifying element
for the country. With the death of Mao Zedong and the reconfiguration of
the Communist ideology to incorporate capitalism, the power of ideology
as a unifying force for the state weakened. Also, although the country was
unified politically under the Communist Party after the revolution, the
inability of the Communist Party to provide a lasting political definition
of national identity that included all parts of China led to weak national
unity. Parts of China that did not associate themselves either politically
with the Communist Party, or culturally with the majority Han culture,
such as Taiwan, Tibet, or Xinjiang, represented a risk to Chinese state
unity by perceiving themselves as not being included in the Chinese state.
Parts of the population and lagging regions that did not feel gains from
the economic reforms were perceived as questioning the validity of CCP
leadership and the state. State unity was constantly endangered as a result
of a weak concept of national identity. Thus respondents thought the Chinese state was obliged to place a premium on defending territory and sustaining economic growth to maintain Party and state legitimacy in order
to preserve the unity of the state.

Globalization and State Sovereignty

Both Chinese and Indian elites agreed that as a result of the forces of
globalization, increasing their nation's comprehensive national strength
was critical for successful pursuit of the national interest. The

comprehensive national strength includes a combination of both economic and military strength in order to allow a nation to have greater leverage in all negotiations. Both sets of respondents viewed economic strength in terms of the capability to adjust to the globalized world through trade and the ability to compete internationally with other economies. As a result of the forces of globalization, a country cannot expand economically without adapting to the market economy and market standards. Globalization also altered views of military strength. As military technology and weaponry have increased in quality and become internationalized, it is impossible to increase military strength without competing with international standards of military technology. Consequently, the People's War concept for China could no longer be a feasible defense strategy, and the Non-Aligned Movement certainly could not ensure security for India. Respondents repeatedly cited Iraq and Kosovo as examples not to follow in this respect. Both India and China felt that without accepting modernization, they would be forgoing future military strength, decreasing comprehensive national strength, and ultimately eroding their state sovereignty.

Both countries' respondents also felt that a nuclear capability was necessary in order to maintain or increase comprehensive national strength and protect state sovereignty. The Chinese respondents noted that China's existing nuclear capabilities were necessary for providing nuclear deterrence. In addition, they said that China's initial nuclear tests were done to avoid strong-arming by Western countries during the Cold War and to protect their sovereignty of decision making. However, given that the concept of sovereignty in China was focused mainly on territorial sovereignty, the goal of increasing comprehensive national strength was for preservation of China's territorial integrity. The nuclear capabilities were also part of a larger deterrence strategy that included conventional capabilities. China's military capabilities would have to be greater than Taiwan's in order to protect Taiwan as an integral part of China, and capabilities would also need to deter any assistance Taiwan might receive from the United States.

For India, the nuclear and missile capabilities were also meant to improve its military strength and provide nuclear deterrence. However, the nuclear capability was not meant to be used in warfare. Instead, Indian respondents perceived the power gained from a nuclear capability to be fungible. Rather than for use in combat, the deterrent power of nuclear weapons, along with increasing economic power, would increase overall negotiating power. The purpose of increasing comprehensive national strength was to maintain sovereignty of decision making in various international political and economic arenas, thereby protecting India's ability to develop in the future.

Conclusion

The pursuit of similar policies by countries often leads to the assumption that the ultimate goals of these states are also identical. However, an empirical analysis of national-interest formation in China and in India reveals that policies do not predicate the primary interests of the state. Although both countries have pursued an economic reform and defense modernization program, perceptions of state priorities are different.

Diverse approaches to the formation of national interest by states are indications of different underlying internal and external challenges. For states that have yet to institutionalize norms and solidify state identity, the basic internal goals of preservation of political stability, state legitimacy, and territorial consolidation may be the primary interests, whereas states with secure identities and strong institutions can focus on the preservation of state sovereignty in the external economic or political spheres. In either case, these countries may find economic reform and defense modernization useful policy paths to adopt in order to increase their comprehensive national strengths relative to other nations.

Both China and India have come to very similar conclusions on how to pursue their national interests in selecting economic reforms and defense modernization as the optimal policy choices for increasing comprehensive national strength. However, the reasons these two countries have chosen such similar policy paths are different. Though both India and China ultimately want to preserve their sovereignty of decision making, India is focused on sovereignty for political and economic issues, whereas China is interested in protecting territorial sovereignty and state legitimacy. These divergences necessitate a deeper analysis of national identity and political institutions in China and India. Whereas the Indian definition of national identity is politically defined and fosters little debate, the Chinese definition is disputed from within. The problems embedded in state unity lead the Chinese state to focus far more on territorial consolidation and place a secondary focus on protecting the political and economic interests of the country.

In terms of foreign-policy implications, viewing territorial consolidation as the critical national interest implies a higher priority for China on maintaining Taiwan and other disputed regions as Chinese territory, even at the risk of damaging the nation economically. It does not necessarily imply expansionist tendencies. For India, placing the premium on sovereignty of decision making in international political and economic issues indicates the centrality of obtaining economic and political influence within the international system in the future, particularly through international organizations. For the developed world, understanding the dynamics of national-interest formation in these rapidly growing states is essential if cooperation rather than conflict is to be the future in Asia.

Overview

Both China and India have pursued similar capabilities in the defense modernization and economic reforms programs, but for different reasons. China's primary national interest is in maintaining territorial and social unity, whereas India's primary interest is in protecting sovereignty of decision making in the international economic and political spheres. Chapter 2 outlines the similarities between the Chinese and Indian economic reforms and defense modernization programs, starting from Indian independence and the Chinese Communist Revolution. It discusses how both countries in the past two decades have adopted remarkably similar policy programs to pursue their national interests. Chapter 3 discusses the relationship between the concept of national identity in China and India and the formation of the national interest. National identity crises lead to the need for policies that can preserve the unity of the state. The state can play a critical role in providing a political definition for the nation that overrides centrifugal forces. Chapter 4 analyzes the relationship between globalization and state sovereignty. Globalization is increasingly viewed by China and India as a force that can erode state sovereignty. Thus, increasing comprehensive national strength is necessary to protect state sovereignty and pursue national interests. Chapter 5 discusses the political system of each country, positing that political institutions affect national-interest prioritization. Weak institutions and threatened political legitimacy can create conditions where policies are pursued in order to preserve the stability and legitimacy of the system. Chapter 6 discusses how the national interests of each country affect their bilateral ties. Similar interests in economic development and resolution of tensions are drawing the two countries into a more cooperative relationship. Chapter 7 provides conclusions and implications for the analysis of national-interest formation in other countries and for foreign policy.

Notes

1. For further discussion of the national security interpretation of the national interest, see Hans J. Morgenthau, *In Defense of the National Interest: A Critical Examination of American Foreign Policy* (New York: Alfred A. Knopf, 1951). As the title indicates, according to Morgenthau, national interest should be examined as a foreign policy. Also, see Hans J. Morgenthau, *Politics Among Nations: The Struggle for Power and Peace*, 6th ed. (New York: Alfred A. Knopf, 1985), 5; Kenneth N. Waltz, *Man, the State, and War: A Theoretical Analysis* (New York: Columbia University Press, 1959), 238; and The Commission on America's National Interests, *America's National Interests* (The Commission on America's National Interests, July 2000), 5.

2. Globalization here refers to a combination of market forces, technological change, increased communications, and increased international integration of goods and services. See Martin Wolf, "Will the Nation-State Survive Globalization?" *Foreign Affairs* (January/February 2001): 178.

3. National identity here refers to how the citizens of a nation perceive and define the identity of their nation as well as how they define their own nationality. Respondents in this study were asked to define what was the meaning of "China" or "India" and what did it mean to be "Chinese" or "Indian," respectively. For further discussion of national identity, see Walker Connor, *Ethnonationalism: The Quest for Understanding* (Princeton, NJ: Princeton University Press, 1994).

4. Shashi Tharoor, *India: From Midnight to the Millenium* (New York: HarperPerennial, 1997), 13.

CHAPTER 2

Similarities between China's and India's Pursuits of National Objectives

In the years immediately following revolution and independence, both China and India suffered from devastating poverty and possible territorial fragmentation. The threat of imminent dismemberment or collapse in both countries caused leaders to focus upon a development path that emphasized economic unity and independence with growth and a military tailored to quell insurgency and separatism. Although increasing national strength was thought to be in the national interest as defined by both nations, the ideology and methods used by leaders in each country to attain these goals were different. China under Mao Zedong relied heavily upon revolution in both the military and economic arenas to overthrow imperialists and bourgeoisie. India under Jawaharlal Nehru and later Indira Gandhi relied at first upon nonalignment and pan-Asianism as a security path, and a Socialist economy to lift the country from poverty.

Though both countries came from these differing perspectives, there was a common reliance upon Socialist theory in some form as a valid economic and military development path. The parallels between the two countries increased in the 1980s and 1990s when both China and India drastically changed their economic and defense policies. In their respective conceptual transformations away from Communism (in the case of China) and Socialism (India), both countries' policies reflected similar ideological shifts. Attaining an increased comprehensive national strength in order to pursue the national interest required a new set of policies underpinned by a different ideological basis. Both have adopted economic liberalization as the new path to economic strength, and Western technology-based, outward-focused defense programs to ensure security. The economic liberalization program signified for both countries a new acceptance of social and economic inequalities in exchange for rapid growth. It also showed a new willingness to allow foreign influences into the economy, along with the accompanying vulnerabilities to the vagaries of the world economy. In terms of domestic political structure, it reflected a willingness of highly centralized governments to devolve some economic powers to other authorities, as well as to the private sector.

In this chapter, I broadly outline the conceptual shift in the economic sphere and in the political sphere of both countries in order to highlight similarities in their new policy paths. Although many differences exist between the specifics of particular policies adopted by both countries, this chapter focuses on the similarities in the general direction of policy programs, rather than attempting to draw detailed parallels. The existence of policy similarities in the two major fields of economics and security lead to questions about the underlying determinants of these similar policy decisions in China and India. In particular, how do the factors of national identity, globalization, sovereignty, and political institutions combine to create similar policy paths? Also, why have these countries adopted similar programs, despite the existence of extremely different political institutional structures? Finally, are these policies driven by the same national objectives? These questions are addressed in the subsequent chapters, for which this chapter provides the historical overview.

Conceptual Shift in Economic Models of China and India

Both China and India began as new nations by adopting similar economic ideologies in order to help them achieve their respective national goals of rapid economic growth. China enlisted a radical form of Socialism in a revolutionary movement to communize all of Chinese society. Egalitarian society was to be attained through the elimination, by economic and violent means, of the middle and upper classes and the exclusion of foreign influence. India, also accepting Socialism as a valid and expedient path to development, selected the more moderate form of Fabian Socialism. This ideology appealed to people to democratically promote egalitarianism through state Socialist economic policies and also exclusion of foreign goods. However, China in 1978, and India in 1991, both concluded that Socialist economic policy was not the most effective path for rapid growth. Rather than egalitarianism and self-sufficiency as economic ideals, both countries began promoting privatization, rapid growth without regard to equity, and acceptance of foreign goods in their markets. This rapid and remarkably similar transition in China and India reflected new philosophies adopted by decision-making elites for addressing state economic challenges.

Socialist Economic Model in China

As a large, impoverished nation, China under Mao Zedong was attracted by the claims of the Socialist revolution. It promised egalitarian results with growth, and independence from imperialism, an attractive combination in the aftermath of World War II. Leninist economic theory stated that public ownership through state control of the economy could play a dual role by creating rapid economic growth while representing the interests of the people.[1] Mao's ideas and leadership combined this concept with an emphasis on constant revolution in all spheres of society to attain the goals of Marxism-Leninism and the ideological purity of the people. Mao's revolution can be divided into three main phases: the Communist Revolution of 1949, the Great Leap Forward of 1958–1961, and the Great Proletariat Cultural Revolution of 1966–1976. Each of these three encompassed a somewhat differing model of how to pursue Socialism according to Mao; however, all three were underpinned by Mao's main ideals of revolution, exclusion of foreign influence, grassroots participation, state ownership of production, collective agricultural ownership, and egalitarianism in plain living.

Mao's economic vision for China after the revolution was a version of the Soviet model transformed for use by China with two main modifications: (1) the concept of China as a nation oppressed by foreign imperialist economic aggression and (2) the necessity for the Chinese revolution to be mainly agrarian led rather than urban led; both differed from Lenin's model, where the primary concern was an urban proletarian revolution against a national bourgeoisie. The fact that the Chinese people as a whole had been oppressed by imperialists meant that the entire nation was, in fact, analogous to the urban proletariat oppressed by the bourgeoisie in Lenin's model. In explaining the implications of the imperialist system for Socialism, Mao wrote the following in August 1949:

> Imperialist aggression stimulated China's social economy, brought about changes in it and created the opposites of imperialism—the national industry and national bourgeoisie of China, and especially the Chinese proletariat working in enterprises run directly by the imperialists, those run by bureaucrat-capital and those run by the national bourgeoisie. To serve the needs of its aggression, imperialism ruined the Chinese peasants by exploiting them through the exchange of unequal values and thereby created great masses of poor peasants, numbering hundreds of millions and comprising 70 percent of China's population.[2]

The implications of this perception were that foreign corporations and other representations of foreign countries were not to be tolerated unless they were a part of the Communist Revolution, such as the Soviet Union, or a "friendly" country. Trade with foreign countries would be virtually nonexistent as a result, as would foreign investment.

Also, whereas Marxism-Leninism promoted an urban proletarian-led revolution, Mao initially believed the largely agrarian society of China would be better suited to a grassroots rural Communist revolution. Thus, the revolution in China was to begin in the countryside and then move to the cities. In 1927, Mao expected the peasants soon to "sweep all the imperialists, warlords, corrupt officials, local tyrants and evil gentry into their graves."[3] The fundamental role of the peasantry in China's Communist Revolution meant an emphasis on communization of land early on and the extension of central government control into the social and economic lives of all the people. The concept of grassroots revolution would remain a central element of Mao's economic and social direction until his death.

Mao outlined in his plans for the new economy that the state would own all large banks, industrial and commercial enterprises, railways, and airlines. However, as of 1940, he maintained that a somewhat gradual transformation in the countryside could be accommodated; peasants would own the land until cooperative based Socialist agriculture could be fully implemented.[4] By 1949, the revolutionary base was broadened from the peasantry to include the entire urban and rural working class as a move meant to restore and develop production, combat imperialism, and change China from an agricultural to an industrial country.[5] This modification ensured that the Socialist economic principles of public ownership being promoted in the countryside would be adopted in the urban centers as well and that a united front would exist politically for their implementation. However, even in 1949 Mao advocated that four types of ownership could coexist: the state owned sector, the cooperative economy, the private sector, and the state-capitalist sector.[6] This moderate approach was meant to provide only a transition period to a truly socialized economy.

By confronting the conflict of interests within China among the rich peasants, the middle peasants, and the poor peasants, rural society would be transformed. Mao viewed the inability of the Party to account for the needs of the poor as a fault that would inevitably lead to greater polarization of society and a destruction of the worker peasant alliance. His solution was thus:

> To bring about, step by step, the socialist transformation of the whole of agriculture simultaneously with the gradual realization of socialist industrialization and the socialist transformation of handicrafts and capitalist industry and commerce; in other words, it means to carry out co-operation and eliminate the rich peasant economy and the individual economy in the countryside so that all the rural people will become increasingly well off together.[7]

The three years from 1949 to 1952 were a transition period setting the stage for more radical Socialism. By 1953 and 1954, respectively, socialization of the private sector in urban areas[8] and the formation of agricultural producer cooperatives (APCs) began.[9] By December 1955, Mao claimed that more than 60 percent (70 million) of China's peasant households had already joined "semi-socialist agricultural producer's co-operatives" in response to the Central Committee of the CCP's suggestion, an increase of 50 million in only three months. As a result, he projected that the moderate pace of reforms to date was insufficient to the task. Instead of the original blueprint (September 1955) recommending three, five-year plans for the Socialist transformation, he stated that by 1959 or 1960 (three to four years) full transformation into Socialist cooperatives could be completed.[10] The basic conversion from a four-sector economy to all production under state or collective ownership was completed by 1956.[11]

At this point, the majority of the country had been folded into a socialized system with state ownership predominant in production, and the focus shifted largely from agriculture to heavy industry. Remaining agriculture was collectivized. Industry was socialized with private industry accounting for 63 percent of industrial output in 1949, but only 16 percent in 1955. State-owned industry in the same period increased its share in gross industrial output from 35 percent to 68 percent.[12] The weight of agriculture in the economy declined drastically. Whereas agriculture comprised 58 percent of national income in 1952 to industry's 24 percent contribution, by 1979, the numbers were 37 percent and 50 percent, respectively.[13]

The Great Leap Forward (1958–1961) extended and deepened the socialization of China, with communization of land, mass participation in heavy industry production, and primary emphasis on advanced collectivized agricultural production. A total of 740,000 advanced APCs combined into 26,000 communes in 1958.[14] In this undertaking, Mao again emphasized the importance of "plain living and hard struggle" as critical in achieving the ends of rapid economic growth.[15] Private property of the peasants was confiscated during this period for use by the state. The state shut down small markets used by the peasants for exchange of goods because they were perceived as being opposed to Communist ideology.[16] Wages and benefits of workers and peasants, as well as prices for producers, were all set by the state, and all profits accruing to industry and agriculture were the property of the state. China largely continued these economic policies through the Cultural Revolution (1966–1976). During that period, the Party also insisted upon implementing greater ideological purity through the elimination of any remaining private ownership and collective enterprises. Though there were 9,000,000 individual workers in the cities and towns of China in 1953, by 1978 there were only 150,000.[17]

During this phase of history, the Chinese Communist Party under the guidance of Mao stated that public ownership, in the form of socialized industry and communized agriculture, was the most effective method in achieving the national goal of increased power and wealth. China's economic growth during the period from 1949 to 1978 was indeed solid, and from 1952 to 1978 growth averaged 6 percent.[18] The industrial base overall expanded from the 1950s to the 1970s, particularly in the sectors of electric power, cement, and steel. Because of ideological bias against foreign borrowing, China also had relatively little foreign debt.

However, public discontent was widespread from decades of Socialist revolutionizing of the economy. The economic and human costs from mismanagement and bad policy were extreme.[19] Growth fluctuated vastly; for example, negative rates of 29.7 and 6.5 in 1961 and in 1962, respectively, were followed by positive growth rates of 16.5 and 16.9 in 1964 and in 1965, respectively.[20] The inability of prices to adjust to the realities of production and demand led to insufficient quantities for domestic consumption both in food grains and light industry consumer goods. Uneven increases in production without concomitant increases in necessary infrastructure led to severe bottlenecks and waste. Also, centralized planning without effective distribution led to disastrous results. More than 30 million died in the Great Leap Forward from famine, which resulted from a combination of shortages and a waste of grain. After the devastation of the Great Leap Forward, China took a more moderate path in production during the 1960s. Thus, as China entered 1978, the economic situation was not in crisis. In 1977, China sustained 7.8 percent growth, accelerating to 11.7 percent in 1978.[21] The anomalies embedded in China's economy during the Mao era beg the question, What was the impetus for reform, economic or other factors? In any case, this economic system reigned until the next ideological shift was to transform the Chinese method of pursuing their national interests.

China and the Economic Reforms of 1978

At the Third Plenum of the Eleventh Party Congress in 1978, Deng Xiaoping initiated a sweeping reform program that essentially changed the direction of Socialism in China. These reforms can be divided into several phases,[22] but for simplicity they are divided into two main time periods for this study: the first stage from 1978–1992, where incremental reforms were initiated, and the second stage from 1993–2000, where economic institutions and reforms were deepened.

By advocating Mao's slogan, "Seek truth from facts,"[23] Deng was able to begin a radical conceptual shift in the approach to development of the economy. Using Mao's own words, he repudiated the current doctrine upheld by the Hua Guofeng–led Maoist faction, the "two whatevers," which stated that whatever Mao said, did, or endorsed should determine all action.[24] Instead, by seeking truth from facts and integrating Marxism-Leninism with the historical practice of Chinese revolution, Deng said that the correct path is in actuality quite different from what they had been pursuing for many years. He defined following Mao Zedong Thought as taking account of present reality and advantage of conditions to reach the objectives of the four modernizations,[25] which were originally promoted by Mao.[26] This set the stage for acceptance of further reforms on specific functional areas, such as the economy, military, and political behavior, in order to fulfill the objectives of the modernizations.

On the economy, Deng advocated a devolution of power and allowed the use of material incentives in order to increase productivity and efficiency, a reversal of the highly centralized ideal of Mao's Communism. This implied greater powers of decision making to the provinces, municipalities, and autonomous regions in the areas of economic planning, finance, and foreign trade. At the microeconomic level, it meant broadened decision-making powers for mines, factories, other enterprises, and production teams.[27] The implications for society were even more drastic. Individuals and families were able to reestablish authority and increase their power relative to the commune and the Party. This led to an improved lifestyle for Chinese families in general. Also, whereas the ideal society under Mao had no class distinctions, wage differences, or material benefits for increased production, Deng's concept allowed more pay for more work and individual material benefits as incentives. He said the following in December 1978:

> I think we should allow some regions and enterprises and some workers and peasants to earn more and enjoy more benefits sooner than others, in accordance with their hard work and greater contributions to society. If the standard of living of some people is raised first, this will inevitably be an impressive example to their "neighbors", and people in other regions and units will want to learn from them. This will help the whole national economy to advance wave upon wave and help the people of all our nationalities to become prosperous in a comparatively short period.[28]

In dealing with the seemingly inherent contradictions between maintaining a Socialist society and a market economy, Deng said that, in fact, no contradiction really exists. By using capitalist methods in its operation and management, China could develop its productive capabilities under Socialism. In defense of this conceptualization he said, "As long as learning from capitalism is regarded as no more than a means to an end, it will not change the structure of socialism or bring China back to capitalism."[29]

The reforms initially provided guidelines for two, five-year plans covering the period 1976–1985 (adjusting the five-year plan beginning 1976), with the goal of quadrupling China's net national product by the year 2000.[30] Deng's new policy program allowed for private use of agricultural land in the rural agricultural responsibility system and an open policy with special economic zones (SEZs) established for increased trade.[31] Development of infrastructure was to receive particular attention; also the emphasis was to shift from heavy to light industry, industry to agriculture, and investment to consumption.[32] Attention was to be given to population reduction, and technology development and importation as well. The reforms can be divided into four main areas: industrial and public sector, trade sector, financial sector, and the agricultural sector. A broad description of the reforms is provided below.

Industrial and Public Sector Reform

Industrial reform was undertaken in 1978 with the quotas for production lowered to allow the sale of excess products at prices as much as 20 percent higher than the fixed state price.[33] As the reforms progressed, the limits on prices were eased, and the number of products subject to fixed state prices was reduced. In 1982 enterprises were authorized to set prices for 160 commodities, and 350 more items were freed from price controls in 1983.[34] However, all large enterprises such as electric power, communications, and transportation remained under state control during this period.

State-owned enterprise (SOE) reform faced severe difficulties in this first set of reforms. Income inequality was viewed as non-Socialist, and remaining price distortions made distinguishing effective firms difficult.[35] These complications led to the continued support of sick firms, and thus no penalties for poor progress. In an effort to provide incentives for efficiency, in 1983, the state adopted a type of responsibility system, relinquishing automatic profit transfers to the state in favor of direct taxes.[36] This policy enabled producers to retain some profit. The responsibility system was followed in 1986 by the contract responsibility system (CRS), which reduced the level of government intervention in the activities of the enterprises. The CRS gave targets for performance, production quotas for the state, and financial obligations to the government.[37] In 1988 an Enterprise Law was passed to encourage the transition of SOEs into autonomous enterprises that could be held liable for their own profits and losses. The state issued regulations for its implementation in 1992.[38] Despite these changes, production quotas were maintained for various products, as was government support for failing firms, creating a drain on state resources. Nonetheless, the direction of changes in the public and industrial sectors reflected the change from a fully state-controlled industrial sector to a decrease of state intervention in production and a greater emphasis on efficiency and competition.

Trade Sector

With the 1978 reforms China began a new Open Door Policy, opening the economy to foreign trade, investment, and borrowing.[39] Prior to reforms, fewer than 16 foreign trade corporations were able to trade in

China, maintaining monopolies on their products.[40] Tariffs and pricing were unnecessary, as calculations of needs and quotas rather than market mechanisms determined production and procurement. Trade reforms aimed to create greater competition and decrease inefficiency and distortions in the production and procurement of goods. The four main components of trade reform included increasing the number and the type of trading enterprises, adopting trade policy instruments such as licenses and tariffs, reducing exchange rate distortion, and instituting price reforms.[41] Four special economic zones were established in 1979 to spearhead reforms and advance in the foreign trade sector. In 1980, 17 new import-export corporations were established successfully, followed by foreign trade corporations in other provinces. By 1987, industrial ministries and provinces had set up a total of 1,900 foreign trade companies.[42] Tariffs and nontariff barriers that had replaced the monopolistic foreign trade corporations were gradually reduced over the reform period. As a result, from 1978 to 2003, trade as a percent of gross domestic product (GDP) rose sharply, reflecting the greater openness of the Chinese economy. Imports and exports increased from 5.5 percent and 5.2 percent of GDP, respectively, in 1978 to 31.8 percent and 34.3 percent, respectively, in 2003.[43] Trade reforms reveal the shift from a relatively closed economy in China to one that has opened significantly to global trade and is increasingly dependent upon exports for income.

Financial Sector

Prior to reform of the economy, the People's Bank of China (PBC) controlled two other banking institutions, the Bank of China (BoC), which supervised foreign exchange transactions, and the People's Construction Bank of China (PCBC), which supervised investment spending from the state budget (fiscal spending).[44] Macroeconomic decisions were under PBC control through these three arms. The reforms were meant to devolve economic power to lower levels of the state, enterprises, and individuals. The state adopted newer policy mechanisms for regulation of the economy after the reforms, such as taxation, interest rates, tariffs, and prices.[45] In 1979, China initiated banking sector reforms with the "Four Transformations and Eight Reforms." These reforms began the use of interest rates as a financial tool in the Chinese economy, although the interest rate remained subject to political manipulation. In 1979, the Agricultural Bank of China (ABC) was established to oversee rural cooperatives and rural lending. The Industrial and Commercial Bank (ICB)[46] was then established in 1983 to raise deposits and distribute credit for urban industrial and commercial enterprises.[47] The PBC further decentralized by initiating branch banking in 1984.[48]

China opened stock exchanges in Shanghai in 1990, and in Shenzhen in 1991, with different share classes for domestic and foreign investors.[49] A shares are available for Chinese residents and are denominated in renminbi, whereas B shares are foreign currency denominated and available to nonresidents. In 1994, the foreign-exchange rate was unified from what had been two rates, the official and market rates, into a single rate. This was followed in 1996 by current account convertibility of the renminbi.[50]

Financial sector reform included diversifying and opening the banking sector, previously dominated only by the PBC. In 1995, the Central Bank Law was passed, restricting the functions of the People's Bank of China and making it primarily a central bank. The PBC was no longer allowed to directly finance government budget deficits.[51] Expectations of greater financial responsibility were reflected in the ability of financial institutions to fail, "Before 1998, the state always bailed out troubled financial institutions, but for the first time in 1998, several high profile banks and investment companies, such as Hainan Development Bank and Guangdong International Trust Investment Company, closed down or went bankrupt."[52] However, the PBC still could not function independently of the State Council, and monetary policy remained influenced by politics rather than by economic principles. The four main banks, BoC, PCBC, ABC, and ICB, are considered to be "technically insolvent".[53] According to Nicholas Lardy, the problems of the PBC can be traced back to corruption, "In China the weakness of the central bank reflects the extreme reluctance of powerful political leaders, especially at the provincial and local level, to relinquish their power to direct loan funds to specific industries and firms."[54] Despite the slow pace of reform in the banking and financial sector, the direction of reforms in this area has been to increase accountability and incentives for both domestic and foreign investment in China.

Agricultural Sector

In rural areas, most collectivized farms reverted to family farms under the household responsibility system by 1982. The government encouraged diversification and specialization of crops and raised procurement prices.[55] Though the state still reserved a bulk of agricultural production for sale to the state according to quotas, excess production could be sold for profit at market prices. By 1985, they modified even these remaining quotas into limited targets, allowing meat, fish, poultry, and vegetables to be sold at market prices. As a result, average agricultural output rose from 4 percent during 1971–1978 to 13 percent during 1982–1986.[56] However, fiscal subsidies absorbed the increase in producer prices in order to reduce the costs to the urban consumer. As subsidies increased in the early 1980s, the government shifted from a mandatory purchase quota system to a procurement contract system.[57] By 1991–1992, the increasing fiscal burden led the state to raise the urban sales prices up to the procurement prices. Subsequently, grain prices were freed in most areas.

Another aspect of agricultural reforms was the rise of township and village enterprises (TVEs). These enterprises were able to receive credit from rural credit cooperatives and sell products at market prices. By reinvesting profits, they were able to offer incentive-based wages to members and improve productivity.[58] The existence of these enterprises provided a successful example of rural transition to a market economy for other sectors and regions.[59] The general direction of agricultural reforms was to decrease the role of the state in production and introduce profit incentives in order to spur efficiency and production.

Economic reforms in China beginning in 1978 reflected a fundamental change in the priorities outlined by the Party in achieving its stated national interest of rapid economic growth. The shift from an ideologically Socialist ideal of society with egalitarian, simple living and indigenous production to that of unequal but effective growth with openness to the world was parallel to the shift that occurred in India. Analyzing the reasons for the similarities between these transformations can yield significant insights into national interest formation in both China and India.

Socialist Economic Model in India

The immediate postrevolutionary societies were both based on Socialism, revolutionary Socialism in China and democratic Socialism in India. However, the Socialist similarities between the two nations are overshadowed by their differences in political system, leadership, and culture. The difference between China's and India's political systems affected greatly the extent and manner in which Socialist ideals could be implemented in these societies. Mao used mass mobilization to communize Chinese society as a whole, whereas public opinion and constitutional processes limited Nehru's pursuit of Socialism. The powerful role of the state in directing the economic plans of both countries is similar, however. State involvement in the industrial sector through SOEs, state control of industry, public ownership of banking, use of price controls, and limited involvement in the international economy all are similar facets of prereform China and India. With the advent of economic reforms, the state modified its involvement in these areas in both countries in the direction of liberalization and openness.

Early Indian leaders Jawaharlal Nehru and Mohandas K. Gandhi, in particular, incorporated many Socialist tenets into the political economy of India. Prime Minister Nehru was drawn to the writings of Karl Marx, particularly the Socialist lessons outlined in Marx's thoughts of British rule in India.[60] Committed to the ideals of Socialism, Nehru nonetheless rejected the necessity for the use of violence to achieve Socialist goals. In a speech in 1955, he said thus:

> The communists tell us that the basis of society is class struggle and therefore the people must be trained for class struggle and for destroying the upper classes. I also want a classless society in India and the world. I do not want any privileged classes. I do not want a great deal of inequality among people. The point is how we are to proceed about it. Even recognizing the conflict between classes, the right way of liquidating that conflict is to put an end to it by peaceful methods.[61]

Gandhian thought and spirituality proved to be highly influential in forming the economic philosophy of India during this period as well. An avowed believer in moral Socialism,[62] he emphasized the need for egalitarianism and the need for poor nations to develop independence from foreign rule through economic self-reliance. He warned that revolution would occur if income inequality were not eradicated through voluntary generosity by the rich.

> The contrast between the palaces of New Delhi and the miserable hovels of the poor laboring class nearby cannot last one day in a free India in which the poor will enjoy the same power as the richest in the land. A violent and bloody revolution is a certainty one day unless there is a voluntary abdication of riches and the power that riches give, and sharing them for the common good.[63]

The difference between Gandhi and revolutionary Socialists in China, however, was that he did not advocate the violent option of revolution. Rather, he refused to be a part of a revolution that used violence as a method in any way. Gandhi expected man to be perfectable and able to relinquish riches and property through spirituality.

He believed that independence from economic slavery could be accomplished mainly by adherence to *swadeshi*, or indigenous, production. Self-reliance would also contribute to world peace by allowing poor nations to avoid exploitation by industrialized countries.[64] In particular, *swadeshi* production of cloth would be necessary to clothe the poor of India. Indigenous production was considered best if done by hand, using a spinning wheel to produce Indian cloth known as *khaddar* (*khadi*).[65] Through reliance upon individuals and small-scale industry for production, Gandhi believed that India would be able to maintain economic independence and national self-sufficiency for all elements of society. Gandhi's ideas on self-reliance and economic isolationism became the theoretical basis for decades of import restrictions and *swadeshi* bias in industrial policy.

Both Gandhi and Nehru advocated a democratic and peaceful transformation of society into a Socialist ideal, rather than the authoritarian approach used in China. Although all of their methods for the transformation were not necessarily effective, the Socialist ideal remained the guiding force for the state. Despite the fact that the ruling Congress Party was not Socialist, there was still considerable popular support for the democratic, moderately Socialist policies promoted by Nehru. His plan was to implement such policies over time, as supported by the populace.[66]

Nehru's Economic Policies

Nehru set the nation upon the path of modern secular Socialism, with a planned economy, state ownership of major industries, and heavy controls. Among the priorities for the new government were stability, both political and economic, economic growth, egalitarianism, and self-sufficiency. However, the sheer magnitude and diversity of interests within the country made these tasks formidable. The government responded to these challenges by strengthening the power of the center over the states.[67] The result was a highly regulated and stifled economy until beyond Nehru's death in 1964. Planning, both during and after his government, was divided into Five-Year Plans. The Second Five-Year Plan (1956–1962) deserves mention here in particular, as it influenced policies for the decades to come. Also known as the Mahalanobis Plan, the plan emphasized the development of heavy industries and included a dominant role for the public sector in the economy.[68]

India implemented the import-substitution path to industrialization from independence onward to reach the level of industrialization envisioned for the nation in its plans while maintaining national self-sufficiency. The instruments of policy were mainly quantitative restraints, meant to counter both the balance of payments crisis by reducing the demand for foreign exchange while at the same time furthering the goals of import substitution.[69] Ensuring *swadeshi* predominance in production and consumer goods remained of the utmost importance. To this end, state-owned enterprises retained considerable power regardless of huge inefficiencies. Export subsidizing policies augmented the import restricting strategies from 1962 onward. Though governments succeeding Nehru attempted some moderate reforms,[70] political drag and natural disasters colluded to sustain the existing system.[71]

After independence, although Nehru was committed to land and agriculture reforms to reduce inequalities, policies were not implemented well due to many of the state-governing elites overriding interests in the properties. A major element of reforms was to transform the *zamindari* feudal system of land holdings into a more modern, efficient one that gave farmers more entrepreneurial freedom.[72] The *zamindari* was outlawed over the 1950s, and in stages, the government implemented reforms to limit the maximum size of land holdings and regulate tenancy rights.[73] According to Shalendra Sharma, the existence of these moderate reforms after independence had deep political implications for Congress rule and was a method to weaken the strength of the Communist Party in India. "Winning over the peasants by satisfying their ubiquitous land hunger was one way the Congress political elites hoped to neutralize and undermine the call of the Communist Party of India for militant mobilization of the peasantry for an eventual Chinese-style agrarian revolution."[74] The limited reforms undertaken after independence changed the fundamental legal structure of the *zamindari* and land holdings but was incomplete in that there was no large-scale transfer of land from elites to the peasantry over this period.

Indira Gandhi and the Economy

Indira Gandhi, Nehru's daughter, maintained close ties with the Soviet Union both economically and militarily and upheld many of Nehru's economic policies. The state retained a large influence over the economy via industrial policy. Indira nationalized even more industries, including many banks.[75] However, in agriculture, a radical change was wrought through the Green Revolution, and a technocratic model initiated by Prime Minister Lal Bahadur Shastri (prior to Indira Gandhi's term) replaced the Socialist model for agriculture.[76] The new agricultural policies created food surpluses for India, and agricultural production more than doubled after their implementation in the mid-1960s.[77]

India and the Economic Reforms of 1991

After many years of a highly socialized economy, India undertook reforms that changed the ideological basis upon which the economy was built. Rajiv Gandhi put forth the first set of economic reforms in 1985, but these ultimately proved unsustainable. In July of 1991 Prime Minister Narasimha Rao announced radical plans for stabilization and structural reforms, initiating a broad conceptual and policy shift away from the decades-old Socialist system.[78] Similar to Deng's reforms, Rao implemented policies that allowed market competition and a decrease in central government control over the economy. The main elements of Indian initial reforms were in investment and production in most industries: (1) loosening of control over business; (2) the delicensing decisions on location and technology transfer; (3) lifting import controls, except for consumer goods; (4) lowering of tariffs; (5) encouragement of foreign direct investment; (6) opening of power, steel, oil refining, air transport, telecommunications, ports, mining, and pharmaceuticals, among others to private investment; (7) liberalization of capital markets, allowing entry of private mutual funds and foreign institutional investors; and (8) simplification of the tax system, with lowering of rates.[79]

These reforms, though by no means complete, were successful in increasing investor confidence. Issues of note can be divided into four categories: public sector and investment, trade sector, financial sector, and agricultural sector.[80]

Public Sector and Investment

Public enterprises have held a powerful role in the Indian economy since the Nehruvian era. Providing 7 million jobs in 1961, the Indian public sector had grown to a total of 19 million jobs by 1990. Reforms aimed to reduce the size of this sector and provide more opportunity for competition and efficiency. The reforms' purpose in the public sector can be summarized in five areas[81]: (1) privatization of SOEs, (2) reducing subsidies and monopoly privileges to SOEs, (3) partial divestiture of SOEs, (4) creating incentives for accountability through increasing use of market mechanisms, and (5) the 1991 establishment of the National Renewal Fund to finance the retraining or retirement of 60,000 workers in 40 public enterprises.[82] Sectors opened to private investment included power, steel, oil refining and exploration, road construction, air transport, telecommunications, ports, mining, and pharmaceuticals.[83] Despite these advances, the public sector, even after reforms, has remained a large and inefficient drag on the economy. These enterprises have suffered from low profitability and poor management. In addition, the large role of the public sector in the economy has led to crowding out problems through large amounts of public borrowing, thereby driving up interest rates and creating a shortage of available credit for private investment. However, political realities have necessitated glacial movement in sales and reforms of public enterprises.

Indian investment prior to 1991 suffered from a stifling set of controls. Licensing greatly limited entry, and foreign direct investment (FDI) was hindered by regulations banning companies with more than 40 percent foreign equity from borrowing or raising deposits in India, taking over business interests, acquiring physical assets in India, and from using their trademarks without Reserve Bank of India clearance.[84] A monopolies law that restricted the growth of large firms, and preferences for the public sector enterprises, exacerbated the problems of limited entry. The 1991 deregulation of the investment regime included removing many of these licensing restrictions in the industrial sectors. The government amended antitrust legislation to allow expansion and diversification and gradually reduced the areas reserved for the public sector. Theoretically, infrastructure projects are open to private investors; however, actual investment has been slowed by various regulatory problems such as licensing procedures and an absence of a viable commercial framework for investment. Public sector and investment reforms in India, nonetheless, reduced the size of the state-owned sector and decreased overzealous regulation. The result has been greater incentives for production and efficiency, leading to the rapid growth of formerly nonexistent sectors, such as information technology, and the opportunity for competition in other industries.

Trade Sector

The realization that the past restrictive policies toward imports had inhibited export growth led to reform policies more open and conducive to trade. Devaluation of the rupee led to a 15 percent depreciation of the real effective exchange rate in 1991–1992.[85] In February 1993, this policy culminated in the change to a floating rupee on trade accounts. In 1994, the rupee became convertible on the current account.[86] Trade policy finally moved away from the import substitution strategies of the past, and most quantitative restraints on imports of capital and intermediate goods were removed. For the 1997–2002 export-import policy, quantitative restraints overall were lowered, and quantitative restrictions were removed as part of India's commitment to the WTO.[87] A certain small amount of consumer goods was also allowed to be imported through particular types of licenses. Also, most nontariff barriers were abolished. Tariffs were lowered substantially, from a maximum rate of 200 percent pre-1991 to a maximum rate of 40 percent by 1998. Export controls, formerly exerted over 439 items, were reduced to 210 items, and export taxes were completely abolished. Export subsidies were also eliminated. [88] India's trade reforms show that the direction of reforms in this arena is also similar to those of China. Decreased quotas and tariffs and other regulations have led to a larger role for trade in the Indian economy and a greater integration into the international economy.

Financial Sector

Prior to 1991, the state controlled the financial sector heavily through interest rates and general meddling in financial markets. The state fixed interest rates according to loan size and sector categories and maintained interest rate floors. Also, the government preempted much of the bank reserves via the cash reserve ratios (CRR) and statutory liquidity ratios (SLR).[89] Bank credit was directed to priority sectors at concessional interest rates, and the interest rates on government securities was controlled. These policies created serious distortions in savings and the demand for credit. Last, state controls highly restricted entry into the banking market.

The government determined that deregulating the financial system, banks, and capital markets was critical for the success of reforms.[90] After 1991, interest rates were deregulated and rate floors on loans over

Rs. 200,000 were eliminated. The CRR was lowered to 10 percent in 1997.[91] By 2005, the CRR had come down to 5 percent.[92] India curbed directed bank credit and developed money markets. For government securities, auctions replaced controls. Restrictions on the opening of new bank branches were loosened, and guidelines for new entry were formulated. In addition, measures were taken to increase supervision on bank balance sheets. The government aimed the reforms to improve efficiency of the markets, curb unfair trading practices, and implement an effective regulatory framework.[93] Since 1994, several new banks have been licensed, including foreign banking institutions.[94] In addition, in 1992 the Securities and Exchange Board of India was established to reform the capital and securities markets, increasing regulation and surveillance of stock market activities.[95] Even the Bharatiya Janata Party (BJP), originally thought to be a protectionist party, opened the financial, insurance, and telecommunications sectors to foreign competition during its term in office.[96] Although reforms have been slow, the direction has been toward creating incentives for competition and investment, from both domestic and foreign sources.

Agricultural Sector

Indian agriculture was never socialized as was the Chinese agricultural sector. After independence it remained semifeudal for the first few decades, with much agricultural land under the control of elites. India implemented the most significant agricultural reforms in the 1970s and the 1980s, prior to the reforms of 1991. However, after 1991 moderate further changes were instituted to reduce the role of the state in the agricultural sector, such as decreasing regulation of product markets in wheat, rice, sugar, cotton, and edible oils; lessening controls in the markets for inputs, such as machinery, seeds, electricity, and irrigation water; and reducing subsidies and controls for fertilizers.[97] However, price supports in agriculture remain, and the agricultural market needs further opening to imports.

The New Logic of Economic Reform in China and India

Both countries adopted an open door, liberalized their economies, and revealed unexpected similarities in the direction of their new policies. Although implementation of the details of all of these reforms has proved to be a political challenge for both countries, forward movement on reforms of most fronts is visible. Whereas before, Socialist policies with strict emphasis upon egalitarianism, eradication of poverty, independence from foreign economic influence, public ownership, and heavy industry-led growth determined the economic policies implemented, reforms reflected a fundamental philosophical change. In order to implement the new economic reforms, both countries had to accept a radically different concept of domestic economic growth, including large income differentials both individually and regionally, privatization, and an influx of foreign-made products and investment. Various other factors had to be accepted as well, such as foreign ideas, vulnerabilities to the vagaries of the market, and diversified paths for domestic investment and production.

Conceptual Shift in Military Doctrine in China and India

In addition to adopting similar policy directions as a result of economic reforms in the 1980s and the 1990s, China and India both embarked upon new strategies for their defense programs. In China, defense changed from a grassroots concept of a people's army fighting a guerrilla war toward the goal of creating a modern, professional military with high-technology weaponry. India also changed its policies and outlook from those of a primarily ground-based army to that of a modernized defense with a nuclear option. Though India's military organization was that of a conventional military force, based upon the British tradition and extremely different from China's guerrilla military organization, a convergence of military ideals can be seen in both countries' modernizations programs as they enter the 1980s. Both countries opted for technology and weaponry that provide increased force projection capabilities. The changes in equipment and weaponry procurement reflected a new conception of military strategy needed to face new threats.

China and a Grassroots Military Concept

Several factors characterized the military concepts of China under Mao. The primary focus was on revolution and its many aspects as they applied to liberating China. A secondary goal of Mao's defense concept was to foment Communist revolution in other countries. The struggle against imperialism needed to be fought as a united front both internally in China and externally around the world. By uniting people internationally, U.S. and other imperialism could be resisted and world peace would be safeguarded.[98] Underpinning both goals was a dedication to the efficacy of guerrilla warfare and protracted war in a revolution against technologically superior adversaries.

To be successful in the revolution, the state expected the military to function as a multirole force in both fighting and building society in order to ensure the security of the vast territories of China that first had to be liberated, then administered. The various roles and aspects of military doctrine were integrated in that the People's Liberation Army's (PLA) strength came from its close relationship to the people, "The richest source of power to wage war lies in the masses of the people."[99] Mao repeatedly criticized the Japanese and Kuomintang armies for their morally inferior position as imperialists and their bourgeois inability to integrate with the people. In contrast, he constructed a role for the army that was tightly connected with the people through its role as a working force and through its dependence on the people for its military strength. He outlined for the military a broad social role in China. Rather than being only a fighting force, it was a fighting and a working force, according to the needs of the nation. In 1949, he wrote the following in reference to urban work:

> The army is not only a fighting force, it is mainly a working force. All army cadres should learn how to take over and administer cities. In urban work they should learn how to be good at dealing with the imperialists and Kuomintang reactionaries, good at dealing with the bourgeoisie, good at leading the workers and organizing trade unions, good at mobilizing and organizing the youth, good at uniting with and training cadres in the new Liberated Areas, good at managing industry and commerce, good at running schools, newspapers, news agencies and broadcasting stations, good at handling foreign affairs, good at handling problems relating to the democratic parties and people's organizations, good at adjusting the relations between the cities and the rural areas and solving the problems of food, coal and other daily necessities and good at handling monetary and financial problems.[100]

The military was to be incorporated with the masses in every way, also in agricultural production in the rural areas, and in cultural affairs. This extremely broad role for the military was meant to unite the people and the army as one,[101] enhancing the strength of both. However, while being necessary for the success of a grassroots-based, revolutionary army, the multitasking required of the military precluded the existence of a professional, Western-style military with the capability of fighting a war with high-technology weaponry. Time spent in economic, cultural, and ideological work replaced training, and the close identification with the civilian population negated the existence of a separate military ethic. Without the ability to form a separate identity and ethic, professionalization of the troops was difficult if not impossible.

Guerrilla Warfare and Protracted War

To address the problems of fighting a revolutionary war, whether against the Japanese, the Kuomintang, or the United States, the effective strategy was determined to be that of guerrilla warfare and protracted war. This strategy made use of China's relative advantages vis-à-vis the enemy, whether it be the Japanese, the Kuomintang, the United States, the Soviets, or otherwise. With reference to Japan, Mao viewed China as a relatively weak country that was inferior to the enemy in "military, economic and political-organizational power."[102] These fundamental weaknesses would mean that in a conventional war in which massed soldiers were to face one another in battles, China would be unable to compete. However, China's inability to defeat Japan quickly underscored the importance of fighting a protracted war. China's rich resources in land, population, and number of soldiers reinforced the plausibility of China's being able to emerge victoriously in a prolonged war against an enemy who did not have these resources. The People's Army would be able to avoid sustaining heavy losses by amassing their forces upon the enemy over a prolonged period of time. In addition, the "just character of her war" would translate into international support for China. The various attributes in China's favor led to three main conclusions: (1) protracted war would be necessary, (2) the revolution would have to retreat to the countryside to form bases and obtain supplies, and (3) guerrilla warfare would be the key to success.[103]

Mao describes guerrilla warfare in the following points: "Divide our forces to arouse the masses, concentrate our forces to deal with the enemy. The enemy advances, we retreat; the enemy camps, we harass; the enemy tires, we attack; the enemy retreats, we pursue. To extend stable base areas, employ the policy of advancing in waves; when pursued by a powerful enemy, employ the policy of circling around."[104] These concepts reflect a strategy that enables a weaker military to inflict damage upon a stronger adversary through waiting for the appropriate moment, using advantages of time and space rather than sheer force, and basically attacking the enemy's weaknesses. The principles of flexibility, the ability to conduct offensives within the defensive, and exterior-line operations within interior-line operations would allow the guerrillas to keep the upper hand in otherwise impossible situations.[105] The guerrilla forces could obtain the offensive by using surprise attacks and amassing large forces of guerrillas against a small section of the enemy. The guerrilla forces could also defeat the enemy's encircling exterior lines by encircling parts of their forces and destroying that part of the enemy's exterior lines that was encircled.[106] Mao described the process as, "Taking advantage of the enemy's shortage of troops (from the viewpoint of the war as a whole), the guerrilla units can boldly use vast areas as their fields of operation; taking advantage of the fact that the enemy is an alien invader and is pursuing a most barbarous policy, the guerrilla units can boldly enlist the support of millions upon millions of people."[107]

Necessary for the success of this strategy was a strong network of bases in the countryside. These bases were the foundation upon which a protracted war could be fought and were seen as the rear of guerrilla operations. When confronted with a superior military force, the guerrilla forces could retreat to the bases in the countryside and await the appropriate time for attack. Bases were composed of armed, trained guerrillas and the people (peasants, youth, women, children, etc.) and were of necessity located over wide expanses in order to allow freedom to maneuver.[108] After the enemy was weakened by sustained guerrilla attacks, the People's Army would be able to launch the final stage of the war, the strategic counteroffensive. This counteroffensive would use regular army fighting tactics, because the Chinese forces would have military superiority at that time. Incremental successes could lead to the ultimate defeat of the enemy.

The last main characteristic of Mao's concept of revolutionary, protracted, and guerrilla warfare was the nature of the command structure. Because guerrilla warfare relied heavily upon taking the initiative in attacks through surprise over large areas, command was necessarily decentralized. Though strategic command was centralized, command of campaigns and battles was decentralized to allow for greater flexibility. A decentralized command structure also prevented paralysis from lack of communication, as was very possible in the countryside of China under the centralized command structure of regular warfare.[109]

Exporting Revolution

Though internal revolution and Chinese sovereignty were the primary goals for Mao's revolution, he also firmly believed in exporting Communist revolutions to other oppressed countries. Lin Biao, Defense Minister in 1965, stated the following argument for these policies:

> Taking the entire globe, if North America and Western Europe can be called "the cities of the world," then Asia, Africa, and Latin America constitute "the rural areas of the world." ... In a sense, the contemporary world revolution also presents a picture of the encirclement of cities by the rural areas. In the final analysis, the whole cause of world revolution hinges on the revolutionary struggles of the Asian, African, and Latin American peoples who make up the overwhelming majority of the world's population. The socialist countries should regard it as their internationalist duty to support the people's revolutionary struggles in Asia, Africa, and Latin America.[110]

The united front concept was enacted in Korea, Vietnam, as well as other nations. Mao said of the Vietnamese in 1967 that "their struggle is our struggle," and China's territory was their rear area.[111] Though these wars were fought abroad, they retained Mao's main precepts of the primacy of guerrilla warfare and protracted war. The exception is in Korea, where they engaged in mass warfare at enormous costs. For Mao, the road to military success, whether in China or externally, was people's war. Lin Biao commented on military modernization in 1965:

However highly developed modern weapons and technical equipment may be and however complicated the methods of modern warfare, in the final analysis the outcome of a war will be decided by the sustained fighting of the ground forces, by the fighting at close quarters on battlefields, by the political consciousness of the men, by their courage and spirit of sacrifice.... The spiritual atom bomb which the revolutionary people possess is a far more powerful and useful weapon than the physical atom bomb.[112]

Nuclear Policy

One anomalous aspect of Mao's defense concept during this period was his view of nuclear weapons and their role in national defense. Though people's war was considered superior to atom bombs, Mao believed that a nuclear-weapons capability was in China's interest, resulting in the nuclear tests of 1964 and 1965. This understanding resulted from his experiences with nuclear threats from the United States during the Korean War and over Quemoy and Matsu in 1954 and 1955.[113] The primary form of defense remained guerrilla warfare and protracted war, but nuclear weapons and missiles were intended to prevent hegemonistic foreign nuclear powers from exerting influence on China.

China and the Military Modernization of 1985

After several decades of guerrilla warfare with a central role for the People's Army as the reigning strategy for facing the adversary, China undertook a radical transformation in its approach to its military forces and war fighting. First, moderate modernizing changes were instituted during the 1970s, with the PLA's role in the Cultural Revolution.[114] After the adoption of the four modernizations in 1978, new strategic concepts were gradually formulated and implemented, and the necessity of modernizing the military gained support. Rather than a dispersed guerrilla army relying upon space and time to gain the advantage over a superior adversary, the Communist Party under Deng Xiaoping decided to form a modern, high-technology military that would be capable of fighting against enemy forces in a modern, regular war.

Deng in the early 1980s first initiated an intermediate move toward "people's war" under "modern conditions," an idea that did not seem markedly different from the previous strategy, but in actuality was the first step in forming a professional military to repulse threats at or beyond China's borders.[115] In 1985, China began the shift in its military policies. In a speech to the Central Military Commission, Deng stated that modernization of the military is a necessary goal and part of the four modernizations, but that the process of modernization must be subordinate to economic development.[116] In order to implement the modernization, a troop reduction of 1 million men would be necessary, and modernization of army equipment would have to wait. The priority was as follows: "[W]hen we are strong economically, we shall be able to spend more money on updating equipment. We can also buy some from abroad, but we should rely on ourselves to conduct research and design superior planes for the air force and equipment for the navy and army. If the economy develops, we can accomplish anything…. That is the most important thing, and everything else must be subordinated to it."[117]

Two main points encompassing China's changed understanding of the world environment explained the necessity of these sacrifices. First, unlike before, China did not see war as inevitable and imminent. Rather, world forces for peace were growing, and therefore there was no imminent danger. Second, relations between China and the United States and between China and the Soviet Union had both improved. The result of these two changes was that modernization could be embarked upon without fear, and China could absorb foreign influences to that end.[118]

Adopting a New Military Strategy

In terms of war fighting strategy, the new military concepts promoted forward defense rather than drawing the enemy in to divide and conquer. Keeping combatants on the periphery of the nation became the optimal strategy, and recognition of the enhanced importance of technology in gaining military superiority led to new operational concepts. China implemented combined arms-warfare training in the 1980s, using integrated armor, artillery, and air defense to develop the capability to repel an enemy attack.[119] The hierarchy of the military services in national defense also changed drastically. Whereas under the people's war doctrine the PLA was dominant and an extended land war was the optimal strategy, the modernization brought with it a new importance to the navy and air force. The PLA embarked upon a fundamental shift from continental to peripheral defense.[120] "Today and toward 2000 the PLA is attempting to implement a doctrine of flexible response for multiple missions based on high-technology weapons and a diversified-yet integrated-force structure."[121] Called "active defense," the new strategy required "a high level of readiness and willingness to fight and win, so as to deter war in peacetime. It also means strategic defense with operational and tactical offensive operations in wartime."[122] According to a Chinese military official, "The Chinese military is transforming itself from one which is only superior in quantity to one which is also superior in quality, and from one which is manpower-intensive to one which is technology-intensive."[123] Under the new, more offensive strategies, the navy and air force gained importance as part of an integrated force for fighting forward deployed positions.

The shift to modern warfare necessitated adoption of new, highly centralized command and control systems and a reorganized force structure. Field armies were restructured into group armies that combined armor, infantry, artillery, and other ground force branches in a single command.[124] In 1983, internal security forces of the PLA were separated into the People's Armed Police so that the main body of the PLA could prepare for foreign threats. Defense Minister Zhang Aiping outlined the new concept in stating that "the sophisticated nature of our military equipment, [and] the quality of our personnel who use the equipment" were critical in achieving a military victory.[125]

The retirements of 40 senior general staff officers were followed by cuts in the military budget, further retirements of 47,000 officers (in 1986), and conventional force reductions of 1 million men. The army redistributed money to technological modernization of weapons systems and professional training for the officer corps. In addition, the nonegalitarian tradition of rank insignia was reinstated.[126] Rapid reaction ground forces called "Fist Formations" were also created to address both external and internal threats.[127] The new emphasis was on a younger, educated, professional military with high-technology weaponry, a radical shift from the grassroots people's army concept of the Cultural Revolution. From a total of 3.9 million in 1985, the armed forces had been reduced to approximately 2.25 million by 2004.[128] The defense budget in the same time frame increased from $30 billion to $56 billion, according to The International Institute for Strategic Studies (IISS) estimates.

The new military concept included expanded roles for the PLA Navy (PLAN) and the PLA Air Force (PLAAF) for integrated operations, reflecting a wider conception of China's security interests. Rather than an air force and a navy that could defend a limited perimeter of China's borders, the new PLAAF and PLAN were to have an extended reach into the Pacific and Indian oceans and along China's land borders.

In structuring the modernization, Deng Xiaoping denoted the air force as a priority area for investment, over the army and navy.[129] The air force gradually shifted from a strictly subordinate position in the military, as support only, to an independent strategic role. In doing so, its primarily defensive strategy began a transformation into a more offensive strategy requiring air superiority.[130] Numbers of aging aircraft were retired, and implementation of a smaller, more modern force was initiated. In pursuit of a more rapidly upgraded force, the PLAAF purchased 200 Su-27s as well as 38 Su-30MKKs in 1999 and 28 Su-30MK2s in 2003 from Russia and reached an agreement on joint production of the fighter aircraft.[131] The air power–led victory of the Gulf War provided much support for this conceptual change and highlighted the need for further technological advances.

Deng expanded the role of the PLA Navy to include protection of territorial waters outside of China's coastline, particularly the South China Sea, Taiwan, and trade routes.[132] Whereas prior to reforms, the Navy's role was coastal defense to 200 km from the coast, modernization required that it take on an offensive role and increase to a blue-water naval capability, out to 2,000 km from the coast.[133] The PLAN's focus was on developing an aircraft carrier and expanding its submarine fleet. The initiative to develop the aircraft carrier is known as Project 9935. The carrier is being modeled after the Russian *Admiral Gorshkov,* and China has plans to build up to three of these carriers.[134] The implications of this array of new weapons is that China's naval reach has been expanded in its ability to defend against foreign navies, in particular, through a wide spectrum of cruise missiles that can be used against enemy ships. The strategic goal is to have a blue-water capability out to the Kuriles, the Bonin and Marina islands, and Papua New Guinea by the year 2020.[135]

Nuclear Forces in China

Nuclear forces do not appear to be a primary focus of the Chinese defense modernization. This may be because the strategic goal of "minimum deterrence" has already been accomplished by the development of nuclear weapons and credible delivery systems.[136] According to The Stockholm International Peace Research Institute (SIPRI) data, China possesses approximately 400 deployed nuclear warheads and several delivery systems, including aircraft and both medium- and long-range missiles.[137] The Chinese nuclear capabilities are not considered a main part of the modernization program, as they were tested and incorporated into defense strategy since 1964. However, China has continued to test its nuclear weapons in order to modernize and increase the accuracy of capabilities.[138] The conceptual basis for the nuclear deterrent in China remains the same as in Mao's era, to prevent hegemonistic foreign powers from exerting influence over China. However, these goals and the Intercontinental Ballistic Missile (ICBM) delivery systems for the nuclear warheads are in accordance with the high-technology, peripheral defense strategy of the military modernization program.

China's shift to a modern, professional military equipped with high-technology weaponry reflects a new direction in its defense program and implies a new set of national priorities. Correspondingly, India's defense strategy and policies changed from those of a primarily land-based military prepared for territorial defense to one that is undergoing a gradual transformation into a modernized, more technologically proficient force with nuclear capabilities.

Military in India and Grassroots Defense

The philosophical basis for Indian security and defense was largely formed by the success of nonviolent resistance as a strategy led by Gandhi against the British. As the concept of guerrilla warfare had proven effective for Mao in China's case, Gandhi believed that a form of nonviolent resistance was necessary for India. However, the effectiveness of Gandhi's strategy relied upon civil disobedience and popular participation in nonviolent resistance in opposing British imperialism rather than military strategy. This strategy was also a revolution, albeit a nonviolent one. Mass participation in the nonviolent civil-disobedience campaign was required for its effectiveness. In order to reach the broadest possible group of individuals to join in the campaign, Gandhi considered the spread of the spiritual bases for the movement of the utmost importance. In explaining this necessity, Gandhi wrote thus:

> I realized that before a people could be fit for offering civil disobedience, they should thoroughly understand its deeper implications. That being so, before re-starting civil disobedience on a mass scale, it would be necessary to create a band of well-tried, pure-hearted volunteers who thoroughly understood the strict conditions of *Satyagraha*.[139] They could explain these to the people, and by sleepless vigilance keep them on the right path.[140]

Nonviolent civil disobedience became the practical and philosophical basis for all security concerns, internal and external, because its strength derived from individual spiritual transformation. If people could be perfectable, then violent means would not be necessary for the attainment of political or military ends. Gandhi's philosophy had a deep and enduring influence on the thinking of Indians of all religions and classes and led many to have faith in nonviolent methods as an alternative to a traditional military-led defense. The effectiveness of the nonviolence movement in liberating India from British rule thus undermined the notion of a strong, modern military as necessary for the country's national defense in the public consciousness.

After independence, India under Jawaharlal Nehru followed a strategy of nonalignment in order to avoid entangling India's fate with the ongoing Cold War rivalries and to avoid dependence on other countries.[141] As a poor nation, the focus of the Indian government was on internal development and economic issues. In terms of foreign policy, Nehru viewed Asia as a type of family of nations working together against imperialism, writing, "There is some meaning when we say that we stand for the freedom of Asian countries and for the elimination of imperialistic control over them,"[142] revealing some similarity with the worldview of China in the same time period. Nehru assumed that in the postcolonial period, Asian nations would work together and thus a strong defense strategy would be unnecessary for India. Nonalignment would ensure the ability of each nation to pursue its interests without imperialist or other (Cold War) intervention. Nations would be able to peacefully resolve problems big or small. Peace as a strategy was made explicit in the concept of *panchsheel*, or the Five Principles of Peaceful Coexistence, which he promoted internationally, and which China concurrently adopted in 1955 in Bandung. This concept underpinned the Non-Aligned Movement (NAM) with five basic principles: (1) mutual respect for each other's territorial integrity and sovereignty, (2) mutual nonaggression, (3) mutual noninterference in each other's internal affairs, (4) equality and mutual benefit, and (5) peaceful coexistence.[143] Overall, Nehru rejected the military perspective in formulating a strategy for national defense. He believed that the Indian National Army had a role in protecting India's sovereignty but that its role need not be more expansive than that. Nehru perceived alliances such as Central Treaty Organization and Southeast Asia Treaty Organization as detrimental and overly militaristic.[144]

A concentrated focus on the principles of nonviolence, nonalignment, and peaceful coexistence resulted in a marginalization of the military after independence. Recognized was the need for a military to ensure the safety of borders and a paramilitary force to tame civil unrest. However, the Indian leadership did not view professionalization of the military and acquisition of modern weaponry as essential to the limited goals set out for Indian defense.

The military was initially primarily focused on the threat from Pakistan, which had had a war with India at independence. The nature of the threat necessitated a large ground army with some air and sea capabilities. During this period, Nehru did not view China as a threat. Nehru believed in a pan-Asian concept of peace that precluded war with the Chinese. A prevalent phrase reflecting the Indian view of China in the 1950s was "Hindi-Chini bhai-bhai," meaning that Indians and Chinese are brothers. However, rising tensions over Tibet and border demarcation led to war in 1962 between the two countries. India was defeated soundly. In the aftermath, Nehru and the Indian defense establishment were forced to reassess the threats and the necessary strategies. In 1964, China's first nuclear test also had an impact on Indian strategic thought. Coming so soon after their defeat by China, the nuclear tests forced the Indian leadership and strategic community to begin reconsidering a nuclear option. Soon after, Pakistan initiated an attack in 1965 as an unsuccessful attempt to take Kashmir. The combined effect of these encounters with its neighbors led India to pursue a more aggressive weapons procurement and development policy in the following years. Ideological and diplomatic leanings translated into large purchases from the Soviet Union. In the next few decades, India began a moderate increase in military procurements. During the period from 1964–1989, India was able to procure, among others, more than 200 MiG-21, with licensed production of 140 more, 135 MiG-23, 65 MiG-29, and 140 Su-7 fighters, several submarines and destroyers, several hundred T-55 and T-72 main battle tanks, and thousands of surface-to-air missiles (SAMs) and air-to-air missiles.[145] At the same time, India continued to buy weaponry from France, Britain, and the United States, albeit in smaller quantities, to avoid complete dependency on the Soviet Union for supplies.[146]

Although this buildup was marked in comparison to the original Nehruvian defense concepts, it was directed primarily toward the regional and border threats to India. A limited capability was established to repel any further threats from Pakistan while simultaneously being able to hold the Chinese at bay, or vice versa. The Indian military and weaponry was not intended or expected to address threats far from India's borders or from any advanced nations.

Nuclear Weapons

Nehru was deeply committed to the nuclear nonproliferation movement. In 1961, he stated in response to the Soviet decision to test, "I am against nuclear weapons at any time in any place."[147] In 1947, Nehru admitted the need for India to begin nuclear research, but the intended goal was energy rather than weaponry.[148] Throughout the 1950s, Nehru supported several initiatives for disarmament in and out of the United Nations. Total disarmament through dismantling of bombs, ending of tests, and public declaration of all not to manufacture nuclear weapons was his intended outcome.[149] However, his concession to its use for peaceful purposes led to the existence of further nuclear research in India. A nuclear energy program with the help of CIRUS (Canada-India and U.S. Research Reactor) was begun in 1960 with a 40 MW thermal reactor meant only for "peaceful" purposes. Because there were no formal safeguards and decision making remained decentralized, the spent fuel was reprocessed by Homi Bhabha, head of India's nuclear program, to extract plutonium eventually used in the 1974 test.[150]

After China's victory in 1962 and its nuclear test in 1964, however, the nuclear establishment in India became more aggressive as India became less and less enthusiastic about the possibility of global disarmament. Despite these pressures from the nuclear establishment in India, Prime Minister Lal Bahadur Shastri in 1965 and Prime Minister Indira Gandhi in 1968 both declined the option of pursuing weaponization. Finally in 1974, Indira Gandhi conducted the "peaceful nuclear explosion" and then consistently denied its use for weapons or any other aggressive use: "We in India have condemned and will continue to condemn military uses of nuclear energy as a threat to humanity," and "There are no political or foreign policy implications of this test."[151] The Indian public received the

1974 test poorly, and the subsequent government of Morarji Desai (1978) did not lend its support to the program. The general antinuclear weaponization policy remained in effect until the late 1980s and changed in tandem with a shift in military perspective, both of which would reflect an increase in the depth and the scope of India's defense strategy.

India and the Conceptual Shift to a Modern Defense

Similar to the transformation occurring in China's defense policies, India began a shift to a modern, expansive defense with high-technology capabilities aimed at deterrence of major powers. By the mid-1980s, Indian defense planners and elites had started to move toward a different definition of security for India. Rather than a limited concept encompassing the areas immediately surrounding the country, a blue-water navy, new aircraft carriers, nuclear submarines, long-range missiles, and nuclear capabilities all became imperative. The Indian defense establishment exhibited this push for new development and procurements in three main ways: high technological capabilities, extended reach, and effectiveness against threats from developed as well as less developed countries.

The transition from a more limited concept of Indian defense to one with expanded geographic and technological capabilities has been described as a shift from a "minimalist" to a "maximalist" strategy. The former Indian minimalist strategy was based upon the threat from China and Pakistan, and the maximalist policy of the 1980s and the 1990s included the Middle East, the Indian Ocean, and Southeast Asia.[152] India's more expansive geographic area of military interest can be seen clearly through its increasing procurement of extended-reach advanced weaponry systems in the army, the navy, and the air force, as well as by its new reliance upon nuclear-weapons capabilities.

The Indian Army from the 1990s onward placed greater emphasis on development of the indigenous missile programs for the short-range Prithvi (150 km/500 kg) and the intermediate-range Agni II (2500 km/ 1000 kg).[153] During the previous decades, missiles with shorter range were considered sufficient because of their capability to bring all of Pakistan into range. The expanded definition of security, however, has translated into these IRBMs (intermediate-range ballistic missiles) that can bring parts of the western part of China into range. Further missile development is certainly possible: "India has the technical expertise to pursue an ICBM capability. It has successfully launched both the Polar Space Launch Vehicle and the Geo-Synchronous Space Launch Vehicle, which could serve as a technological springboard for an ICBM capability."[154] In 2000, the Indian Army acquired 310 Russian T-90 tanks, with 124 imported directly and the remainder produced under license.[155] They concurrently increased production and modernization of the T-72 tank.[156]

The Indian Air Force gradually upgraded its forces during this time period, with procurement of several advanced aircraft. The Indian Air Force in 2000 bought 140 Russian Su-30MKI strike aircraft, to be made under license by Hindustan Aeronautics Limited.[157] They also ordered 10 Mirage 2000H fighter aircraft from Dassault Aviation, to be delivered by 2004 to add to the 38 Mirage 2000Hs in service.[158] In addition, the air force version of the Agni II ballistic missile has a range of 250 km for a 500–750 kg payload.[159] India's nuclear capable aircraft included the Jaguar, with a capability of 900–1400 km/1000 kg, the Mirage 2000, the Su-30, as well as the MiG-27 and MiG-29.[160] Air-refueling tankers, the Il-78, have been purchased to extend the range of the Su-30 to 5000 km. Creation of India's "credible nuclear deterrent" relies upon a combination of the nuclear capable aircraft in the air force, as well as on land-based missile capabilities. Nonetheless, the air force fighter aircraft are considered more reliable for delivery of nuclear weapons than the developing missile capabilities. In addition to these advances, India in 2003 signed a major deal with Israel for three Phalcon airborne early warning systems.

The Indian Navy also expanded its role by increasing the geographic area and the nature of the threat that must be covered in order to ensure India's security interests. Whereas in the past the threat was primarily seen as military, it has since the 1990s defined the threat as both military and economic, "In view of the geo-political situation, the Indian Ocean Region has attained immense significance. Also, to provide protection to our trade, it is necessary to have the requisite Naval capability."[161] These ideas translated into the necessity for a blue-water navy with nuclear submarines and new aircraft carriers. In 2004, India signed an agreement for the *Admiral Gorshkov* aircraft carrier and MiG-29 carrier-based fighters from the Russians. Chief of Indian Naval Staff Admiral Sushil Kumar also outlined a new naval doctrine with plans to acquire a blue-water navy with two aircraft carriers by the year 2010.[162] However, the navy would have to repair and refit the *Admiral Gorshkov* and replace the retired *Viraat* aircraft carrier in order to achieve this goal. The *Admiral Gorshkov* is expected to take five years to refit. Also, the Indian Navy does not have a submarine-launch ballistic missile capability or a nuclear-powered submarine, although they are under development.[163]

India's Nuclear Tests

India's concept of a modernized defense capability has also included its recently tested nuclear capabilities and weaponization. Although the first nuclear test was conducted in 1974, India did not state that the purpose was to weaponize at that time. Rather, Indira Gandhi claimed the test was a peaceful nuclear explosion.[164] In marked contrast, the tests conducted by the BJP government in May of 1998 were an explicit message to the international community that India was a nuclear power. The adoption of a nuclear deterrent as part of India's defense strategy is also significant in that it is a radical departure from Nehruvian and Gandhian concepts of peace, nonviolence, and opposition to nuclear weapons.

The transition to an aggressive nuclear posture can be seen both through India's decision to conduct the tests in May of 1998 and in the government's actions to acquire delivery systems for nuclear material. Initial signs to the international community that the government of India was considering testing nuclear weapons came in 1995. In advance of the coming into effect of the CTBT (Comprehensive Test Ban Treaty), Prime Minister Narasimha Rao prepared to test at Pokhran but was deterred when the United States discovered the plans and international furor erupted as a result. In 1996, during the brief coalition government of the BJP under A. B. Vajpayee, nuclear testing was considered but rejected on the grounds that the government had a tenuous hold on its majority in Parliament. In 1997, Prime Minister Gujral considered testing but deferred. The hawkish BJP government under P. M. Vajpayee finally actually conducted the tests in May of 1998, with considerable popular support. Prime Minister Manmohan Singh subsequently continued support for India's nuclear-weapons capability. The change in popular and political support for a nuclear-weapons option in India from the 1980s to 2005 reflected a fundamental shift in the Indian view of national security and requirements for national defense. According to SIPRI data, India in 2005 was estimated to possess approximately 30–40 nuclear warheads.

In addition to the new acceptance of a nuclear option as necessary for national defense, the Indian government began acquiring delivery systems for offensive, long-range operations. Nuclear-capable missiles, aircraft, and submarines were procured, or are being procured by the services. The IRBM Agni could provide a delivery system for the nuclear material, and the short-range Prithvi is configured for the same. In the Indian Air Force, the Dassault Aviation Mirage 2000H fighters and the British-made Jaguar are capable of carrying nuclear weapons, and the Russian MiG-27 Flogger and the Su-30 as well have the capability. The change in popular and political support in India for a nuclear-weapons option and delivery systems from the 1980s to 2005 reflected a fundamental shift in the Indian view of national security and requirements for national defense: that higher technology capabilities and extended reach would be increasingly necessary to protect India's interests.

In terms of command and control, overall authority remains the prime minister's, aided by the Cabinet Committee on Security (CCS). The members of the National Security Council, which include the Strategic Policy Group, the National Security Advisory Board, and the Joint Intelligence Committee also provide input. The National Security Council's role is to help frame security policy, while taking into consideration both military and nonmilitary threats, and to increase the input of the service chiefs in the decision-making process. These changes in command and control are meant to strengthen the power and the efficiency of the military and security infrastructure. Whereas under Nehru, the powers of the military and security apparatus were thought best proscribed, the new concept expands the role of defense and allows for greater defense influence on foreign policy through the CCS. The establishment of the CCS and National Security Council as an institution for processing and developing national security policy, in conjunction with the pursuit of advanced missile and nuclear technology, has been another example of a new strategic thinking in India.

Conclusion

China and India as new nations embarked upon apparently differing paths designed to enhance their economic development and national security. China under Mao followed a path of revolution, both economic and military, to attain the goals of a Socialist, Communist society. India under the leadership of Nehru and Gandhi pursued the path of nonviolence and peaceful cooperation in the security realm and a moderate Socialism as the economic model. A similarity in the focus of both nations was the acceptance of the Socialist goal as a practical and ideal development path. However, the implementation and extent of the Socialist ideas varied dramatically between India and China.

As both countries entered the 1980s and the 1990s, they adopted reforms with respect to the economy and defense, which amplified the similarities in approach. China and India undertook radical economic reforms requiring liberalization, opening to foreign goods, and selling of state-owned enterprises. Ideologically vastly different from the Socialist models followed for decades, the new economic reforms in both countries required acceptance of income inequality, unemployment, and vulnerability to the vagaries of the international economic system in exchange for rapid economic growth.

China and India subjected their security concepts to similarly drastic reforms. Whereas China under Mao had relied upon a guerrilla-type, protracted war concept for effecting revolution and defeating a superior enemy, and India under the direction of Nehru and Gandhi utilized peace concepts against the British and a minimalist military against Pakistan to emerge victorious, by the late 1970s, a transition to increasingly similar policies was under way. Both nations changed to a similar defense doctrine in the 1980s and the 1990s, looking to new technology and to geographic necessities as the basis for future strategy. Rather than maintaining forces for basic territorial defense, China and India have adopted security strategies for modern war, force projection, and offensive operations, and a similarly broader definition of the geographic area of maximum concern.

China's and India's similarities in the two major fields of economics and security provide an opportunity for understanding the manner in which policy decisions are determined. Although both countries have pursued parallel paths in reforming their economies and defense capabilities, it is necessary to study whether these changes were made for the same reasons. The ultimate purpose for these fundamental changes reflects the changing national goals held by the decision-making elite in each country. By analyzing these elites' perceptions of the importance of national identity, globalization, sovereignty, and the role of political institutions in each country, valuable insights into the formation of these national interests can be drawn. The following chapters will investigate the process by which perceptions of the national interest are formed in each country.

Notes

1. Feng Chen, *Economic Transition and Political Legitimacy in Post-Mao China: Ideology and Reform* (Albany: State University of New York, 1995), 24.

2. Mao Tse-tung, "Cast Away Illusions, Prepare for Struggle," 14 August 1949, in *Selected Works of Mao Tse-tung* (Peking: Foreign Languages Press, 1961), 4:426.

3. Mao Tse-tung, "Report on an Investigation of the Peasant Movement in Hunan," March 1927, in *Selected Works of Mao Tse-tung* (Peking: Foreign Languages Press, 1965), 1:24.

4. Mao Tse-tung, "On New Democracy," January 1940, in *Selected Works of Mao Tse-tung* (Peking: Foreign Languages Press, 1965), 2:353–354.

5. Mao Tse-tung, "Report to the Second Plenary Session of the Seventh Central Committee of the Communist Party of China," 5 March 1949, in *Selected Works of Mao Tse-tung* (Peking: Foreign Languages Press, 1961), 4:364–365.

6. Mao Tse-tung, "Report to the Second Plenary Session of the Seventh Central Committee of the Communist Party of China," 5 March 1949, in *Selected Works of Mao Tse-tung* (Peking: Foreign Languages Press, 1961), 4:369; Feng Chen, *Economic Transition and Political Legitimacy,* 26.

7. Mao Tse-tung, "On the Cooperative Transformation of Agriculture," 31 July 1955, in *Selected Works of Mao Tse-tung* (Peking: Foreign Languages Press, 1977), 5:202.

8. State capitalism was defined as the regrouping into "joint state-private enterprises," where former owners became state employees who collected interest payments from the state based upon the state's estimate of the value of their shares in the enterprise. (See Feng Chen, *Economic Transition and Political Legitimacy,* 27.).

9. Feng Chen, *Economic Transition and Political Legitimacy,* 27.

10. Mao Tse-tung, "Prefaces to Socialist Upsurge in China's Countryside," 27 December 1955, in *Selected Works of Mao Tse-tung* (Peking: Foreign Languages Press, 1977), 5:235-241.

11. Feng Chen, *Economic Transition and Political Legitimacy,* 29.

12. Paul Bowles and Gordon White, *The Political Economy of China's Financial Reforms* (Boulder: Westview Press, 1993), 68. See also Feng Chen, *Economic Transition and Political Legitimacy,* 28, for full statistics.

13. Bowles and White, *The Political Economy,* 69.

14. Feng Chen, *Economic Transition and Political Legitimacy,* 29.

15. Mao Tse-tung, "The Chinese People Have Stood Up!" 21 September 1949, in *Selected Works of Mao Tse-tung* (Peking: Foreign Languages Press, 1977), 5:18.

16. Feng Chen, *Economic Transition and Political Legitimacy,* 30.

17. Feng Chen, *Economic Transition and Political Legitimacy,* 30–31.

18. Michael W. Bell, Hoe Ee Khor, and Kalpana Kochhar, *Occasional Paper 107: China at the Threshold of a Market Economy* (Washington, DC: International Monetary Fund, 1993), 6.

19. Economic data for this period is also incomplete and somewhat questionable, due to the insular nature of Mao's China. This adds to the difficulty in discerning the true nature of the economic system in the pre-reform era.

20. *China Statistical Yearbook, 1992.* (Beijing: State Statistical Bureau).

21. Ibid.

22. The phases are as follows: from 1979–1983 the shift to economic development as an indicator of success, inception of special economic zones; 1984–1988 market and planned economy mixed, contract responsibility system, banking reforms; 1989–1992 retrenchment after Tiananmen incident, 1992–1997 Deng's southern tour, building market institutions, privatization of SOEs; 1997–2000 emphasis on private ownership after the 15th Party Congress, forming legal structure to support market economy.

23. Deng Xiaoping, "Hold High the Banner of Mao Zedong Thought and Adhere to the Principle of Seeking Truth from Facts," 16 September 1978, in *Selected Works of Deng Xiaoping: 1975–1982* (Beijing: Foreign Languages Press, 1984), 141.

24. Deng, "Hold High the Banner of Mao Zedong Thought," 141.

25. The four modernizations are the modernization of China's industry, agriculture, national defense, and science and technology.

26. Deng, "Hold High the Banner of Mao Zedong Thought," 143.

27. Deng Xiaoping, "Emancipate the Mind, Seek Truth from Facts and Unite as One in Looking to the Future," 13 December 1978, in *Selected Works of Deng Xiaoping: 1975-1982* (Beijing: Foreign Languages Press, 1984), 157.

28. Deng, "Emancipate the Mind, Seek Truth from Facts and Unite as One in Looking to the Future," 163–164.

29. Deng Xiaoping, "We Can Develop a Market Economy under Socialism," 26 November 1979, in *Selected Works of Deng Xiaoping,* vol. 2 (http://english.people.com.cn/dengxp/contents2.html).

30. Penelope Hartland-Thunberg, *A Decade of China's Economic Reform* (Washington, DC: CSIS, 1989), 4.

31. Richard Baum, "The Road to Tiananmen," in *The Politics of China: The Eras of Mao and Deng*, ed. Roderick MacFarquhar (Cambridge: Cambridge University Press, 1997), 376.

32. Gordon White, "The Chinese Developmental State in the Reform Era," in *The Chinese State in the Era of Economic Reform*, ed. Gordon White (Armonk, NY: M. E. Sharpe, 1991), 3.

33. Hartland-Thunberg, *A Decade of China's Economic Reform*, 22.

34. Hartland-Thunberg, *A Decade of China's Economic Reform*, 22.

35. Hartland-Thunberg, *A Decade of China's Economic Reform*, 30.

36. Bell, Khor, and Kochhar, *China at the Threshold of a Market Economy*, 19.

37. Bell, Khor, and Kochhar, *China at the Threshold of a Market Economy*, 19.

38. Bell, Khor, and Kochhar, *China at the Threshold of a Market Economy*, 19.

39. Jude Howell, "The Impact of the Open Door Policy on the Chinese State," in *The Chinese State in the Era of Economic Reform*, ed. Gordon White (Armonk, NY: M. E. Sharpe, 1991), 119.

40. William Martin and Christian Bach, "State Trading in China," in *State Trading in the Twenty-First Century, World Trade Forum, Volume I*, ed. Thomas Cottier and Petros C. Mavroidis (Ann Arbor: The University of Michigan Press, 1998), 289.

41. Martin and Bach, "State Trading in China," 290.

42. Jude Howell, in *The Chinese State in the Era of Economic Reform*, ed. Gordon White (Armonk, NY: M. E. Sharpe, 1991), 123.

43. *World Development Indicators*, World Bank China Data Profile, http://www.worldbank.org/data/countrydata/countrydata.html (accessed May 24, 2005); Ligang Song, "Trade Liberalisation and Development of China's Foreign Trade," in *China's Entry to the WTO*, ed. Peter Drysdale and Ligang Song (New York: Routledge, 2000), 67.

44. Bowles and White, *The Political Economy of China's Financial Reforms*, 58. During the Great Leap Forward and the Cultural Revolution, the PBC was under supervision of the Ministry of Finance.

45. Bowles and White, *The Political Economy of China's Financial Reforms*, 72.

46. The ABC, ICB, PCBC, and BoC became known as the specialized banks.

47. Bowles and White, *The Political Economy of China's Financial Reforms*, 75. The China International Trust and Investment company (CITIC) was also established in 1979 to encourage foreign investment and joint ventures.

48. Bowles and White, *The Political Economy of China's Financial Reforms*, 75.

49. Baizhu Chen, J. Kimball Dietrich, and Yi Feng, *Financial Market Reform in China: Progress, Problems, and Prospects* (Boulder, CO: Westview Press, 2000), 16.

50. Qian Yingyi, "The Institutional Foundations of China's Market Transition," The World Bank, ABCDE Conference (Washington, DC: The World Bank, 1999), 27.

51. Baizhu Chen, Dietrich, and Feng, *Financial Market Reform in China*, 7.

52. Qian Yingyi, "The Institutional Foundations of China's Market Transition," 29.

53. James Kynge, "China's Liabilities," *Financial Times*, 22 January 2002, 14.

54. Nicholas Lardy, "China and the Asian Financial Contagion," in *Financial Market Reform in China: Progress, Problems, and Prospects*, ed. Baizhu Chen, J. Kimball Dietrich, and Yi Feng (Boulder, CO: Westview Press, 2000), 29.

55. Bell, Khor, and Kochhar, *China at the Threshold of a Market Economy*, 16.

56. Hartland-Thunberg, *A Decade of China's Economic Reform*, 21.

57. Bell, Khor, and Kochhar, *China at the Threshold of a Market Economy*, 17.

58. Bell, Khor, and Kochhar, *China at the Threshold of a Market Economy*, 17.

59. In 1992, TVEs were estimated to employ more than 100 million workers out of a rural labor force of 430 million. See Bell, Khor, and Kochhar, *China at the Threshold of a Market Economy*, 17.

60. Marx had written, "It was the British intruder who broke up the Indian handloom and destroyed the spinning wheel. England began with driving the Indian cottons from the European markets … and in the end inundated the very mother country of cotton with cottons … British steam and science uprooted, over the whole surface of Hindostan, the union between agricultural and manufacturing industry." M. N. Das, *The Political Philosophy of Nehru* (New York: George Allen & Unwin, 1961), 128.

61. Das, *The Political Philosophy of Nehru*, 157.

62. Das, *The Political Philosophy of Nehru*, 135. Gandhi said, "Even when I die, you will have to admit that Gandhi was a true socialist."

63. Das, *The Political Philosophy of Nehru*, 147.

64. Rashmi-Sudha Puri, *Gandhi on War and Peace* (New York: Praeger Publishers, 1987), 204–206.

65. M. K. Gandhi, *Gandhi's Autobiography: The Story of My Experiments with Truth* (Washington, DC: Public Affairs Press, 1948), 588–589.

66. Das, *The Political Philosophy of Nehru*, 164.

67. Vijay Joshi and I. M. D. Little, *India: Macroeconomics and Political Economy, 1964–1991* (Washington, DC: The World Bank, 1994), 9.

68. T. N. Srinivasan, "Planning and Foreign Trade Reconsidered," in *Foundations of India's Political Economy*, ed. Subroto Roy and William E. James (New Delhi: Sage Publications, 1992), 115.

69. Srinivasan, "Planning and Foreign Trade Reconsidered," 138.

70. In 1966, the rupee was devalued by 36.5 percent along with other measures designed to help India qualify for increased aid from the World Bank and the International Monetary Fund (IMF). (Joshi and Little, *India: Macroeconomics and Political Economy*, 49). Controls on the exchange rate were loosened somewhat, licensing restrictions were loosened on imports of intermediate and capital goods, and some import competing goods (148).

71. Srinivasan, "Planning and Foreign Trade Reconsidered," 140.

72. Shalendra D. Sharma, *Development and Democracy in India* (Boulder, CO: Lynne Rienner Publishers, 1999), 95.

73. Sharma, *Development and Democracy in India*, 101.

74. Sharma, *Development and Democracy in India*, 101.

75. Sharma, *Development and Democracy in India*, 196.

76. Sharma, *Development and Democracy in India*, 126.

77. Sharma, *Development and Democracy in India*, 144.

78. By the end of the 1980s, the fiscal improprieties of the government had surpassed the benefits of moderate liberalization, resulting in a severe balance of payments crisis in 1990 and 1991. The public debt to gross national product ratio by 1990 was almost double the figure from 1980. The main cause of this was the phenomenal rise in foreign borrowing, leading to more resources allotted to debt servicing and plummeting foreign reserves. The IMF extended loans to India with the

requirement that India undertake structural reforms and reduce the budget deficit.

79. Martin Wolf, "India: Slow Reforms Promise Better Times," *Financial Times*, 19 September 1997.

80. Ajai Chopra, Woosik Chu, and Oliver Fratzscher, "Structural Reforms and the Implications for Investment and Growth," in *India: Economic Reform and Growth*, Occasional Paper 134 (Washington, DC: International Monetary Fund, 1995), 54.

81. Sharma, *Development and Democracy in India*, 224.

82. Javad Khalilzadeh-Shirazi and Roberto Zagha, "Economic Reforms in India; Achievements and the Agenda Ahead," *Columbia Journal of World Business* 29, no. 1 (22 March 1994): 65.

83. The Economist Intelligence Unit, *India Country Profile 2001* (London: The Economist Intelligence Unit, 2001), 24.

84. Khalilzadeh-Shirazi and Zagha, "Economic Reforms in India," 24.

85. Chopra, Chu, and Fratzscher, "Structural Reforms," 54.

86. Sharma, *Development and Democracy in India*, 224.

87. The Economist Intelligence Unit, *India Country Report* (London: The Economist Intelligence Unit, 2002), 37.

88. Sharma, *Development and Democracy in India*, 225.

89. Cash Reserve Ratios refers to the required percentage of reserves by banks; large reserved percentages are considered to preempt resources that could be used for investment.

90. Khalilzadeh-Shirazi and Zagha, "Economic Reforms in India."

91. The World Bank, *India: Sustaining Rapid Economic Growth, A World Bank Country Study* (Washington, DC: The World Bank, 1997), xv.

92. "RBI's Guarded Approach to Interest Rate Changes," *The Hindu*, 2 May 2005.

93. Khalilzadeh-Shirazi and Zagha, "Economic Reforms in India."

94. Sharma, *Development and Democracy in India*, 226.

95. Sharma, *Development and Democracy in India*, 226.

96. The Economist Intelligence Unit, *India Country Profile 2001* (London: The Economist Intelligence Unit, 2001), 23.

97. Sharma, *Development and Democracy in India*, 227.

98. Mao Tse-tung, *Mao Tse-tung: On Revolution and War*, ed. M. Rejai (Gloucester: Peter Smith, 1976), 382.

99. Mao Tse-tung, *Mao Tse-tung: On Revolution and War*, 234.

100. Mao Tse-tung, "Turn the Army into a Working Force," 8 February 1949, in *Selected Works of Mao Tse-tung* (Peking: Foreign Languages Press, 1961), 4:337.

101. Mao Tse-tung, "Notes on the Report of Further Improving the Army's Agricultural Work by the Rear Service Department of the Military Commission," 7 May 1966, *Long Live Mao Tse-tung Thought* (http://marxists.org/reference/archive/mao/selected-works/volume-9/mswv9_57.htm).

102. Mao Tse-tung, "On Protracted War," May 1938, in *Selected Works of Mao Tse-tung* (Peking: Foreign Languages Press, 1965), 2:124.

103. Mao Tse-tung, *Mao Tse-tung: On Revolution and War*, 235.

104. Mao Tse-tung, "A Single Spark Can Start a Prairie Fire" 5 January 1930, in *Selected Works of Mao Tse-tung* (Peking: Foreign Languages Press, 1965), 1:124.

105. Mao Tse-tung, "Problems of Strategy in the Guerrilla War Against Japan," May 1938, in *Selected Works of Mao Tse-tung* (Peking: Foreign Languages Press, 1965), 2:82.

106. Mao Tse-tung, "Problems of Strategy in the Guerrilla War Against Japan," 2:83–86.

107. Mao Tse-tung, "Problems of Strategy in the Guerrilla War Against Japan," 2:86.

108. Mao Tse-tung, "Problems of Strategy in the Guerrilla War Against Japan," 2:97–99.

109. Mao Tse-tung, "Problems of Strategy in the Guerrilla War Against Japan," 2:111.

110. Mao Tse-tung, *Mao Tse-tung: On Revolution and War,* 383.

111. Mao Tse-tung, *Mao Tse-tung: On Revolution and War,* 399.

112. Lin Piao, "Long Live the Victory of People's War!" in *Mao Tse-tung: On Revolution and War,* ed. M. Rejai (Gloucester: Peter Smith, 1976), 413.

113. Robert A. Manning, Ronald Montaperto, and Brad Roberts, *China, Nuclear Weapons, and Arms Control: A Preliminary Assessment* (New York: Council on Foreign Relations, 2000), 16.

114. Paul H. B. Godwin, "Party-Military Relations," in *The Paradox of China's Post-Mao Reforms,* ed. Merle Goldman and Roderick Macfarquhar (Cambridge, MA: Harvard University Press, 1999), 81.

115. You Ji, *The Armed Forces of China* (London: I. B. Taurus & Co., 1999), 4.

116. Deng Xiaoping, "Speech at an Enlarged Meeting of the Military Commission of the Central Committee of the Communist Party of China," 4 June 1985, *Selected Works of Deng Xiaoping,* vol. 3 (http://english.people.com.cn/dengxp/contents3.html).

117. Deng Xiaoping, 6 June 1985, *Selected Works of Deng Xiaoping,* vol. 3 (http://english.people.com.cn/dengxp/contents3.html).

118. Deng Xiaoping, 4 June 1985, *Selected Works of Deng Xiaoping,* vol. 3 (http://english.people.com.cn/dengxp/contents3.html).

119. Paul H. B. Godwin, "The PLA Faces the Twenty-First Century," in *China's Military Faces the Future,* ed. James R. Lilley and David Shambaugh (Washington, DC: American Enterprise Institute, 1999), 46.

120. David Shambaugh, "China's Military: Real or Paper Tiger?" in *The China Reader: The Reform Era,* ed. Orville Schell and David Shambaugh (New York: Vintage Books, 1999), 437.

121. Shambaugh, "China's Military: Real or Paper Tiger?" 437.

122. Military Official, "China's Defense Policy" (paper presented at the Foreign Affairs College, Beijing, 29 May 2001).

123. Military Official, "China's Defense Policy."

124. Godwin, "The PLA Faces the Twenty-First Century," 47.

125. Godwin, "The PLA Faces the Twenty-First Century," 47.

126. Baum, "The Road to Tiananmen," 377–378.

127. The International Institute for Strategic Studies, *The Military Balance 2001* (London: Oxford University Press, 2001), 172.

128. The International Institute for Strategic Studies, *The Military Balance 2004–2005* (London: Oxford University Press, 2004).

129. You Ji, *The Armed Forces of China,* 146.

130. You Ji, *The Armed Forces of China*, 124.

131. The International Institute for Strategic Studies, *The Military Balance 2004–2005*; You Ji., *The Armed Forces of China*, 157–159.

132. You Ji., *The Armed Forces of China*, 161.

133. Ehsan Ahrari, "China's Naval Forces Look to Extend their Blue-Water Reach," *Jane's Intelligence Review* 10, no. 4 (April 1, 1998): 31.

134. The International Institute for Strategic Studies, *The Military Balance 2004–2005*.

135. John Downing, "Maritime Ambition China's Naval Modernisation," *Jane's Navy International* 103, no. 4 (May 1, 1998): 8.

136. Michael Nacht and Tom Woodrow, "Nuclear Issues," in *Strategic Trends in China*, ed. Hans Binnendijk and Ronald N. Montaperto (Washington, DC: NDU Press, 1998), 82.

137. SIPRI, *SIPRI Yearbook 2005: Armaments, Disarmament, and International Security* (London: Oxford University Press, 2005), 579.

138. Shambaugh, "China's Military: Real or Paper Tiger?" 432.

139. *Satyagraha* means nonviolent resistance.

140. M. K. Gandhi, *Gandhi's Autobiography: The Story of My Experiments with Truth*, 576.

141. Jawaharlal Nehru, *India's Foreign Policy: Selected Speeches, September 1946–April 1961* (Bombay: The Publications Division, Ministry of Information and Broadcasting, Government of India, 1961), 24–29.

142. Nehru, "Non-Alignment," in *India's Foreign Policy*, 24.

143. Nehru, "The Concept of Panchsheel," in *India's Foreign Policy*, 99. The five principles of peaceful coexistence were first introduced in the agreement between India and China on Tibet, signed 29 April 1954.

144. Nehru, "A False Conception of Security," in *India's Foreign Policy*, 97.

145. Chris Smith, *India's Ad Hoc Arsenal* (New York: Oxford University Press, 1997), 237–238.

146. Smith, *India's Ad Hoc Arsenal*, 100.

147. Praful Bidwai and Achin Vanaik, *New Nukes: India, Pakistan, and Global Nuclear Disarmament* (New York: Olive Branch Press, 2000), 59.

148. At a speech inaugurating the National Physical Laboratory at New Delhi, he said, "Presently we may have to follow other countries in having a great atomic energy research institute also, not to make bombs, I hope, but nevertheless I do not see how we can lag behind in this very important matter, because atomic energy is going to play a vast and dominating part, I suppose, in the future shape of things. Already it is known that radioactive elements that are produced can be used for therapeutic purposes but in regard to other matters too it will make power mobile and this mobility of power can make industry develop anywhere." Jawaharlal Nehru, "The Necessity of Atomic Research in India," *Selected Works of Jawaharlal Nehru* (New Delhi: Jawaharlal Nehru Memorial Fund, 1984), 377–378.

149. Jawaharlal Nehru, "Towards Disarmament," 2 September 1957, in *India's Foreign Policy*, 199–200.

150. Bidwai and Vanaik, *New Nukes*, 61.

151. Bidwai and Vanaik, *New Nukes*, 61–63.

152. Raju G. C. Thomas, "The Growth of Indian Military Power," in *India's Strategic Future: Regional State of Global Power?* ed. Ross Babbage and Sandy Gordon (New York: St. Martin's Press, 1992), 41.

153. Joseph Cirincione, Jon B. Wolfsthal, and Miriam Rajkumar, *Deadly Arsenals, Tracking Weapons of Mass Destruction* (Washington, DC: Carnegie Endowment for International Peace, 2002).

154. Cirincione, Wolfsthal, and Rajkumar, *Tracking Proliferation*.

155. IISS, "India's Military Spending: Prospects for Modernisation," *IISS Strategic Comments* 6, no. 6 (London: IISS, 2000).

156. The International Institute for Strategic Studies, *The Military Balance 2004–2005.*

157. The International Institute for Strategic Studies, *The Military Balance 2004–2005.*

158. Rahul Bedi and J. A. C. Lewis, "India to Buy 10 Mirage 2000Hs," *Jane's Defense Weekly* 34, no. 11 (September 13, 2000).

159. Cirincione, Wolfsthal, and Rajkumar, *Deadly Arsenals.*

160. Cirincione, Wolfsthal, and Rajkumar, *Deadly Arsenals.*

161. Ministry of Defence, *Annual Report, 92–93*, (New Delhi: Ministry of Defense, Government of India), 19.

162. IISS, "India's Military Spending: Prospects for Modernisation."

163. Cirincione, Wolfsthal, and Rajkumar, *Deadly Arsenals.*

164. George Perkovich, *India's Nuclear Bomb: The Impact on Global Proliferation* (Berkeley: University of California Press, 1999), 178. See also Ved Mehta, *A Family Affair* (New York: Oxford University Press, 1982), 158–160.

CHAPTER 3

National Identity and National Interest

Introduction

National identity plays a central role in creating ideas of a society's purpose. Without a notion of who we are, it is difficult to conceptualize what we should be doing as a group. Erik Erikson, in pioneering research on identity, noted the importance of identity and ideologies in establishing the parameters of individual behavior.[1]

Conversely, individuals, groups, and institutions also affect the definition of national identity. As society and institutions change, traditions and norms adjust, shifting the parameters of the national identity. With this shift, national interests are recalibrated to reflect the values and goals of the polity. However, in times of rapid change, schisms may form between institutions and goals, leading to challenges to the national identity. If national identity is in question, national unity can be challenged. Ultimately, if the state is to survive, national unity must become the national interest. Thus, investigating how national identity is perceived is critical to understanding the dynamics of national interest formation.

There are various ways to approach the study of national identity and national interest. One is to recount historical notions of identity and what others have written in the past. This method provides a depth of background knowledge concerning long-standing concerns and entrenched ethnic problems. However, the historical method is dependent upon the conceptualizations of those intellectuals who have written on the subject. I propose to listen to the voices of Indian and Chinese decision makers and intellectuals to hear what they believe. Through interviews with elites in both countries, it is possible to compare perceptions of national identity and its relation to the national interest at a moment in time when both nations are experiencing vast economic, social, and political changes.

In deciding that defense modernization and economic reform programs are necessary for furthering the national interest, Chinese and Indian respondents differed in their conceptualizations of why and how these programs would address the critical issues faced by their respective countries. Whereas Chinese respondents perceived national unity to be critical in determining the need for defense modernization and economic reforms, Indian respondents focused far more on their geopolitical status and the effects of globalization in choosing these programs. These differences in the more inward-oriented perceptions of China and the outward orientation of India can be traced back to how each country perceives its national identity.

In the interviews with government officials, scholars, and journalists conducted for this research, respondents listed three main facets of national identity: (1) cultural/geographic, (2) economic, and (3) political. In China, all three facets of national identity were viewed as problematic in that each contained forces that challenged the unity of the Chinese state. Although the official definition of the state in China includes all of territorial China, the common cultural definition of the nation held by respondents conflicted with the definition held by the peoples of some regions, such as Taiwan, Tibet, and Xinjiang. Most relevant, Chinese respondents believed that the inability to deal with these separatist regions could lead to problems for the state as a political entity; i.e., the separation of Taiwan, Tibet, or Xinjiang could mean the loss of legitimacy of the Party and the state as a whole. Economically, growing disparities of income between regions and classes led to challenges to political stability and state unity from disaffected sections of the population. Respondents stated that politically, the Chinese Communist Party's (CCP's) position was precarious in that its legitimacy rested upon the successful maintenance of the first two problems. The three sets of divisive forces in China led to a sense of national identity crisis, a deep sense that state unity was threatened by these challenges. Respondents viewed defense modernization as critical to protect state unity from both external and internal threats. In addition, economic reforms were necessary to ensure rapid economic growth primarily to maintain political stability and state unity.[2]

The Indian respondents offered a definition of India's national identity that was more politically defined than cultural and, therefore, less threatened by centrifugal societal forces. Cultural/geographic and economic issues were facets that challenged the unity of the Indian state as they did in China. However, emphasis on a federal political system with great regional autonomy allowed varied groups to feel included in the Indian state. Separatist groups exist, nonetheless, in Kashmir and areas of the northeast. The critical difference between the separatist movements in China and India is that whereas Chinese respondents viewed these movements as fundamentally threatening the unity of the state, Indian respondents did not view similar separatist threats as a challenge to the unity of the state. Respondents characterized the Indian political system as a unifying force more permanent than any of the admittedly existent divisions. The unifying effects of the political system were considered stronger than the divisive cultural and class issues. Indian respondents also did not perceive state unity as fundamentally threatened by either political or economic divisions.[3] Consequently, threats to national identity were not viewed as critical in deciding defense modernization or economic reforms. Instead, globalization and its effects on geopolitics and sovereignty became the deciding factors (to be discussed in Chapter 4).[4]

National Identity

Before looking at Chinese and Indian perceptions of their national identities, it is important to define the concept of a nation and national identity. In common usage, the term "nation" is often confused with state, or nation-state. However, these terms are not identical. Scholars have described the concept of the nation variously, but with a common understanding that a nation requires individual belief in its existence. A. D. Smith has defined a nation as, "a named human population sharing an historic territory, common myths and historical memories, a mass, public culture, a common economy and common legal rights and duties for all members."[5] Walker Connor defines the nation as "a psychological bond that joins a people and differentiates it, in the subconscious conviction of its members, from all other people in a most vital way."[6] Ernest Gellner adds to these by saying that people are of the same nation if they share the same culture and if they recognize each other as part of the same nation.[7] The simplest definition of a nation may be that a nation is a group of people who believe that they are a nation.

In comparison, the state is defined by Ernest Gellner as "that institution or set of institutions specifically concerned with the enforcement of order (and whatever else they may be concerned with).[8] Connor simply phrases it as "the major political subdivision of the globe." The most critical element of this difference is that the concept of nation incorporates the psychological aspects of the people and their perceptions of their identity, whereas the state is considered the political framework of a country. As such, it is clear that the nation and the state do not necessarily overlap. A multitude of nations may be included in the territorial framework of the state, some nations may cross state boundaries, or, on occasion, the nation and the state may be roughly identical. Connor cites 1971 data supporting this showing that of 132 states, only 12 were homogeneous nation-states. Of the remainder, 25 contained an ethnic[9] group that accounted for 90 percent of the population, 25 held an ethnic group that accounted for

75 percent to 89 percent of the population, in 31 states the dominant ethnic group represented only 50 percent to 74 percent of the population, and in 39 cases the largest group was not even half of the state's population.[10]

Most important in this analysis is that the definition of a given nation is dynamic, not static. Though there may be a myth of common descent, this is not necessarily the primary reason for a feeling of common identity within a nation. Political factors may, in fact, have a greater role. Max Weber emphasized this relationship, "It is primarily the political community, no matter how officially organized, that inspires the belief in common ethnicity."[11] The reciprocal nature of nationality/ethnicity and politics of the state is further outlined in his definition of national identity, "Differences in the economic and social structure and in the internal power structure, with its impact on the customs, may play a role, but within the German *Reich* customs are very diverse; shared political memories, religion, language and, finally, racial features may be a source of the sense of nationality."[12] In this definition, the inclusion of shared historical memories is critical. It is possible to infer that a state that is able to politically successfully incorporate a multitude of nationalities can create an overarching single national identity coterminous with the state.

Conversely, when the state is unable to accommodate the economic, social, and territorial diversity of its peoples and is unable to provide an acceptable national identity, an identity crisis will emerge. This identity crisis will ultimately manifest itself in the state's interests and actions.

> National identity theory merely posits that the more closely the inclusion/exclusion criteria of national self-identity (however the state chooses to draw them) comport with the constituent emotional and symbolic elements of national self-definition, the firmer the national identity; the more secure the national identity, the more predictable the state's behavior.[13]

Illuminating this argument, Lucian Pye describes four fundamental types of identity crisis: (1) territorial/geographic problems dealing with who should administer particular territory, (2) class divisions, (3) ethnic divisions that occur when groups feel a greater sense of allegiance to their ethnicity rather than to the state, and (4) strain from rapid social change and modernity.[14] Pye also notes, "if a polity is to resolve its identity crises through more effective governmental performance and a rise in political capabilities, it must also resolve any issues of legitimacy."[15]

Though both China and India contain all four of Pye's problem areas listed above, interviews with Chinese and Indian respondents reveal that the Chinese state has had difficulty providing an acceptable political national identity to the country, whereas the Indian state has been relatively successful in providing a political definition of national identity acceptable to the majority of its population.[16] These differences in perceptions of political identity in both countries have had an effect on national interest formation. Whereas Indian respondents perceived the national interest in the external sphere, protecting the state against infringements on economic and political sovereignty, the Chinese respondents viewed the national interest as internally focused, protecting the state against disunity and collapse.

The divergent views of political identity reflect in part that the existence of political participation in elections in India fosters the sense that the government is beholden to the people of India. Thus, the question of political legitimacy of the CCP was raised with regard to the People's Republic of China (PRC), but not with regard to the Indian government. The differing exigencies of state authority and legitimacy have led to diverse conceptions of why a particular policy should be included in pursuit of the "national" interest. The role of state institutions and legitimacy will be addressed further in Chapter 5. Although the definition of nation and state has been clarified, the phrase "national interest" has commonly been used to refer to state interests rather than the interests of the various nations involved throughout the interviews and this research.

China

In China, the inability of the state to provide an acceptable, inclusive definition of national identity verges upon a crisis of national identity. Various groups of people within the Chinese state have responded to cultural, geographic, economic, and political feelings of disaffection by resorting to separatist insurgencies and protests against the government. Respondents stated that these disturbances could destabilize the Party, and the state. In order to handle these challenges to state unity, Chinese respondents viewed a military modernization program to strengthen the state's defensive capabilities, and an economic reforms program to decrease economic disaffection and bolster the regime's legitimacy as critically necessary.

The State and the Nation in Communist China

Since the Communist Revolution, the Chinese state has by ideology and mandate defined the nation and state to be synonymous. The Chinese Communist Party viewed service to the party to be service to the state and considered both to be done in the name of society.[17] This is not unique to China, as Communist parties around the globe faced the paradox of integrating a proletarian internationalist ideology with nationalist sentiment. Connor posits that "[T]here is an evident conflict between an ideology that maintains that the most significant cleavages are those that divide mankind horizontally into socioeconomic classes and one that maintains that the most significant cleavages are those that divide humanity vertically into national compartments."[18] In the Marxist-Leninist paradigm, nationalism was a force that could tear apart the social contract required for Communism to be successful. Marxists viewed nationalism as a tool of the bourgeoisie to further their own interests by defining their own class interests to be the nation's.[19] In this light, it was necessary for the Chinese Communist Party to formulate a definition of the nation that was satisfactory both to the ideology and to the various peoples of China, at least at the country's inception. As stated in the constitution, this definition is, "the People's Republic of China is a unitary multinational state, created in common by its various nationalities."[20] However, this statement can be viewed as an idealized history. The minority ethnicities of western and northern China were led to believe that self-determination for all nationalities would follow their support of the Communist cause during the war against the Kuomintang (KMT). In reality, statements issued by the CCP were hazy declarations of the fact that no such self-determination would be allowed. The difference in the statements can be seen in the following lines, both contained in the same 1931 resolution:

> This means that in districts like Mongolia, Tibet, Sinkiang, Yunnan, Kwei-chow, and others, where the majority of the population belongs to non-Chinese nationalities, the toiling masses of these nationalities shall have the right to determine for themselves whether they wish to leave the Chinese Soviet Republic and create their own independent state, or whether they wish to join the Union of Soviet Republics, or form an autonomous area inside the Chinese Soviet Republic ... .
>
> In the fundamental Law (Constitution) of the Chinese Soviet Republic it shall be clearly stated that all national minorities within the confines of China shall have the right to national self-determination, including secession from China and the formation of independent states, and that the Chinese Soviet Republic fully and unconditionally recognizes the independence of the Outer Mongolian People's Republic.[21]

This statement, which appears to support self-determination, in actuality supports this right only for "the toiling masses," in Communist discourse referring only to the proletariat. Thus, groups who subsequently supported self-determination could be dispelled by the state being classified as bourgeois elites. In 1949 and in subsequent years, those who attempted to further the self-determination argument were charged with counter-revolutionary behavior and treason.[22]

In addition to the official government statement of what constitutes the Chinese national identity, various scholars have addressed the question from different perspectives. According to Michael Ng-Quinn, Chinese national identity was traditionally tied to the state, irrespective of the ethnic balance.[23] Nan Li documents that a shift occurred from a revolutionary internationalist proletarian identity to one of conservative nationalism in China, but he does not define the boundaries of the new nation.[24] Lynn White and Li Cheng outline one framework that divides Chinese national identity into several parts, "between Han and minority areas, between north and south, and … between coast and inland."[25] Although each of these definitions addresses some aspects of China's national identity or identities, they are not comprehensive.

Three Aspects of National Identity

Chinese respondents, in the interviews conducted for this research, listed three main aspects of national identity, which are often overlapping: (1) cultural/geographic, (2) economic, and (3) political. Culturally, respondents most often defined China as Han and Confucian, while admitting that geographically it includes many cultures that are not Han. Economically, there was no class that Chinese respondents felt was representative of China, in contrast to the Maoist proletarian era. Politically, they defined China as a Communist state that represented many nationalities and many classes within certain geographic boundaries.

In each of these areas, however, Chinese respondents noted problems of maintaining unity. In the cultural/geographic aspect, territories such as Taiwan,[26] Tibet,[27] and Xinjiang[28] posed a separatist threat. This may be related to the fact that most respondents felt that the Confucian, Han culture is the actual Chinese culture, but they admitted that Tibet, Xinjiang, and various other areas were not traditionally Confucian. They stated that often exacerbating these cultural and regional differences were the effects of economic reforms. Great class and economic disparities resulting from these reforms challenged Chinese national unity and deepened the differences among regions, creating destabilizing parallel cleavages in society. Respondents viewed the state's inability to provide a strong political impetus for unity as the problem that underpinned many of these other issues. The problems of corruption and regime legitimacy were eroding Chinese state unity and, ultimately, the threat to state unity could require a military response to hold the country together. Respondents stated that in order to be prepared for separatism, insurgency, and rebellion, a defense modernization would be necessary. Following a brief overview of respondents' perceptions of the cultural, economic, and political aspects of China is an analysis of how these factors necessitate economic reforms and defense modernization in China.

Culture and Geography. The Chinese respondents saw cultural and regional differences as challenging state unity because of a combination of factors including the ethnic, geographic, and political diversity among the regions. These factors, which emphasized the differences among the various regions of China, created a situation where many nationalities demanded greater political autonomy or independence.

The respondents perceived the cultural definition of China in a traditional light, rather than the definition provided by the Party. They felt that the Communist ideology no longer reflected the ethos of the state or economy. The Chinese language, the way of thinking, and the influence of Confucian ideology defined Chinese culture. They viewed the current state as under the control of the Han Chinese.[29] A CCP official described China as the Middle Kingdom, a country constituted from several smaller countries, "Around the Huanghe River were many little countries. They little by little were introduced to the Chinese culture. So, slowly a China was made over 4000 years. Tibet, before they had relations, but over time through their relations with China, they became Chinese."[30] In this explanation, the interaction with China over time created a reason for Chinese political dominance over other neighboring areas. Through repeated interaction, areas in the periphery of China could be absorbed into the country and would be accepted by the state as an integral part of China, although their cultures may have been radically different from the dominant Han Chinese culture.

The cultural definition of China resulted in a situation where the Taiwan issue became the primary threat to Chinese state unity. Growing differences in living styles and political philosophy between Taiwan and the mainland created a paradox for most Chinese interviewees. Respondents constantly contradicted themselves over the issue of whether Taiwan should be considered part of the Chinese *nation,* while repeatedly stating that Taiwan was an integral part of the Chinese *state.* They noted that traditional Taiwanese culture and mainland culture are the same in that both reflect Han Chinese traditions such as Confucianism and the use of the Chinese language. Confusingly, they often contradicted themselves on the issue of culture and later said that Taiwanese culture is different and that Taiwanese are different from mainland Chinese. Respondents also admitted that many Taiwanese want to separate from the mainland due to differences in the political system and economic system, as well as standard of living. They noted that these divergences appear to have changed Taiwan over the past several decades to the extent that the current Taiwanese culture is no longer the same as the mainland culture, although some similar traditional elements may exist in both areas. "Politics, culture, psychological changes mean that Taiwan and the mainland get further and further apart and economic connections have not led to closer ties between the two societies."[31] The contradictory statements made by Chinese respondents on the issue of Taiwan's identity, both claiming that Taiwan and the mainland have the same culture and identity, then reversing to say that Taiwan is basically different, reflect that a cultural identity crisis may exist on this issue.

Chinese scholars reflected that even in Taiwan, which is widely perceived by the mainland as being of the Han culture, there was a popular sentiment that Taiwan is not included in the Chinese concept of the nation. One Chinese scholar noted, "The Taiwanese say 'We are Chinese, but the Chinese don't see us as part of the nation.' "[32] This underlines the fact that whether the mainland Chinese perceived the Taiwanese as Chinese, or whether the Taiwanese themselves perceived themselves as Chinese, in the end neither the mainlanders nor the Taiwanese felt that they were part of the same nation.

Chinese respondents also noted that the definition of nation commonly held in China creates divisiveness, "Mainly, nationalism in China deals with the Han people and it can hurt the feelings of minority people here. Also, nationalism deals with irrationality, demands that cannot be met by the government. This can lead to disappointment, which can lead to political problems."[33] The tendency to equate nationality in China with Han culture, in particular, can be seen as exacerbating regional tensions in areas such as Xinjiang and Tibet by creating resentment toward the dominant culture. Both Tibet and Xinjiang have separatist movements and also peoples who disagree with the Chinese political system.[34] Respondents noted that external support to the movements exacerbated the problem of divisiveness.

Moreover, the absence of religion as a culturally integrative force in China created a philosophical vacuum in society. An eminent scholar stated, "In a religious society, things are held together by religious groups and churches. In China we do not have that, we have the CCP. You need to have something to hold it together. Before it was Maoism—Now what is it? Capitalism? That can not be a very good future. Humans also want morality, belief, some kind of religion."[35]

Economic. Respondents also viewed the vast economic disparities between the coastal regions and the inland regions of the mainland as a threat to unity of the state. "The government knows the gap between the east and west[36] and that nationalities has become too wide. If we can't narrow the gap, it will be a great challenge, not only economically but also may be politically."[37]

State unity was gradually being weakened through widening economic disparities. A Foreign Ministry official noted, "During the Mao period, I think the country was more unified. Now, with the economic gaps I think the country is less unified."[38] Compounding the disaffection caused by economic disparities was a widespread feeling that rampant corruption was allowing people to unfairly benefit from reforms. "If corruption is not handled well, then dissatisfaction may erupt. Disparity and corruption are related. Now people can accept that my neighbor is richer because he worked hard. But they cannot accept it if he is richer because he used his power."[39] Others commented on the urban-rural divide, "People are not satisfied in the countryside. They can not make money from crops. They're not satisfied with the gap of the rich and poor, also bribery and corruption."[40]

Respondents believed that the state was responsible for addressing the problems of gross income inequalities and corruption. If the state failed to respond appropriately, dissatisfied masses of people facing economic duress would advance upon the government demanding improvement of their situations. If the situation continued to deteriorate, respondents believed the legitimacy of the Party and the legitimacy of the state would come under attack by the people.

Political. Furthermore, many aspects of China's political system are considered weak or unstable. From the theoretical aspect, respondents questioned the compatibility of a Socialist political system with a market economy. "We call this the market economy with socialist characteristics. What does it mean? It just means maintaining the ruling Socialist Party. If a society changes fundamentally its economic system, can its political system remain? No. Even in Marxist Leninist theory, on the basis that the economy changed, the political and social system changed."[41]

Internal political factors such as general dissatisfaction with the effectiveness and fairness of the government posed the greatest threat to China, according to respondents. Social and political instability could lead to a loss of legitimacy for the CCP, endangering the state and national unity.

> Respondent A: The biggest threat in general is internal, from within. It comes from deep in society, it depends on how the CCP can administer and manage society.[42]
>
> Respondent B: The most important challenge comes from within … Whether China can maintain domestic political stability. That is why many Chinese are in favor of political reform, but also in favor of taking cautious steps in reaching that aim. We don't want a chaotic situation.[43]
>
> Respondent C: In the next 10 years in China, the major problem is internal stability.[44]

The many references to internal stability and internal challenge underline the CCP's inability to accommodate the cultural/geographic and economic divisions through the appropriate political solutions. Walker Connor describes state ethnic policies through which various ethnic groups have become a minority in their region in China. "[A] policy of extensive gerrymandering and migration has made the titular national group a certain minority in four of the five autonomous regions and a most probable minority in the other … according to Chinese data, in only eight of the 29 autonomous districts existing in 1965 did the titular group represent a majority of the population."[45] These political moves, meant to weaken the ability for minority groups to assert their rights for self-determination, most likely increased the feelings of resentment toward the cultural majority and the state, thereby decreasing political stability. Economically, the lack of political representation for labor groups means that economic discontent during the transitions of economic reforms can have a limited voice and influence. Again, the lack of a political avenue for addressing economic problems creates conditions for greater political instability.

Defense Modernization and Economic Reforms to Sustain National Unity

The inability of the CCP to provide a sense of strong political unity for the country allows the cultural and economic differences to erode the existing definition of Chinese national identity. As identity is progressively weakened, unity is challenged, and with it the existence of the state as a coherent organization. Consequently, the Party ultimately defines the national interest as the preservation of the unity of the state.[46]

> Respondent A: The Chinese government takes the territorial integrity very seriously. China believes it is a country now not unified, divided at present. So, unification of the country will be a major goal of the Chinese government.[47]

> Respondent B: Now the biggest national interest is national unification. First Taiwan, then the western areas.[48]

The two main policy paths chosen to further this national interest are the defense modernization and economic reforms programs.

Defense Modernization. Respondents believed that the defense modernization program was necessary for protecting national unity from threats: separatist movements with external support and internal general uprisings. Of the separatist movements, Taiwan created the most anxiety, followed closely by concern about the Tibetan and Xinjiang independence movements.

Respondents viewed Taiwan as the primary threat to state unity for two main reasons: the existence of a popular separatist movement on Taiwan and the existence of U.S. support for separatism through advanced weapons sales and possible military intervention. "If Taiwan wants to separate, and if the U.S. wants to separate Taiwan, then for us they are choosing the road or path of war, not peaceful reunification … if there is a war, it is not what we wanted."[49] This thought summarizes concern over Taiwanese separatism and U.S. support. It also reflects the perception that war would include both Taiwan and the United States as potential adversaries. In case of such a contingency, respondents noted that China would have to be prepared to defend against the military might of Taiwan and the United States. Such preparation would require a defense modernization.

When asked what the primary reason is for defense modernization, or what the main defense threat is to China, respondents repeatedly stated variations of this idea. In addition, conventional defense capabilities were a priority in addressing the threat due to the territorial nature of the threat.

> Respondent A: The military wants to modernize and improve their capability. We do not foresee a war or aggression, but the Taiwan issue is a special one. So, this is the biggest potential conflict, Taiwan and theater missile defense as linked to this.[50]

> Respondent B: The main challenge is, the Taiwan issue.[51]

> Respondent C: The issue is still territory, the enemy. The independence of Taiwan is one of these issues.[52]

> Respondent D: The Chinese people are ready to sacrifice everything for unification.[53]

> Respondent E: The key factor is that the possible separation of Taiwan could become an immediate threat. People get the impression here that at the moment we rely more and more on military resort to detain Taiwan from separation because of the political change on that island.[54]

> Respondent F: China's main security challenges are 1) Taiwan, and 2) Separatist movements.[55]

> Respondent G: I think the single most task for Chinese defense is centered around the issue of Taiwan. What comes to mind is sovereignty and territorial defense.[56]

Although clearly subsidiary to the Taiwan threat, respondents also considered Tibet and Xinjiang viable reasons for a defense modernization program. In addition, the positive resolution of the Taiwan independence movement was seen as a critical precedent for a positive resolution of the Tibet and Xinjiang problems.

> Respondent A: In Tibet and Xinjiang, separatist sentiments are strong. These are the issues the military states are necessary for the quick modernization of the military.[57]

> Respondent B: The Taiwan issue is very important, it is our national identity and national unification issue. Taiwanese are Han minorities, but in Xinjiang we have other kinds of minorities. So, if Taiwan has independence, then these areas will also want this. So, we need military power to deal with this Taiwan issue.[58]

The existence of external support to separatist groups, and the necessity to be able to withstand U.S. hegemony, was also central to understanding the danger of Taiwanese, Tibetan, and Xinjiang separatism to Chinese unity. Respondents felt that rising tensions between China and the United States were exacerbating an already tense situation within the country, making defense modernization requisite for maintaining stability.

Respondent A: Now because of tensions between the U.S. and China we feel we should increase investment in this [defense] sector. It is in response to international tension, not because it is our intention to expand.[59]

Respondent B: Now, peace is the main trend but hegemonism still exists. For example, the U.S. is for a theater missile defense, including Japan and maybe Taiwan. So if the U.S. insists on that, it will be a threat to China's national unity and national integrity.[60]

More concretely, respondents believed that the United States wanted to weaken and divide China in order to eliminate China as a future competitor. Again, the ultimate threat was the destruction of the state. A Foreign Ministry official explained the common thinking among respondents on U.S. intentions toward China.

China cannot allow Taiwan independence, or accept this fact. In some sense, they believe the U.S. military will intervene in China's reunification because a lot of (U.S.) military officers do not believe the Chinese territory covers the Taiwan area … . In the next 10 years or so, the U.S. views China as another rising new major power in the world. What does it mean? I believe that a lot of Republicans believe China is another country like the former Soviet Union because the Chinese political system is the same as the Soviet Union and given the population size and the size of the country. So, what is the best way to eliminate the China threat—it is to separate China. So that is why the U.S. is critical of China's human rights, Taiwan, and Tibet. The fundamental reason is to eliminate the China threat. The best way is to separate China. They have done this thing in the Soviet Union. [61]

Quelling internal disorder and chaos was also a critical reason for pursuing a defense modernization, according to respondents. An eminent scholar noted his personal opinion of the three main reasons for military modernization, "First is national defense. Secondly is the integration of Taiwan. Thirdly is internal stability, helping to maintain national stability."[62] This use of military force is qualitatively different from that mentioned for use in case of a conflict over Taiwan or Tibet. The use of military force to suppress internal dissent and political instability has the aim of protecting the supremacy and coherence of the state. Some scholars even noted that the role of the military in China has always been to provide security for the emperor and that there were a large number of soldiers stationed in the capital city expressly for that purpose. Constitutionally, the People's Liberation Army (PLA) provides the function of the protector of the Communist Party, rather than the state. Thus, the PLA could be called upon to buttress the stability of the CCP in case Party authority or legitimacy is in question.

Economic Reforms. The economic reforms initiated in the 1980s and 1990s caused both strong economic growth and wide economic disparities in China. As the Communist ideology lost its luster in the face of market principles, the CCP increasingly relied upon economic growth as an indicator of its political legitimacy. As such, respondents said that the failure of economic reforms to provide widespread prosperity to all corners of the populace was an element that could undermine the Party's legitimacy. Paradoxically, although economic reforms were generating problems for the Chinese state, respondents stated that further economic reforms and additional political reforms were the appropriate solution. The original reforms had created rapid growth and large amounts of wealth for a small percent of the population. They had also forced millions of Chinese workers out of their jobs as a result of the closing of state-owned enterprises and other inefficient industries. The great number of unemployed workers expected the Chinese government to create new employment on their behalf, a feat that could be managed only by further reform measures.

The main purpose for continuing economic reforms in China was political stability and state unity, according to respondents. They noted that great disparities in income both between regions and between the urban and rural sectors were fomenting political discontent. Also, growing corruption was becoming a serious problem. The disaffection engendered by these economic factors was being directed at the government, or more precisely, at the CCP. The result was declining legitimacy of the Party and weakened cohesiveness of the state. Respondents concurred that since the primary integrative force for the Chinese nation was the CCP, a deterioration of its authority could mean widespread chaos and possible fragmentation of the country.

Chinese respondents noted that many people felt left behind by the economic boom, which created a feeling of discontent. Further economic reforms would address this issue. By continuing economic reforms, economic growth could be generated, spreading benefits more widely across society. The added wealth from reforms could be critical in closing existing income differentials and quelling social unrest.

> Respondent A: Those who have not become better off feel they are getting poorer though in reality they are getting richer. So, this results in criminal activities and unrest. So, the reforms have to be carried out with determination[63]

> Respondent B: The biggest problem is the issue of how to eliminate the disparity between the rich and poor of different areas and peoples because our objective is to have common prosperity. So, if there is a disparity for a long time, this will pose a serious problem to us. If their livelihood does not improve, the poor will complain, and this will have a negative affect on our political stability.[64]

Chinese respondents also felt that economic reforms necessitated political reforms and that without these critical reforms more instability would be forthcoming. Without reforming the political institutions, endemic corruption would continue. In the transitional economy, the ability to translate political power into economic power was great, as politicians took advantage of rents and bribes. Corrupt business people were able to use high political connections to their personal benefit. Political reforms, including legal reforms, would have to be instituted in order to break the existing corrupt cycles. However, respondents noted that taking these steps toward political reform could also lead to political instability; therefore, the process would have to be gradually instituted. In addition, they perceived these political reforms as necessary in rooting out the endemic corruption, but the reforms also entailed a risk of political instability as traditional authority was undermined by the same reforms.

> Respondent A: Definitely we need political reform, but because of the political sensitivities of adopting Western policies we don't often directly say political reform "*zhengzhi gaige*," we say political system reform "*zhengzhi tizhi gaige*." But they are the same thing.[65]

> Respondent B: Economic reforms call for simultaneous political reform. How else can you get rid of corruption? If you want to get rid of corruption, you need to take some fundamental steps to promote your political system. This is a dilemma for China. You need political reforms, but there is concern that this will lead to a situation out of control or chaos.[66]

The threat to state unity posed by economic problems was brought to the fore by the decline of Maoism as a defining philosophy and the subsequent inability of the CCP to provide a political definition of national identity that was acceptable to the country. The CCP ultimately was forced to rely upon economic growth as a legitimizing force to sustain political legitimacy and retain its hold on power. Continued economic growth meant increased support for the government, regardless of their policies in other areas.

> Respondent A: The government needs legitimacy. The key factor for today's government legitimacy is the progress of the whole society, living standard improvement or any progress related to national dignity. The CCP knows that nationalism is an important source of legitimacy because the party is the symbol of the nation.[67]

> Respondent B: The legitimacy for the party to govern the people is through growth and welfare. If there is much unemployment, there is a problem.[68]

> Respondent C: The people say, okay, even though we cannot have freedom, at least our life is better.[69]

In the absence of any other compelling political or cultural unifying force for the state, economic legitimacy became compulsory for the continued political stability and legitimacy of the CCP.

Chinese respondents felt that through implementation of a defense modernization program and the economic reforms program, the territorial mass of China and the legitimacy of the CCP could be maintained. China would protect its territorial integrity by keeping Taiwan, Tibet, and Xinjiang from separating from the mainland. By creating economic growth and prosperity for the people, and quelling domestic unrest, the stability and legitimacy of the state would be preserved.

India

In India, respondents did not perceive national identity to be in crisis. Although cultural/geographic issues and economic issues were also challenges to the unity of the state, respondents credited the flexible democratic system for providing a strong political definition of identity that was acceptable to most of the various ethnicities and classes within the Indian state. The parliamentary democracy in India provided a greater unifying force than the effects of admittedly divisive issues. Consequently, political and economic forces did not threaten state unity or legitimacy, and Indian respondents did not point to national identity or national unity as a significant reason for pursuing a defense modernization program or the economic reforms program. However, they viewed both the defense modernization program and the economic reforms program as policies to bolster the popularity of the current political party and policies that were likely to be continued into the future.

The State and the Nation in India

The establishment of the Indian state in 1947 was inextricably tied to the fact that it was independence from the British Empire. Independence for the Indian nationalist movement meant a democratic system in which Indians would be active participants in all levels of political administration, as seen in stark contrast to the British Raj where Indian political participation was an extension of the British Empire's rule, and seen as subjugation. As such, independence and democracy were created of a moral-political philosophy put forth for the country by Gandhi and Nehru. R. S. Khare has described the intrinsic relationship between morality and democracy in the foundation of the Indian state:

> The two founders of modern democracy in India, Gandhi and Nehru, recognized democracy not only as a justified form of government but also as an uncompromising social value for a whole nation. If democracy started as a political strategy of the colonized for seeking freedom, it became a moral conviction and nationally accepted just procedure with Gandhi and the Indian National Congress. Hence justification of democracy in India essentially preceded rather than followed political independence, and it was at once moral and political at the hands of Gandhi.[70]

Gandhi's philosophy indeed fundamentally linked spiritualism to political thought and direction, "I am told that religion and politics are different spheres of life. But I would say without a moment's hesitation and yet in all modesty that those who claim this do not know what religion is."[71] Thus democracy became a necessary and integral philosophical foundation of the Indian state and a basis for state identity. Jawaharlal Nehru explained to the population of India via radio address at the first general elections the importance of the democratic approach to the building of the Indian Republic:

> It is right that each one of you should take an interest as citizens in this great democratic process which is taking place on a scale yet unknown to history. It is also important that you take interest as citizens of the Republic of India, the future of which will, no doubt, be affected by these elections. Democracy is based on the active and intelligent interest of the people in their national affairs and in the elections that result in the formation of governments.[72]

He also explained at this occasion the importance of separating the nation-state from any individual political party by limiting the use of the national flag to the emblem of the state, "It should always be remembered that the National Flag must not be used or exploited for party purposes … . It must not be used for any election purpose."[73] This is in marked contrast with the CCP in China, where the Party forms the state, and combination is reflected in the fact that the symbols of one are the symbols of the other.

Upon independence the Indian state absorbed more than 500 princely states into the parliamentary democracy. By doing so, smaller nations were subsumed into a larger definition of the Indian nation that was the Indian democratic state. Maya Chadda describes the role of this political structure in the construction of India's identity, "In the postindependence period, modern democratic institutions have served to reconcile India's vast heterogeneity. However, their other priority is to protect national unity. Both are the constitutive principles of the modern Indian state."[74] Kanti Bajpai goes further to say that democracy was necessary for Indian unity, "An India that was not democratic would probably not have remained as united and stable as it has been since 1947."[75]

One of the basic structural strengths of the Indian democracy was the high level of autonomy given to the states and various ethnicities. This is reflected in the 1956 reorganization of states along linguistic lines, which gave recognition to the various ethnicities that had been absorbed into the Indian state.[76] India further refined the state language policy by 1967 with the adoption of the three language system in which Hindi was the official national language, states could use their own official languages, and English would be the link between the central government, the states, and state-to-state communications within India.[77] The language policy is reflected in current daily usage within the central government. Despite the dominance of Hindi as a north Indian language, respondents and others in the government consistently communicated in English as the common language. This custom may be a reflection of the high levels of non-Hindi speakers within high positions, as well as a reflection of constructed norms within society to accommodate the vast cultural and linguistic differences.

Having established democratic institutions, the Indian leadership was nonetheless unwilling to allow separatism, regardless of how the demands were submitted. Instances in which more authoritarian measures were used to protect territorial unity were also allowed. This approach proved less effective, however, in promoting a sense of state unity. In India, according to Paul R. Brass, "no secessionist movement will be entertained and that any group which takes up a secessionist stance will, while it is weak, be ignored and treated as illegitimate, but, should it develop significant strength, be smashed, with armed force if necessary."[78] Kanti Bajpai notes that the use of military force by the Indian government in dealing with separatism has had a negative effect and should be curtailed:

> If taken to extremes, centralization and the use of force can produce the very effects that they are intended to control. Devolution and democracy are the best long-term basis for ethnic justice and peace. When the central and state governments have made an effort to share power and when they have been sensitive to public—often group—opinion, they have done much to promote peaceful ethnic relations.[79]

Other scholars on Indian national identity have also noted the importance of a definition of political identity, though they may differ on their conclusions. David Taylor posits that the political identity existing in India is not powerful enough to withstand the divisive forces in the face of a crisis, "Whether the attachment of its citizens to the notion of an Indian state would survive the total collapse of central authority is perhaps doubtful, for except among a relatively small elite, the concept of a specifically Indian political identity is still in its infancy."[80] However, Taylor's interpretation may be a reflection of the era in which he was writing. In 1979, India had recently reestablished democratic norms after Indira Gandhi's 1975–1977 authoritarian Emergency. Since then, democratic processes have been followed and strengthened. Malcolm Yapp states that democracy has been of central importance in negotiating the linguistic and religious differences in India, "Democracy creates the most favorable conditions for the formulation and expression of political identity. The electoral process encourages groups to identify themselves politically so that they may exert a greater influence both within constituencies and within parliament."[81]

The Three Aspects of National Identity in India

Indian respondents' views on the issue of Indian national identity can also be classified along the lines of the three aspects of national identity mentioned earlier: cultural/geographic, economic, and political. Culturally, although respondents noted that Indian culture is inclusive and a medley of many subcultures, separatist movements on the periphery of India exist, particularly in Kashmir,[82] Assam, and Nagaland.[83] The difference was that Indian respondents did not perceive these separatist struggles to be a threat to India's unity as a state. Similarly, although they viewed economic inequality as a challenge for India in the coming decade, inequality was not a threat to the legitimacy of the state. Two of the primary reasons for the difference in perceptions between China and India on these identical issues are (1) the absence of a clearly dominant ethnic group in India comparable to the Han Chinese in China and (2) the existence of a democratic political structure in India that provides an acceptable and flexible political identity for the country and appropriate political outlets for popular dissatisfaction.

Cultural/Geographic. Respondents were unanimous in their beliefs that India was a multicultural and multinational state. Although the existence of such a variety of cultures translated into the same forces for divisiveness seen in the Chinese case, the fact that no one culture could claim absolute dominance in the state meant that all cultures were forced into negotiations with each other through the center. These crosscutting rather than parallel social cleavages decreased the ability of groups to effectively destabilize the state. As described by Kanti Bajpai, "This demographic profile does, however, point to one source of stability: the absence of a nationwide cleavage along ethnic lines. Religious, caste, tribal, linguistic, and regional differences do not converge along a single fault line. As a result, ethnic crises tend to be localized and are therefore more easily contained by the government."[84] Indian decision makers agreed with this analysis, noting that the religious group with the greatest number of Indian followers, the Hindus, were divided along various ethnicities, regions, and languages, decreasing their political power.

In describing the cultural identity of India, respondents generally discounted the importance of any particular language, religion, or ethnicity but noted the difficulty in handling state-to-state relations inside India.

Respondent A: The country endowed with vast diversity, many languages, religions, different geographical terrains. It is still displaying an astounding internal unity.[85]

Respondent B: India is a culture, it is not religiously based. Language and religion are not necessary.[86]

Respondent C: It is more civilizational than religious. The milieu is generally tolerant and loose. There are very few rigidities. That gets reflected in our approach. Maybe we are too elastic.[87]

Respondent D: We have unity in diversity. Whenever it threatened by external aggression, such as Kargil, I have never seen more support for anything more than this. India is just like the joint family system—together against threat and divided at peace.[88]

Respondent E: In India, every state has been built according to language. So, many times people think in terms of their own state. Not that they are an Indian, but that they are a Bihari, etc. Only in calamity do we have a national feeling, such as Kargil or the earthquake. In these cases, they think about India. Otherwise, they fight amongst themselves over water between states.[89]

Respondent F: India is a multinational multi-cultural entity. Each region has its own culture. The fact is that people realize the fact that they belong to the nation of India. That is the national identity. I won't give up my language just because the BJP [Bharatiya Janata Party] says so. Cricket and things like this are the things that show that India is together. You see people celebrating all over the country after a cricket match.[90]

Alternatively, an economist from Bihar disputed the claims that a national identity even exists in India, "Most Indians don't know that they are an Indian. They don't know the boundaries of the country. Only their subregion, they think 'Yes, this is our country.' Most Indians are still illiterate. What concept there is that exists in India is from the educated class."[91] This statement reflects the sentiment of the various Indian separatist movements as well. There exist separatist groups in Kashmir and in the northeastern states such as Nagaland and Mizoram who feel that their ethnic identity supersedes their identity as Indians. However, some important methods used by the Indian government to deal with these ethnic groups have been different from those used by China in dealing with ethnic separatism. Through central government policy, the Naga tribes have maintained control of Nagaland, with little in migration from other Indian ethnic groups to change the ethnic composition of the region.[92] In the case of Kashmir, the Indian government has used force to quell separatism, with less success. A respondent noted, "We didn't make those in Kashmir feel satisfied."[93]

Nonetheless, separatist tensions from Kashmir and Nagaland do not spell the same threat to Indian unity as do Taiwan, Tibet, and Xinjiang to China. Indian respondents felt that a negotiated solution was possible on the Kashmir issue, due to growing political consensus inside India for a solution. Economic concerns took precedence over the Kashmir issue as well. The lack of anxiety caused by the Kashmir issue largely reflected the fact that no Indian respondent believed that the state or the unity of the rest of India was threatened by secession of any given territory. The absence of a tangible threat to the state, then, led to a belief that economic considerations weighed more heavily upon the state than the Kashmir issue and that a gradual cooperative resolution of the issue was preferable.

> Respondent A: Even the Kashmir issue can be resolved by SAARC [South Asian Association for Regional Cooperation], through the influence of trade issues.[94]

> Respondent B: Jammu and Kashmir is a process moving on its own time.[95]

> Respondent C: If our internal stability is continually disrupted, that will make it difficult for us to get investment, with terrorist bombs going off in India. We want Kashmir to be resolved because we don't want it to affect our economic growth.[96]

> Respondent D: I think India's foreign policy is post-Kashmir. The elite establishment is waiting for a solution to emerge. This will rule out a plebiscite in Kashmir. But if there is an arrangement where Pakistan, India, and the Kashmiri militants agree to get something and lose something, this will be the optimal solution. If you take the political parties of India, apart from communal opinion and the RSS [Rashtriya Swayamsevak Sangh], I can't think of a set which will reject this. Earlier, the Indian position was fundamentalist, that Kashmir is an inalienable part of India. Now India sees the futility of this position.[97]

Economic. Similar to the Chinese respondents, the Indian respondents felt that uneven distribution of wealth was a challenge for state unity. Prime Minister Manmohan Singh, who pioneered the Indian economic reforms as Minister of Finance, saw this as the main element of Indian national identity:

> We can strengthen the cohesiveness, unity and integrity of India by having a development that is inclusive, reaches all parts of India, to all communities. This is how we can become a cohesive proud country. This is the challenge, not only to work for accelerated economic and social growth, but to see that the benefits of growth are distributed equitably among regions and among the various classes … . The share of Agriculture in the economy has fallen from 50% to 25%. So, the disparities between urban and rural India have increased. All of this creates tensions in the system. This has led to greater divides in society.[98]

The Indian Finance Secretary agreed that equitable growth posed a serious economic challenge to India, a fact that is exacerbated by the vast population of the country. "The first problem is that of the population, with about 1 billion people, it is very large. As economic prosperity grows, we expect it to stabilize. 26% are below the poverty line. We brought it down from 34% to 26% in the past 10 years. We need to get them above the poverty line. We need to get them employment."[99] However, as with the territorial issues, no Indian respondent perceived the economic problems of India to possibly erode the legitimacy of the state. Respondents widely viewed the economic disparities as a national problem that must be solved, but not as an issue that could derail the fundamental basis for the state.

Political. Indian respondents most ardently argued that in the political sphere, Indian democracy and federalism had been able to provide a powerful unifying force for the state that was able to counteract the divisiveness of cultural/geographic problems and economic disparities. I. K. Gujral, former Prime Minister of India, and other senior officials emphasized the stability of the political system in India and the role of Indian democracy in maintaining state unity, noting that Indian governments have all been a result of democratic elections:

> Respondent A: It is unity in diversity, we have a plethora of languages, cultures, and religions. It is the success of India that we have all stayed together democratically. We only need not have uniformity.[100]

> Respondent B: Of all the countries in this region, India is an ocean of stability. The changes have always taken place via the ballot box, not the bullet. What ever happens, it is stable. It is a true democracy.[101]

> Respondent C: Democratic rights of the people have become much more important to the people than they were 40 years ago under Nehru. After 50 years of democracy, people are more conscious of their rights. Independence groups were more tolerant because they saw the British. After that, people became more critical of their government.[102]

Whereas for Chinese respondents, the political sphere posed the greatest problem to Chinese national unity, Indian respondents perceived the political system to be a factor adding to national unity in the face of other challenges to the state.

Defense Modernization and Economic Reforms in Indian National Politics

Defense Modernization. A result of this relatively optimistic view of Indian national identity and national unity was that Indian respondents did not view defense modernization necessary for protecting national unity. A defensive capability was considered critical to facing threats in Kashmir and the northeast, but a modernization was not necessary to fight separatism. Although India certainly has had problems of ethnic separatism in Kashmir and the northeast similar to China's problems in Tibet and Xinjiang, Indian respondents were markedly less concerned about these issues. Respondents did not cite the separatist movements in Kashmir, Nagaland, Mizoram, and Assam as the reason or even a plausible reason for pursuing a defense modernization program. They viewed these issues as best dealt with via diplomatic means. In the case of

Kashmir, appropriate conventional weapons were needed to address the threat, but a defense modernization was not necessary in order to defeat Pakistan. The Indians interviewed commented that the Indian military would be able to defeat Pakistan in a war over Kashmir without the help of a military modernization. However, they emphasized that they did not think that a full-scale war over Kashmir was necessary or useful in resolving the situation. Rather, they intended to continue low-intensity conflict in the region until a political/diplomatic solution became available.

In terms of using the military modernization to face internal political threats destabilizing to the state, again respondents did not find this necessary or desirable. Although the Indian military maintained paramilitary forces to provide support for the police forces and individual state paramilitary forces, these military forces were not needed to protect the state from internal attack on institutions, or collapse. Because of the nature of the parliamentary democracy, if internal disorder were to erupt, rather than endangering the state itself the party in power would suffer. The military, as a tool of the state but not of any particular political party, could not intervene on behalf of a political party in case of a loss of confidence in the party's legitimacy by the people. If the BJP were to fall from power, the state would still exist and not be threatened by the change of the ruling party. The fact that the military remained under control of the central government and not any political party and that the stability of the state itself was not threatened by political transition meant that a military modernization was certainly not necessary to maintain state unity.

Nonetheless, a few respondents viewed political parties as politically benefiting from the added national prestige that accrued to India as a result of the defense modernization program, particularly the Indian nuclear tests of 1998. An Indian army officer cynically noted, "The BJP did it [the tests], because they had promised it on their agenda. Secondly, they did it to get the vote back. They wanted to remain in power."[103] However, this subsidiary reason for pursuing a defense modernization program is not military in its purpose, but political.

Economic Reforms. Indian respondents felt similarly about the importance of economic reforms in maintaining state unity. Although they did not fear that the Indian state would collapse as a result of poor economic performance, a few respondents said that without economic reforms the political party in power would be forced out. Prime Minister Manmohan Singh criticized the BJP for first campaigning against economic reforms, but then after coming to power and realizing that economic reforms were necessary for continued growth, turning around and pursuing the same economic reforms. After the BJP realized that economic reforms had been the engine of growth during the 1990s, it came to the conclusion that not continuing economic reforms could be deleterious to its hold on political power. This may also have been the result of a gradual realization on the part of the BJP that there was a wide political consensus across the country in favor of continuing reforms.

> Respondent A: They were accusing us [the Congress Party] of selling India to America, selling India to the multinationals, but they did not believe it. They were doing it simply to win votes. But now that they are in office, they are doing the same thing.[104]

> Respondent B: If they had not opened up, they would have been finished. All the political parties realized this. The basic reason is to remain in power.[105]

Again, the primary concern of political actors was for maintaining the popularity of the political party, not for maintaining the unity of the state. However, even these views cited above, stating that economic reforms were pursued for political purposes, were in the minority. The dominant sentiment regarding economic reforms was that reforms were necessary to continue economic growth, gain efficiency, and compete internationally as a country.

Conclusions

Chinese and Indian respondents concurred that defense modernization and economic reforms were necessary for pursuing their national interests. However, divergent views of national identity and national unity meant that the objectives for these programs were fundamentally different. Although both states faced similar challenges to national unity, only the Chinese respondents felt that the challenges were threatening to the existence of the state. Therefore, Chinese respondents felt that the main purpose of defense modernization and economic reforms was to protect the unity of the state. As the Indian respondents did not believe that state unity was threatened, they did not find defense modernization and economic reforms relevant for maintaining state unity.

The Chinese respondents felt that their state unity was under attack from the internal factors of separatist movements and economically disaffected workers, and from the external factor of foreign assistance to separatist movements in Taiwan and Tibet. To meet the military threats to the unity of the state posed by the internal and external factors, respondents said that a defense modernization program was necessary. According to respondents, continued economic growth through economic reforms was also critical for maintaining the legitimacy of the CCP. Without the economic reforms, public dissatisfaction with the performance of the CCP could undermine the legitimacy of the state. As a result, the Party and the state could face the possibility of collapse, with dire consequences for the unity of the country. Chinese respondents believed that both programs were critical in sustaining state unity.

Conversely, the Indian respondents perceived their state to be durable and flexible and not likely to collapse. Crediting the democratic system, they stated that internal dissent had other avenues for realizing goals, such as elections. Although political parties could suffer as a result of poor economic policies, the state itself was not under threat. In addition, the democratic system provided a political identity that served as a unifying force more powerful than the threats to state unity.

Perceptions of national identity contribute significantly to knowledge of national goals. Although countries may pursue similar policies, or face similar challenges, ideas of the national objective could be disparate. National identity forms the bridge to understanding these differences in ideas and perceptions of the national interest. Ilya Prizel maintains that national identity is the underpinning for the formation of national interests:

> [T]his emotional, albeit irrational, sense of nation and national identity plays a vital role in forming a society's perception of its environment and is an extremely important, if not driving, force behind the formation of its foreign policy because national identity helps to define the parameters of what a polity considers its national interests at home and abroad.[106]

As the largest political group encompassing people in an identity, the nation must consolidate the definition of the nation and state in order to protect national unity. Otherwise, the national interest will become increasingly inward focused, toward the necessity of state integration and formation of a new identity.

Notes

1. Erik Erikson, *Identity: Youth and Crisis* (New York: W. W. Norton & Co., 1968), 190.

2. These are the opinions of the majority of the Chinese respondents.

3. No Indian respondents viewed Indian state unity to be fundamentally threatened.

4. These are the opinions of the majority of Indian respondents.

5. Anthony D. Smith, *National Identity* (Reno: University of Nevada Press, 1991), 14.

6. Walker Connor, *Ethnonationalism: The Quest for Understanding* (Princeton, NJ: Princeton University Press, 1994), 92.

7. Ernest Gellner, *Nations and Nationalism* (Ithaca, NY: Cornell University Press, 1983), 7.

8. Gellner, *Nations and Nationalism*, 4.

9. For the purposes of this research, I will use Max Weber's definition of "ethnic group" as "those human groups that entertain a subjective belief in their common descent because of similarities of physical type or of customs or both, or because of memories of colonization and migration; this belief must be important for the

propagation of group formation; conversely, it does not matter whether or not an objective blood relationship exists." As such, the "ethnic group" is generally the same as the nation. See Max Weber, *Economy and Society,* ed. Guenther Roth and Claus Wittich (New York: Bedminster Press, 1968), 1:389.

10. Connor, *Ethnonationalism,* 29.

11. Weber, *Economy and Society,* 389.

12. Weber, *Economy and Society,* 397.

13. Samuel S. Kim and Lowell Dittmer, *China's Quest for National Identity* (Ithaca, NY: Cornell University Press, 1993), 245.

14. Lucian Pye, "Identity and the Political Culture," in *Crises and Sequences in Political Development,* ed. Leonard Binder et al. (Princeton, NJ: Princeton University Press, 1971), 111–123.

15. Pye, "Identity and the Political Culture," 134.

16. This is based upon the majority opinion of more than 100 interviewees (government officials, scholars, and journalists) in Beijing and New Delhi in 2004–2005 and 2001.

17. Merle Goldman, Perry Link, and Su Wei, "China's Intellectuals in the Deng Era," in *China's Quest for National Identity,* ed. Lowell Dittmer and Samuel S. Kim (Ithaca, NY: Cornell University Press, 1993), 126.

18. Walker Connor, *The National Question in Marxist-Leninist Theory and Strategy* (Princeton, NJ: Princeton University Press, 1984), 6.

19. Connor, *The National Question,* 7.

20. Kim and Dittmer, *China's Quest,* 274.

21. Connor, *The National Question,* 74–75.

22. Connor, *The National Question,* 81, 87–89.

23. Michael Ng-Quinn, "National Identity in Premodern China: Formation and Role Enactment," in *China's Quest for National Identity,* ed. Samuel S. Kim and Lowell Dittmer (Ithaca, NY: Cornell University Press, 1993), 33.

24. Nan Li, "From Revolutionary Internationalism to Conservative Nationalism: The Chinese Military's Discourse on National Security and Identity in the Post-Mao Era," Peaceworks 39 (Washington, DC: United States Institute of Peace, 2001), 18.

25. Lynn White and Li Cheng, "China Coast Identities: Regional, National, and Global," in *China's Quest for National Identity,* ed. Samuel S. Kim and Lowell Dittmer (Ithaca, NY: Cornell University Press, 1993), 164.

26. Taiwan is an island that the PRC contends became a part of China under the Qing dynasty in 1684. Subsequently, the Qing ceded Taiwan to Japan in the 1895 Treaty of Shimonoseki. After 1949, the KMT took control of the territory. The PRC and KMT both claimed sovereignty over Taiwan and the mainland after this time, though only the KMT was recognized by the United States. Subsequently, President Nixon shifted the U.S. stance by visiting the PRC in 1972. President Carter established diplomatic relations with the PRC in 1979. Under Deng Xiaoping, the formula for relations became "one country, two systems." See Jonathan D. Spence, *The Search for Modern China* (New York: W. W. Norton & Co., 1990); and Christopher Hughes, *Taiwan and Chinese Nationalism* (New York: Routledge, 1997).

27. China first intervened in Tibet in 1720, under the Qing dynasty. After the fall of the Qing, Yuan Shikai declared Tibet, Xinjiang, and Mongolia part of China in 1911. In 1950, Chinese Communist troops occupied Tibet. Following a Tibetan

uprising against Chinese rule, in 1959 the Dalai Lama and 80,000 followers fled to India. See Spence, *The Search for Modern China;* also Robert Barnett, ed., *Resistance and Reform in Tibet* (Bloomington: Indiana University Press, 1994).

28. Xinjiang was first incorporated into China by the Qing in 1759. Chinese Communist forces took over Xinjiang in 1949. Rebellion against Chinese rule has persisted since that time. See Spence, *The Search for Modern China;* also Justin Jon Rudelson, *Oasis Identities: Uighur Nationalism Along China's Silk Road* (New York: Columbia University Press, 1997).

29. Scholar (Interview #25).

30. Chinese Communist Party Official (Interview #5).

31. Scholar (Interview #17).

32. Professor (Interview #38).

33. Scholar (Interview #17).

34. Various interviews of Chinese respondents.

35. Scholar (Interview #14).

36. This refers to the eastern coastal regions of China and the western areas.

37. Scholar (Interview #25).

38. Foreign Ministry Official (Interview #4).

39. Scholar (Interview #15).

40. Scholar (Interview #19).

41. Foreign Ministry Official (Interview #7).

42. Scholar (Interview #14).

43. Scholar (Interview #16).

44. Scholar (Interview #22).

45. Connor, *The National Question,* 329.

46. In the interviews, Chinese respondents often use the words nation, country, and state interchangeably to refer to the state.

47. Scholar/Official (Interview #24).

48. Professor (Interview #35).

49. Communist Party Official (Interview #1).

50. Foreign Ministry Official (Interview #4).

51. Foreign Ministry Official (Interview #7).

52. Foreign Ministry Official (Interview #6).

53. Scholar (Interview #18).

54. Scholar (Interview #17).

55. Professor (Interview #32).

56. Scholar (Interview #26).

57. Professor (Interview #32).

58. Professor (Interview #34).

59. Ministry of Finance Official (Interview #3).

60. Foreign Ministry Official (Interview #8).

61. Foreign Ministry Official (Interview #7).

62. Scholar (Interview #23).

63. Scholar (Interview #23).

64. Foreign Ministry Official (Interview #2).

65. Scholar (Interview #14).

66. Scholar (Interview #16).

67. Scholar (Interview #17).

68. Scholar (Interview #19).

69. Scholar (Interview #20).

70. R. S. Khare, *Culture and Democracy: Anthropological Reflections on Modern India* (Lanham: University Press of America, 1985), 26.

71. M. K. Gandhi, quoted in Erik Erikson, *Gandhi's Truth* (New York: W. W. Norton & Co., 1969), 22.

72. Jawaharlal Nehru, *Jawaharlal Nehru's Speeches 1949–1953* (Delhi: Publications Division, Ministry of Information and Broadcasting, Government of India, 1954), 21.

73. Nehru, *Jawaharlal Nehru's Speeches*, 23.

74. Maya Chadda, *Building Democracy in South Asia: India, Nepal, Pakistan* (Boulder, CO: Lynne Rienner Publishers, 2000), 12.

75. Kanti Bajpai, "Diversity, Democracy, and Devolution in India," in *Government Policies and Ethnic Relations in Asia and the Pacific*, ed. Michael E. Brown and Sumit Ganguly (Cambridge, MA: MIT Press, 1997), 38.

76. Chadda, *Building Democracy in South Asia*, 39.

77. Bajpai, "Diversity, Democracy, and Devolution in India," 57.

78. Paul R. Brass, *The New Cambridge History of India: The Politics of India Since Independence* (Cambridge: Cambridge University Press, 1990), 7.

79. Bajpai, "Diversity, Democracy, and Devolution in India," 80.

80. David Taylor, "Political Identity in South Asia," in *Political Identity in South Asia*, ed. David Taylor and Malcolm Yapp (London: Curzon Press, 1979), 265.

81. Malcolm Yapp, "Language, Religion and Political Identity: A General Framework," in *Political Identity in South Asia*, ed. David Taylor and Malcolm Yapp (London: Curzon Press, 1979), 31.

82. The first mention of Kashmir is as a part of the Emperor Ashok's rule (269–232 B.C.). The dispute over Kashmir began with independence from Britain and partition into India and Pakistan in 1947. The Maharajah of Kashmir signed an instrument of accession, ceding the region to India in 1947. Since then, the Muslim majority of the state has meant to Pakistan that the state is naturally an integral part of Pakistan. However, India claims that as a secular country, a state with a Muslim majority proves India's secularism. Wars between India and Pakistan in 1947, 1965, and 1999 have failed to resolve the issue. See Tavleen Singh, *Kashmir: A Tragedy of Errors* (New York: Penguin Books, 1996).

83. Nagaland originated from the state of Assam after independence. In the next few decades, the Indian policy of linguistically organizing the states led to the creation of Nagaland in 1963, as well as several other states. Separatist movements and rebellions in the region have continued since the 1950s. See Sanjib Baruah, *India Against Itself: Assam and the Politics of Nationality* (Philadelphia: University of Pennsylvania Press, 1999).

84. Kanti Bajpai, "Diversity, Democracy, and Devolution in India," 38.

85. Bangaru Laxman, then President of the BJP, in an interview by the author, New Delhi, India, 24 February 2001.

86. Vikrant Pandey, Army Officer, in an interview by the author, New Delhi, India, 17 January 2001.

87. Bharat Karnad, Scholar for the Center for Policy Research, in an interview by the author, New Delhi, India, 2 February 2001.

88. Nil Ratan, Political Scientist for the A. N. Sinha Institute, in an interview by the author, Patna, Bihar, India, 6 January 2001.

89. Pushkar Sinha, Senior News Correspondent for Zee TV, in an interview by the author, New Delhi, India, 7 March 2001.

90. GVC Naidu, Defense Analyst for IDSA, in an interview by the author, New Delhi, India, 8 February 2001.

91. I. D. Sharma, Economist for the A. N. Sinha Institute, in an interview by the author, Patna, Bihar, India, 6 January 2001.

92. Christophe von Furer-Haimendorf, "The Changing Position of Tribal Populations in India," in *Political Identity in South Asia*, ed. David Taylor and Malcolm Yapp (London: Curzon Press, 1979), 244.

93. Lt. Gen. V. R. Raghavan, President of the Delhi Policy Group, in an interview by the author, New Delhi, India, 2004.

94. I. K. Gujral, Former Prime Minister, in an interview by the author, New Delhi, India, 26 February 2001.

95. Manwender Singh, Defense Analyst and Freelance Journalist, in an interview by the author, New Delhi, India, 7 March 2001.

96. Lt. General V. R. Raghavan, President of the Delhi Policy Group, in an interview by the author, New Delhi, India, 2004.

97. Professor Deshpande, Professor of the School of International Studies, Jawaharlal Nehru University, in an interview by the author, New Delhi, India, 13 February 2001.

98. Manmohan Singh [Prime Minister (2004–)], then Leader of the Opposition in Rajya Sabha, in an interview by the author, New Delhi, India, 6 February 2001.

99. Ajit Kumar, Finance Secretary, Former Defense Secretary, in an interview by the author, New Delhi, India, 7 March 2001.

100. I. K. Gujral, Former Prime Minister of India, in an interview by the author, New Delhi, India, 26 February 2001.

101. Senior Navy Official, in an interview by the author, New Delhi, India.

102. Senior Official, Ministry of External Affairs, in an interview by the author, New Delhi, India.

103. Vikrant Pandey, Army Officer, in an interview by the author, New Delhi, India, 17 January 2001.

104. Manmohan Singh [Prime Minister (2004–)], then Leader of the Opposition Congress Party in the Rajya Sabha, in an interview by the author, New Delhi, India, 6 February 2001.

105. Vikrant Pandey, Army Officer, in an interview by the author, New Delhi, India, 17 January 2001.

106. Ilya Prizel, *National Identity and Foreign Policy: Nationalism and Leadership in Poland, Russia, and Ukraine* (Cambridge: Cambridge University Press, 1998), 14.

CHAPTER 4

Globalization, Geopolitics, and Sovereignty

Ruoguo Wuwaijiao—There is no diplomacy for weak countries

—Chinese Proverb

Introduction

In determining why states do what they do, the forces of globalization and geopolitics cannot be ignored. Globalization's increasingly rapid international exchange of information, trade, and technology, along with the accompanying economic interdependence, means that countries must adapt, as never before, and incorporate change or risk becoming obsolete. Competitiveness in these areas translates into power, whether economic or otherwise. The geopolitical implication is that in a world where the most powerful reigns, increased competitiveness leads to improved leverage.

Respondents felt that India and China must acquire international standards of technology and economic might to protect and enhance their state sovereignty as a result of the increased emphasis on international competitiveness in a globalized world, and its impact on geopolitical power dynamics. Chinese and Indian respondents perceived the implied threats of the forces of globalization and geopolitics as critical to the protection of state sovereignty. For instance, both sets of respondents cited the Iraq War and the Gulf War as examples of the use of high-technology weaponry to infringe upon state sovereignty. However, whereas to the Chinese respondents sovereignty referred mainly to territorial issues such as Taiwan, for the Indian respondents, sovereignty in the international political and economic arenas was considered of much higher importance. Both countries' respondents felt that pursuing a defense modernization program and an economic modernization program would lead to greater capabilities to protect their sovereignty in these areas.

For Chinese respondents, globalization meant that defense technology and capabilities were constantly being eroded by new innovations in defense weaponry. According to respondents, if existing capabilities were not upgraded to compete with this new international level of technology, China's sovereignty over Taiwan, Tibet, and Xinjiang could be at risk. The forces of globalization also increased the urgency of furthering economic reforms in China. If economic reforms were not pursued, then China would not be able to integrate into the globalized economy and thus could not continue rapid economic growth. As discussed in Chapter 3, this could undermine the legitimacy of the Chinese Communist Party (CCP) and would derail plans to continue modernizing the military as well. Respondents perceived national unity and ability to defend territorial sovereignty to be endangered by the forces of globalization.

Indian respondents concurred that globalization was a powerful force which could erode state sovereignty. However, Indian respondents stated that sovereignty of decision making on a variety of economic and political fronts such as trade, environmental issues, and labor standards were most important, and they did not mention territorial sovereignty. Although the threats derived from globalization were not perceived to be military in nature, maintaining a nuclear deterrence was considered critical in defending political and economic rights by increasing India's comprehensive national strength. Respondents also stated that globalization was the primary reason for pursuing economic reforms in India. The increasing interdependence of the world economy and the need to build economic competitiveness in the globalized world were seen as necessary for maintaining economic growth and building comprehensive national strength.

This chapter provides the working definitions for globalization, geopolitics, and sovereignty and outlines how globalization is affecting state sovereignty and geopolitics. Then, it discusses the Chinese and Indian respondents' views of globalization and state sovereignty and relates how globalization pertains to the national interests of each country as seen through its pursuit of defense modernization and economic reforms programs.

Defining Globalization, Geopolitics, and Sovereignty

Before continuing, it is important to define the terms *globalization, geopolitics,* and *sovereignty* and to outline the relationship between the terms. Globalization is a word that covers a wide range of factors that have resulted from economic and technological advances in the past several decades.[1] Various authors have included in "globalization" economic, technological, and cultural aspects: "a striking increase in international trade, investment, and capital flows; dramatic progress in communications technology (especially the rise of the Internet); and a considerable enhancement of the role of multilateral institutions, along with a corresponding weakening of state sovereignty in both law and practice"[2] and "the rapid, growing, and uneven cross-border flow of goods, services, people, money, technology, information, ideas, culture, crime, and weapons."[3] A combination of these definitions are used in this chapter in order to provide the broadest possible meaning of the word that encompasses the nuances of the interviewees.

Geopolitics refers to the relationship between the territory and resources of the state and making of policy among sovereign states.[4] To some extent, the meaning of geopolitics is embedded in a time when the possession of territory and resources, physical assets, meant power. However, in the period of globalization, territory and resources have diminished somewhat in value while new economic- and information-based assets have increasingly become features of state power. The existence of globalization has expanded the definition of geopolitics to include the nonphysical resources of the state that can be used to augment state power and can affect the making of its foreign policy. Thus in common use the term geopolitics often encompasses the ideas of realpolitik as well: "the state's interest provides the spring of action; the necessities of policy arise from the unregulated competition of states; calculation based on these necessities can discover the policies that will best serve a state's interest ... success is defined as preserving and strengthening the state."[5] Thus the state is the primary actor and holds the authority to make decisions for the nation or nations it represents in the pursuit of the national interest.

In the comprehensive definition of geopolitics and realpolitik, the centrality of state sovereignty becomes apparent. As the primary unit in the international system, the state uses sovereignty as a basis for its actions in the domestic and geopolitical arenas. Sovereignty, defined as "a final and absolute authority in the political community,"[6] lies in the hands of the state as the highest recognized political community. However, the authority ascribed to state sovereignty can be limited by the decisions of the state itself. According to Kenneth N. Waltz, a sovereign state "decides for itself how it will cope with its internal and external problems, including whether or not to seek assistance from others and in doing so to limit its freedom by making commitments to them."[7] Thus alliances and membership in various international organizations, as well as being party to international agreements, can all place limitations on the exercise of state sovereignty.

Moreover, state sovereignty can be undermined by the lack of state legitimacy, as perceived internally by its citizenry or externally by international standards. The state holds sovereignty over its populace based upon the assumption that it is the legitimate representative of the people and that its authority therefore is superior to that of the individual.

Democratic regimes rest their claim to legitimacy and sovereignty on the will of the majority determined through constitutionalism[8] and electoral processes. Authoritarian regimes, in that they are not elected governments, face pressure from both internal groups who feel that their interests are not being represented and democratic countries that believe the actions of the authoritarian state are an illegitimate representation of the interests of its people.[9] As a consequence, over the past half century states and populations have increasingly viewed electoral democracy as the international standard for state legitimacy.[10] The international community has intervened on behalf of the citizens of an authoritarian state on the basis that there exist individual rights (such as human rights) that supersede the authority of the state. International popular sentiment often supports that concept that the international community has the responsibility to intervene to protect individual rights in the absence of a representative government.[11]

Challenges to Sovereignty in a Globalized World

As globalization increasingly places a premium on modern economic institutions, technology, and information, states must reorganize their priorities to be able to compete in the new world. Developing countries in particular encounter difficulties in juggling the domestic imperatives with the international norms they are expected to follow. Implementation of many of the international rules for expanding growth and competitiveness often simultaneously produces widespread joblessness and political discontent at increasing income inequality. In addition, developing countries view some of the rules as unfair at the outset, and they consider their own ability to adjust these rules in their own favor small. The perception is that the continued existence of these rules as binding on the state's actions will ultimately prove harmful to the state's pursuit of its national interests, and therefore state sovereignty must be protected in some way.

For many, the implications of the new geopolitics is "a new geopolitical order dominated by geo-economic questions and issues, a world where the globalization of economic activity and global flows of trade, investment, commodities and images are re-making states, sovereignty and the geographical structure of the planet."[12]

The forces of globalization have the capability to affect state sovereignty in the economic, political, and military arenas, though most often, significant overlap occurs among these areas. The effects are felt through both domestic and international pressures on the state's ability to make sovereign decisions. Growing wealth inequality leads to domestic political legitimacy problems. Human rights or environmental regulations affect trade and investment relations, and military maneuvers can result in international economic sanctions. The rapid transfer of information and publicity on human rights abuses in another country can result in military action being taken against the transgressing state. In addition, the rapid advance and transfer of military technology to competitors can build the view that state security is being threatened, leading to spiraling international arms races. Globalization creates internal pressures for protection against economic, cultural, and military threats, internal pressures for more rapid change to meet these challenges, as well as external pressures for further opening and adjustment to international standards. Hence, states in the twenty-first century are being forced to make critical choices, either to preserve state sovereignty by walling themselves off from the march of globalization or by adopting policies designed to maximize sovereign power by harvesting the fruits of globalization.

Globalization's ability to create great wealth rapidly has consequences for internal stability and state legitimacy. Increases in income inequality lead to social dissatisfaction and political instability, which can undermine the sovereignty of the state by decreasing state legitimacy: "[G]lobalization offers rising elites and the urban middle class a bigger share of the pie. If this share increases too rapidly, and if the rest of the pie is not made available to others because of monopolies or corruption, the government can lose its legitimacy, as it did in Indonesia."[13] There is ambivalence in these countries as to whether domestic elites should be blamed for the vast inequalities in wealth, or if external forces of trade and investment and iniquitous international rules are the problem.

Among developing countries, there is also a feeling that existing international rules have raised the standards on the developing world and, therefore, are unfairly inhibiting growth by placing limits on state behavior that did not exist earlier for the developed countries. Benjamin R. Barber has summarized the feelings of developing nations with regard to the debate on globalization and the environment, "[E]cological consciousness has meant not only greater awareness but also greater inequality, as modernized nations try to slam the door behind them, saying to developing nations, 'The world cannot afford your modernization; ours has wrung it dry!'"[14] Although existing pollution may have originated in other regions, in the end all states must abide by new environmental rules that make the field more difficult for new players. In addition, opponents of globalization say that it "feeds corporate profits at the expense of workers, undermines democracy, accelerates environmental destruction, lowers health and labor standards, imposes cultural homogeneity, feeds crime, and escalates armed conflict."[15] Increasingly, international engagement implies obedience to international rules and regulations that can be perceived as limiting the sovereignty of the state in pursuing policies in its national interest.

This speaks to a deeper sense in significant parts of the world that globalization has been unjust. There is a perception of unfairness in the rules of the game as well as unfairness in the distribution of the gains. The only solution seems to be strengthening the state's position vis-à-vis the international rule-making community, and the United States in particular, in order to be able to change the future international rules in favor of the state's national interests. Ellen L. Frost explains the importance of the United States in this calculation as a consequence of the dominant U.S. role in international institutions, "Since people in other countries tend to assume that the United States pulls the strings of the World Bank and IMF, financial crises of the Indonesian variety ignite anti-Americanism as well as evoking a legitimate humanitarian outcry."[16] Samuel P. Huntington cites international elites in stating that the leaders of countries with most of the world's population see the United States as their greatest external threat, "They do not see America as a military threat; they see it as a threat to their integrity, autonomy, prosperity, and freedom of action to pursue their interests as they see fit."[17] However, any constraint on autonomy and freedom of action is synonymous with limitations on state sovereignty.

Sovereignty in China and India

The ultimate priority for China and India was the need to preserve state autonomy and the ability to make sovereign decisions. However, each country's respondents emphasized a different set of objectives to be sought by protecting sovereignty. For example, Chinese respondents focused on maintaining territorial sovereignty, particularly with respect to Taiwan, while economic and political issues were of secondary importance. Indian respondents stated that sovereignty on economic and political issues was of prime importance, and territorial sovereignty was not mentioned. These trends emphasize the importance of differing perceptions of the fragility of national unity in the process of formulating national interests in China and India. Moreover, they underline that the absence of national unity in China has led to a deep emphasis on territorial sovereignty to protect the unity of the state, whereas greater confidence in unity in India has allowed the state to focus on more global aspects of political and economic sovereignty.

In both states, respondents viewed an increase of state power (comprehensive national strength) to be the solution to the perceived threat to state sovereignty. State power was defined commonly as the comprehensive national strength, which is comprised of both military and economic power. For China and India, this meant pursuit of a defense modernization program to increase military might, and economic reforms for rapid economic growth. Chinese respondents found that the defense modernization could be useful in militarily protecting territorial interests.

However, Indian respondents did not see the use of military force in protecting territorial sovereignty as effective; modernization of conventional forces and development of nuclear forces were both for enhancing comprehensive national strength and deterrence rather than actual use. Both countries' respondents felt that maintenance of a nuclear option was necessary for protecting state sovereignty because it deterred external threats. In addition, respondents in both countries felt that by increasing comprehensive national strength, a state could improve its position in the international system and have economic, political, and military leverage in shaping rules in favor of the national interest.

China

For Chinese respondents, globalization was a threat to state sovereignty; thus they needed military modernization and economic reforms programs to increase the comprehensive national strength. They believed that defense modernization and economic reforms programs to increase comprehensive national strength would help preserve state sovereignty. The rapid movement and changing nature of military technology brought into sharp focus territorial sovereignty, particularly as pertaining to the protection of Taiwan.[18] Respondents said that the spread of advanced weaponry to Taiwan eroded the PRC's ability to defend its sovereignty over the island, and possible future U.S. intervention in a cross-Straits conflict was a further example of sovereignty infringement. The historical examples of Iraq, the Gulf War, and Kosovo were often cited for illuminating the need to protect territorial sovereignty from external actors such as the United States.[19] Chinese respondents stated that U.S. arms sales and support to Taiwan was analogous to U.S. and other external intervention in Iraq and the Gulf War. Given this example, competing with new military standards set by the international transfer of military technology was integral to defending against Taiwanese independence.

Furthermore, in order to increase its economic power China would need to adapt to the new international rules of market competition and globalization. Globalized markets meant that China could reap great economic benefits from trade through improved competitiveness, or it could face economic strain by not adapting enough. Economic strength could translate into technological and military strength as well, whereas economic weakness could lead to foreign countries taking advantage of China's difficulty.[20] New economic power combined with military strength was valuable for increasing China's leverage in international negotiations and rule making, thereby protecting sovereignty of decision making on a wide variety of fronts into the future.[21]

The Erosion of Chinese State Sovereignty

Chinese respondents viewed state sovereignty as increasingly threatened, particularly by the U.S. dominance in international decision making and U.S. involvement in the Taiwan issue.[22] They stated the U.S. ability to intervene in other states' sovereignty was a consequence of its relatively great economic and military power, i.e., its comprehensive national strength, and its interest in maintaining its premier position in the world. Thus, they saw the dominance of the United States in world politics as a sign of hegemony: "The U.S. capability to change rules, make rules on our control is a result of both its military and economic power. The strong powers make the rules, and the weak observe the rules, and the rules are made in the interest of the strong powers. And that is not fair."[23] The U.S. capability to influence rules and international regimes that affect China was viewed as harmful to China's pursuit of its national interests. Respondents said that because the rules in the international system were heavily influenced by great powers such as the United States, the rules were inherently biased in favor of the more powerful states.[24] Consequently, as all states were forced to accept and abide by these rules, the sovereignty of weaker states such as China would suffer. One senior Communist official said the greatest security problem facing China in the next decade is that possibly "the hegemonists force their will and their opinions on China, and the Chinese people cannot do their own thing, such as the four modernizations. Hegemony or big power is not pointing to a single country, but some coming international aspects, some threats."[25]

Chinese interviewees found the U.S. use of force in pursuing its perceived interests internationally as particularly disturbing. U.S. actions were seen as undertaken in opposition to international norms and therefore illegitimate.

> Ignoring the norms committed by the previous governments, such as the ABM [antiballistic missile treaty] or the Kyoto protocol, the effects may not appear right away. But gradually if they follow this approach, they will run into a counterforce from other countries. The American interests will be hurt in the long run if they continue to do this. The use of military force may be effective against Iraq or Kosovo, but for the bigger countries it may not work.[26]

To respondents, U.S. policies abroad represented intervention in other countries' internal issues and, therefore, infringements of individual states' sovereign rights. The U.S. intervention in Iraq, Kosovo, and the Gulf War were cited repeatedly as examples of U.S. violation of other states' sovereignty.

> Respondent A: Most of the world didn't agree with the Iraq War and preemption. China believed that this policy would lead to anarchy. Any country could attack any country without evidence.[27]

Respondent B: We have had good experience with people's war, but this isn't good enough. Some say in Europe it is Kosovo, in Asia it is Taiwan.[28]

Respondent C: After the Gulf War, people were struck—if we had an attack from the outside what would we do?[29]

Respondent D: Now there is a new type of warfare where the enemy uses precision and guided missiles, laser guided and GPS [global positioning system], cruise missiles, stealth fighters; the whole concept is changing.[30]

The effectiveness of the U.S. military intervention in these conflicts also represented the new technological threat posed by modern weaponry. If the United States, or another country, chose to intervene in China's affairs, China would have to be prepared for the new technological level of warfare.

Comprehensive National Strength: Defense Modernization for Protecting Sovereignty

Chinese respondents viewed the defense modernization program, in conjunction with the economic reforms, as vital to building comprehensive national strength and creating a strong defensive capability that is competitive in the high-tech world. Respondents regarded China's history of facing aggression by other states as a consequence of its relatively weak comprehensive national strength. Without addressing this weakness, China could not be safe. Respondents viewed comprehensive national strength as necessary for a country to protect its sovereignty in making decisions in the national interest and to avoid aggressive bullying by more powerful states. Notably, interviewees expressed concern that without comprehensive national strength, China could face possible coercion by other countries on issues such as human rights, environmental issues, and Taiwan.

> Before, China's comprehensive national strength was weak, so other countries were able to have aggression on China. Fifty years ago, Japan also was able to do this, but now it cannot because China's comprehensive national strength is greater. It has an effect on a countries rank in the world, and helps to protect them. If you have a large comprehensive national strength you can protect your territory. This is not a contradiction; protecting territory is part of comprehensive national strength.[31]

The threat of foreign intervention combined with the high-technology weaponry available to other countries convinced Chinese respondents that a defense modernization is necessary. Chinese respondents emphasized that historical incidences in which Chinese sovereignty was invaded cannot be repeated. They noted that the ultimate goal of Deng Xiaoping's four modernizations, which included both the defense modernization and economic reforms, was to improve China's comprehensive national strength so that these historical incidences would not be repeated. Additionally, comprehensive national strength, in providing the state with fungible power, could also shield China from intrusive actions by other countries on issues that were not essentially military in nature.

> Respondent A: We can not be like the beginning of the century, when the eight powers invaded China and we had to fight the invaders using agricultural era weaponry against industrial era weaponry. We do not want that kind of history to come again, so we must modernize.[32]

> Respondent B: The four modernizations have the purpose of gaining comprehensive power. That will help China play a major role as a major power in the region, so China will not be bullied.[33]

> Respondent C: Better defensive capability can help China protect sovereignty of decision making especially related to the national future such as human rights, environment, and so on. When you are strong, it does not have to be against others, but it can be that you don't force me to do things.[34]

> Respondent D: We need to have deterrence, if we are weaker then we will be bullied.[35]

Maintaining a viable military capability was considered an integral part of comprehensive national strength. Despite its powerful economy, Japan provided an example of weak comprehensive national strength due to its lack of autonomous defense capabilities: "Even Japan has had economic modernization, but it cannot play a leading role like the U.S. because it does not have comprehensive power."[36]

Moreover, the military component of comprehensive national strength could be considered credible only if it were of international high-technology standards. "National integrity will be threatened by national missile defense and theater missile defense because these are very modern systems. China needs modernization for this self-defense."[37] Chinese respondents felt that China's military standards should be similar to those of the most advanced states in the world. The revolution in military affairs meant for respondents that China would need to develop military technology comparable to the highest standards to maintain its standing compared with the greater powers.

> Respondent A: China needs modernization to keep up with the international tide of the revolution in military affairs. Each country has to modernize its military—China does the same.[38]

> Respondent B: After the end of the Cold War, it is not only China, but all the other major powers who are trying to look at military issues from a new perspective. The main reason is technology, particularly high technology. If you look at what the U.S. or Japan is doing, China should do this, if nothing else, to catch up.[39]

Respondent C: The biggest countries are developing their Air Force and Navy. The U.S., Japan, China, France, India are all doing this, otherwise they will fall behind.[40]

Respondent D: Now China needs to modernize the Navy and Air Force because they are very far behind in weaponry. China's defense spending does not have the same quantity or quality as Japan.[41]

Respondent E: India and Russia will put more money to modernize their defense, and there will be another arms race in the world. The U.S. will have a military superiority, so it is a threat.[42]

In consideration of the high-technological standards of military capabilities maintained by its neighbors and competitors, China would of necessity have to upgrade its defenses. The greatest threat cited by Chinese respondents was clearly the United States, as it pertained to the Taiwan issue. They perceived possible U.S. intervention in a conflict between the mainland and Taiwan as a given, with only the extent of U.S. involvement debatable. Therefore, the Chinese military would have to prepare for contingencies involving the United States in order to firmly safeguard territorial sovereignty over Taiwan. A scholar summarized four main reasons for a defense modernization that reflect a strong desire to protect Chinese sovereignty against U.S. contravention:

1) Now the threat perception is more directed to the U.S., because it is more probable that the U.S. might use force against China, especially on the Taiwan Straits. 2) China's military equipment is lagging far behind the equipment of the Western countries, and Taiwan is buying advanced weapons. If China does not develop advanced weapons it cannot deal with this problem. 3) Other countries have developed high technology, so foreign troops will not come to China. They will use high technology weapons. So, if China wants to protect the territorial integrity and security of China, it must develop technologically. 4) China does not want to have an arms race with the U.S. But because its equipment is lagging behind, it must be able to defend itself with a second strike capability. Otherwise it will be like the 1950s and 1960s when China was blackmailed during the Korean War. When the U.S. knew China was developing nuclear weapons, there was discussion of pre-emptive attack.[43]

Other interviewees were similarly apprehensive regarding the threat of U.S. intervention. They reported that trouble regarding sovereignty over Taiwan is "the biggest potential conflict" for China, with the United States as the instigator.

Respondent A: If the U.S. did not intervene, Taiwan would have become a part of China in the 1960s. I think that with the support of the U.S., Taiwan would probably just go for independence and that would lead to war.[44]

Respondent B: We think China must be prepared for a possible conflict that would be high tech. Therefore we would have to selectively beef up our defensive capabilities in case of a contingency that may involve the U.S.[45]

Respondent C: In terms of security threats, the Korean Peninsula, the South China Sea, the Taiwan Straits, three out of four are in China's area. We must prepare for this, or we just have to wait to be bombed. Even on Taiwan, we have to be prepared for the U.S. forces in our planning or we are not good strategists.[46]

Respondent D: The biggest external threat is the U.S., but this is in connection with Taiwan. The U.S. is superior to China in military matters, so we should develop so we have more deterrence on Taiwan.[47]

Respondent E: The typical thinking here relates the Taiwan issue with the U.S. So, the military modernization is directed towards deterring military attacks from the U.S.[48]

Respondent F: China fears a military threat in case the U.S. supports and supplies weapons to Taiwan, but also if it decides to intervene militarily in Taiwan.[49]

Respondents said that a credible nuclear capability was the ultimate deterrence against U.S. infringement on Chinese sovereignty: "Before China developed nuclear weapons, it suffered nuclear blackmail in the 1950s and 1960s. Having nuclear weapons made China's status important today. The fact that China has nuclear weapons makes a difference. When other countries such as the U.S. think of Taiwan, this makes them more cautious."[50]; "The nuclear capability is mainly to deter the U.S. from getting too deeply involved in China's internal affairs, such as Taiwan, Tibet, or Xinjiang."[51]

Economic Reforms: Sovereignty in the Economic and Political Sphere

Chinese respondents viewed globalization as an international force which in and of itself had changed the boundaries of state sovereignty in the economic and political sphere. If the PRC did not adapt its economic infrastructure to accommodate the financial, communication, and technological forces of globalization, China would not be able to procure the investment it needed, and it could not be competitive in international markets. If China did not accept globalization and reform its economy, not only would the economy stagnate, but the CCP could lose legitimacy: "The key factor for today's government legitimacy is the progress of the whole society, living standard improvement or any progress related to national dignity."[52] "They had to have growth and welfare for the legitimacy of the party to govern the people."[53] The loss of regime legitimacy, leading to political disorder and possible chaos would in turn negatively affect China's ability to implement its policies. Economic growth bolstering legitimacy was then also needed to maintain state sovereignty.

Additionally, a slow economy resulting from insufficient reforms would mean scarce budgetary resources for defense, leading to possible future problems deterring foreign states over territorial sovereignty. Any or all of these reasons could lead to a crisis in legitimacy for the CCP. Conversely, strong economic growth resulting from successful reforms would mean enhanced CCP legitimacy and greater comprehensive national strength with which to protect state sovereignty.[54] The exigencies of a globalized economy meant for China that economic reforms would have to be pursued with fervor, both to protect the state from internal strain and from external transgressions.

Therefore interviewees saw globalization as a force that must be accommodated, that attempts to steer clear of globalization would cause more harm than good to the country. They agreed that China must join in the globalized world but must take care to protect China's sovereignty at the same time. A senior Communist Party official outlined the PRC's view toward the effects of economic globalization:

> We want to join globalization. We can get more resources and more investment opportunities from globalization. But we have also found that globalization has its negative sides, things that can hurt the social stability and our economy. We need to participate positively in this globalization, but at the same time protect the sovereignty and interests of our country.[55]

Chinese respondents believed that China needed to join the world economy and learn to be more competitive in order to succeed economically. Increased volumes of trade and higher technological levels would add to the state's economic power. Economic reforms and opening held the key to strength in a globalized world and could ultimately help protect state sovereignty.

> Respondent A: Globalization is a large process that China must join. In face of this process, all countries face both opportunities and challenges ... there is a kind of competition, but this can be just one, a competition of comprehensive national power.[56]

> Respondent B: China has to integrate itself into the world economy if it wants to be an economic giant.[57]

> Respondent C: GATT [General Agreement on Tariffs and Trade] and WTO [World Trade Organization] promoted the process of reform and opening. Because GATT accession has for a long time been the focus of the world, China was encouraged to join the international club and follow international norms. So, we know we need to open the market and reform our economic regime.[58]

> Respondent D: People know from the internet that globalization is occurring, and the country must open for this, and that the growth rate increased as a result of exports.[59]

Interviewees viewed economic reforms as critical for driving China's technological advancement. They believed maintaining international standards of technology was vital to increasing economic competitiveness in manufacturing of consumer electronics, trade, and military hardware. Development and acquisition of high technology, as a central component of the globalized economy, would then lead to greater comprehensive national strength.

> Especially now, high technology is developing quickly in Western countries and developed countries, so people think to develop information technology and high technology is necessary if you want to survive and strengthen your position in economic globalization. China is no exception. If you want your nation to survive in the future, you must have reforms and open-door policy.[60]

Economic globalization has also been an important impetus for defense modernization through the inevitable exchange of technology from the civilian sector to the military sector: "Now the military and civilian technology sector and are easily interchangeable. For example, the computer technology and especially the information technology are providing a strong basis for the military."[61]

By taking advantage of the growth provided by globalization, respondents said that China would be able to protect itself from economic catastrophe in the future and expand the economic component of its comprehensive national strength. In doing so, China would be able to protect its sovereignty so that other countries could not force China to accept decisions or abide by rules that were not viewed as in China's national interest.

> Respondent A: The Chinese think that because China is weak and must depend on the U.S. for its trade relations, even if the U.S. makes some unreasonable steps China must accept it because China is weak. There is a Chinese saying, *"ruoguo wuwaijiao,"* there is no diplomacy for weak countries.[62]

> Respondent B: Because China had bad experiences from historical aggressions, China thought this is a result of a weak economy. If it has economic strength, this will not occur.[63]

> Respondent C: As a developing country, we have a voice but with globalization trends, any country that can't dominate the economy will find that its voice is weaker.[64]

> Respondent D: If openness is low, development will be low. Economic growth and openness can help China have economic dominance in rulemaking in the system, and have a stronger voice and dominance to become an important member of the international club.[65]

> Respondent E: According to Deng's conception of development the economy is the most important in opposing hegemony.[66]

> Respondent F: After 100 years of aggression, China wants to develop.[67]

Thus by improving defensive capabilities and the economic power of the country, China would be able to defend its sovereignty in making decisions in its national interest. In particular, the ability to defend territorial integrity on Taiwan would be enhanced, China's ability to affect international rule making on economic and political issues would be improved, and China would generally not be subject to future infringements on its policies.

India
Sovereignty of Decision Making in the Economic and Political Spheres

For Indian respondents, protection of sovereignty of decision making over a wide area of political and economic issues formed the basis for pursuit of defense modernization and economic reforms programs. They viewed the main purpose as an increase in comprehensive national strength in order to enable India to join in the international rule-making process in India's economic interests and to protect India from international military coercion as seen in the Iraq War, Kosovo, and the Gulf War. Respondents did not see territorial integrity as an issue of concern; only one respondent mentioned this as important. Conversely, they considered India's ability to influence international rules to be of prime importance. Power in the globalized world was more a function of economic power rather than military power to Indian respondents. However, maintaining a nuclear deterrent was critical in that it served as a large component of comprehensive national strength although the nuclear capability's importance was seen as coming from its deterrence value rather than from its actual tactical value in war fighting. Jochen Hippler summarizes this arena for competition:

> The crucial fight today is over control: control of the Third World, control of developments in Russia and the whole of Eastern Europe, control of resources; and control of each other's markets, currencies, and economic and political potential. It is less a fight for territory than to control the structures of the international system, and to set up and control the rules … . This strategy will be based on military means if necessary, but mostly it will be pursued by "peaceful" means, by economic penetration, by economic and political instruments in general.[68]

Integration with the world economy became increasingly vital for gaining and maintaining the economic growth that India needed. "It became very clear to everyone that interdependence was the name of the game. With the information revolution, information technology, it became a global village. If you want sustained growth, you have to integrate and interact with other countries."[69] With the growing significance of economic strength, Indian respondents noted the decreasing influence of territorial issues. "Even Indians think, why are we still arguing with Pakistan and China. Military methods are becoming less important, people don't want to be obsessed with these. The disputes are pretty stupid, if you think of it. Territory is not so important."[70]

However, the end of the Cold War and the importance of interdependence for many Indians meant a new set of insecurities, and new ways of thinking. In the post-Cold War era began a basic change of philosophy from the early Indian international idealism, whereby Indians could through peaceful means and the nonaligned movement implement change, to that of realism, where state power was necessary to deal with the world and security issues.

> The U.S. won the Cold War and over 25 years was not friendly to India. And the Soviets, our friend, lost and collapsed. China and Pakistan seemed to come out on the right side of history. The U.S., China, and Pakistan threw the Indian world view into crisis. India, which had hoped for an end to the Cold War, seemed to come out on the wrong side. Add to that the domestic threats and the economic crisis, and the fall of governments in quick succession. All of these things left a deep impression on the Indian middle class. This is why they have shifted to the right.[71]

The new perspective in Indian political thought had ramifications for every area of Indian policy in that relative power became more important to Indian policy makers. The influence of international organizations and other individual countries in the making of rules that India would be expected to follow meant to respondents that India needed to increase its ability to influence rule making. To accomplish this, Indian respondents said that India needed to spur economic growth and enhance its defensive capabilities. Increasing the country's economic and military power, its comprehensive national strength, gained acceptance as the path to protecting state sovereignty.

In the economic sphere, Indian respondents viewed international institutions as very powerful in their ability to affect India's economic policy and economy. Although most Indian respondents believed that economic reforms were beneficial to India, they noted that some of the changes and rules that India must abide by were implemented under duress.

> Respondent A: In the modern world, influences of the IMF and World Bank should not be underestimated.[72]

> Respondent B: A lot of what was done in economic reforms was also because of requirements from the U.S., from the World Bank, from the IMF. Opening up was thrust on India.[73]

> Respondent C: One of the common disputes in the WTO today is on free trade, applying rules, on non-tariff barriers to protect your own markets. To put these in place without having a fair playing field is not right.[74]

In addition, a military official emphasized that developed and developing countries have a distinct difference in their economic interests that is revealed in their policy preferences: "There are many places where developing countries take the view that is inimical to the developed countries. Today, it is in the interest of the developed countries to keep the price of primary products down and those of value added up."[75]

Indian respondents viewed the U.S. policy toward India's nuclear program as an infringement on their right to sovereign decision making in the sphere of national security interests. A senior military official questioned the appropriateness of the U.S. stand on Indian nuclear testing: "That is the problem we have with the U.S., it is a great and free country, but we don't seem to be able to understand each other. They ask, 'Why did you explode a nuclear device?' We have China on one border, and Pakistan on another. Are we inferior human beings, that we cannot be responsible?"[76]

To the majority of Indian respondents, globalization's gradual erosion of India's ability to make sovereign decisions required a policy response that could enable India to protect state sovereignty. This policy response was the economic reforms program and the defense modernization program, which together formed a comprehensive national strength.

Comprehensive National Strength to Counteract the Erosion of State Sovereignty

Indian respondents viewed increasing comprehensive national strength as vital to protecting state sovereignty in the globalized world. The main components of national power were divided into military strength, as seen mainly in a nuclear deterrent, and economic strength, seen as economic competitiveness and growth in an increasingly globalized world.

Respondent A: This government, when it came to power, had the manifesto in which it was clearly mentioned that we will set up a national security system. The idea behind it was not purely defense or military, but to have a holistic view of national security, which includes food security, energy security, and various other factors.[77]

Respondent B: There has been education and awareness of security matters from the world and our own history. The effect is that people are now very concerned about security and they realize that economic security can't happen without general security and vice versa.[78]

Respondent C: India's position in the world again will depend on its economic capability. The role it can play toward disarmament or economics—our emphasis has been that the rules should be fair and equitable to all, not different criteria for different income countries.[79]

Respondent D: Today, what is national security? It is your ability to take sovereign decisions, so nuclear deterrence is also for that purpose. It is comprehensive, but it is not that we're trying to become proactive. It is defensive.[80]

Respondent E: We should have continued autonomy on decision making at the international level on how we see any issue, whether East Timor, Kosovo, climate, etc. You may find today your interests coincide with some other country, but you should have the capability to take autonomous decisions.[81]

Respondent F: India should have a say in protecting the interests of the developing nations. India has to take a lead in rule making of the WTO and of nuclear issues through the NPT [Nuclear Non-Proliferation Treaty] … India should be for the democratization of the United Nations.[82]

Indian respondents agreed with Chinese respondents that both economic and military might were necessary to have national power. By enhancing India's comprehensive national strength, Indian respondents believed that India's capability to make and defend its decision on issues as varied as human rights, environment, trade, and nonproliferation could be ensured.

Defense Modernization: The Nuclear Deterrent

Indian respondents stated that a strong defensive capability in conjunction with a strong economy was necessary in order to have comprehensive national strength. Although respondents said that a military modernization was needed for conventional forces in order to keep abreast of modern technology, their focus was turned more toward developing India's nuclear deterrent. A nuclear deterrent was considered both economical and effective for protecting state sovereignty. Respondents said that conventional forces were currently needed primarily to deal with the threat from Pakistan in Kashmir and that current conventional forces were sufficient for the job. In addition, an interesting feature is that the vast majority of interviewees did not view China as a serious threat. The warming of relations between India and China in the past two decades through confidence-building measures and diplomatic visits created the sense that China is not an imminent threat to India. Of the respondents who mentioned China, the primary threat cited was the transfer of weapons technology from China to Pakistan:

China will be a competitor, a major player, and there is no reason that it should be a military threat or doing physical threat and harm to India. The Chinese military buildup and modernization is a concern, all countries bordering China are concerned, but even I don't think China will bring a hundred divisions to the border. But military power is a force in being, so you need to do something about it. Why is China a concern to us? Because China helps Pakistan, if there is a war with Pakistan, what will the Chinese do? But it isn't the kind of threat where the Chinese are coming down the Himalayas.

India is trying to build a constructive dialogue where possible, such as the 1993 accord on peace and tranquility on the line of control. The confidence building measures have worked well and the Indian Army has been able to pull back from the border.[83]

To face the long-term threats to India's sovereignty, military capabilities focused on territorial defense of the borders with Pakistan and China were less important, according to respondents. Former Army Chief V. P. Malik explained the transformation of India's security focus from traditional territorial defense to a broader concept of defense: "As our economy improves, ... , along with that you have to build capabilities to protect your national interests. The major change is, now it is more national interest based, whereas before it was territorial integrity."[84]

Indian respondents said that defending the more vague ability to make sovereign decisions on economic and political issues would require a nuclear deterrent. They stressed that in a globalized world where the U.N. Security Council and nations with a nuclear capability have dominant power, India must also maintain such a deterrent to protect its sovereignty. It was viewed as a cheaper alternative to conventional weaponry, but with the benefit of added deterrence. The centrality of a credible nuclear deterrence to enhance India's comprehensive national strength was repeatedly stated:

Respondent A: As far as the major powers have made nuclear weapons a currency of power, you have to keep up with the world. From the late 1970s, China started arming Pakistan. This is part of the globalization process. Whatever arms are produced in the world today, after some time it reaches your neighborhood.[85]

Respondent B: The fact is that China is a full-fledged nuclear weapons power, Pakistan is a nuclear weapons power, so in this environment we are not like Japan or Western Europe. We have no protection of the U.S. umbrella. In order to not be affected by nuclear blackmail, there was a political consensus in India by all political parties that we had to leave the nuclear option open.[86]

Respondent C: The nuclear capability is a kind of deterrent—a deterrent to rectify the imbalance. No country will use it.[87]

Respondent D: If others have them, you need to too ... . Nuclear weapons are a threat saying that we will take interference to an extent, after which we will respond with a nuclear threat to would be nuclear threats. But we have eschewed first use of nuclear-weapons, we have a policy of minimal credible deterrence.[88]

Respondent E: The nuclear capability was essential to counter any threat to its sovereignty and to also tell the world that though this is the oldest nation, that it is not the nation of snake charmers and camel riders.[89]

Respondent F: The U.N. Security Council said you can come in if you have money or the bomb, and money is hard to come by.[90]

Respondent G: To be frank, when China detonated, she became a member of the UN Security Council. In this world, power is appreciated. China is a clear example of it. Why do the U.K. and France need a nuclear capability? I would love to have a garden of Eden, but the world is not like that.[91]

Respondent H: Without nukes, even economically advanced countries are not able to play an influential role in international politics.[92]

The respondents viewed nuclear capability as a defense against interference in Indian sovereignty, particularly in the event of implied or explicit nuclear threats from other countries. As part of India's comprehensive national strength, the nuclear deterrence had spillover effects that enabled India to enhance its leverage in decision making even in the economic field: "In terms of technological advancements, our sphere of interest has to increase if we are to progress economically. We must be able to export much more. Any impediments to trade we must be able to halt. Nuclear capabilities come into play here, they say that please allow us to do our business and don't do an Iraq on us, an Afghanistan on us."[93]

Economic Reforms for Strengthening and State Sovereignty

The Indian government accepted that economic reforms were required for economic growth in the increasingly interdependent world. Economic reforms allowed India to join in competitive markets and expand its economic strength through trade and investment. Indian decision makers were influenced heavily to pursue this path by the examples of the failed Soviet Union and the booming East Asian economies, particularly China. As the only viable remaining path for economic growth, reforms were embarked upon. There were two main purposes for pursuing the reforms, the first and most obvious reason being to eradicate poverty in India and promote development more successfully than the former planned economy model by taking advantage of trade led growth in a globalized economy. The second reason, however, was to increase India's comprehensive national strength in order to help protect India's sovereignty of decision making on a variety of issue areas, such as human rights and the environment. The majority of respondents emphasized the importance of globalization as the main reason for pursuing economic reforms.

Respondent A: Most important are the economic requirements of globalization. The *swadeshi* [indigenous production] chaps can talk, but trade is an important source of finance.[94]

Respondent B: Globalization. We saw the example of the Southeast Asian nations and China which has also liberalized so that they could achieve rapid growth. So we learned our lesson, but late.[95]

Respondent C: The first thing has been the revolution in information technology and satellite TV. At first it was only government TV, now you have all kinds of international information on the outside world, this increases the demand here that we should also reach those levels.[96]

Respondent D: The world was changing around us quickly and was moving more toward a globalized economy. So, sticking to a socialist structure would not have been wise.[97]

Respondent E: People said look at Southeast Asia, Malaysia, Singapore, they are doing extremely well. Especially China, if they can do so well and they had similar policies, then why not us? These changes led to the changes of Indian domestic economic policies.[98]

Respondents also viewed economic competitiveness and economic power as a necessary component of comprehensive national strength in the globalized world. Without economic strength, India could not be considered a developed country or sustain military competitiveness.

Respondent A: Earlier, nationalism was interpreted as self sufficiency. But in the changed world it is the economic power of a country that determines its clout in the world. Therefore, we interpret India's nationalism as an aspiration which is deeply shared in India that India should become a major global player considering its natural resources, mineral resources, human resources, and civilizational heritage.[99]

Respondent B: Economic security is the critical and vital ingredient. If you want military power, it needs to be backed by economic power. And economic power will only come with a galloping GDP [gross domestic product], and foreign capital inflows.[100]

Respondent C: Why did the government push so hard [for economic reforms]? When they looked out and saw what was happening and realized the geopolitical implications, that had international security implications. The China factor—you couldn't get away from the fact that they are doing well.[101]

Through economic integration with other countries, India could become an economic power, thereby increasing its comprehensive national strength. The combination of economic and military power would enable India to influence international rule making in its favor and prevent infringements on its right to make sovereign decisions in its national interest.[102] For India, respondents said that state sovereignty in deciding political and economic issues such as trade rules and human rights was of primary importance.

Conclusion

Both Chinese and Indian respondents stated that globalization was a critical factor in the decision to pursue defense modernization and economic reforms programs. The forces of globalization had eroded the ability of the state to make sovereign decisions in the national interest by changing the nature of state defense through the revolution in military affairs and by increasing the pressure of international rules through economic interdependence. Each country's respondents, however, focused on different aspects of state sovereignty that needed to be protected for the national interest to be served. In the case of China, territorial sovereignty was given the utmost importance.[103] This result corresponded with the respondents' view that protection of national unity was of prime importance, which was discussed in Chapter 3. In the case of India, respondents found that the state's ability to make sovereign decisions regarding its economic and political interests was most significant.[104]

According to the interviewees, the need to counter possible future infringements to state sovereignty induced state leaders of both China and India to follow policy paths that could increase the comprehensive national strength, i.e., the policies of defense modernization and economic reforms. For Indian and Chinese respondents, the main purpose of the economic reforms and defense modernization programs was to increase comprehensive national strength with the ultimate aim of protecting the state's abilities to pursue the national interests. The respondents' hierarchy of goals revealed what they considered most vital to the national interest. Both sets of interviewees considered economic reforms central to sustaining economic growth in a globalized economy. However, for Chinese respondents, the possibility of military conflict over the Taiwan issue required a modernization of defense capabilities for a tangible threat, and nuclear capabilities were vital to preventing nuclear blackmail by other nuclear countries. For Indian respondents a defense modernization, particularly a nuclear capability, was a deterrent against the vague future threat to state sovereignty on political and economic issues.

Notes

1. Paul Krugman defines globalization as originating from "the transfer of technology and capital from high-wage to low wage countries, and the resulting growth of labor intensive Third World exports," in Paul Krugman, *The Return of Depression Economics* (New York: W. W. Norton & Co., 2000), 16.

2. Marc F. Plattner and Aleksander Smolar, *Globalization, Power, and Democracy* (Baltimore, MD: The Johns Hopkins University Press, 2000), ix.

3. Stephen J. Flanagan, "Meeting the Challenges of the Global Century," in *The Global Century: Globalization and National Security, Vol. I,* ed. Richard L. Kugler and Ellen L. Frost (Washington, DC: National Defense University Press, 2001), 9.

4. Gearoid O Tuathail and John Agnew, "Geopolitics and Discourse: Practical Geopolitical Reasoning in American Foreign Policy," in *The Geopolitics Reader,* ed.

Gearoid O Tuathail, Simon Dalby, and Paul Routledge (New York: Routledge, 1998), 79.

5. Kenneth N. Waltz, "Anarchic Orders and Balances of Power," in *Neorealism and Its Critics*, ed. Robert O. Keohane (New York: Columbia University Press, 1986), 115.

6. F. H. Hinsley, *Sovereignty* (London: C. A. Watts & Co., Ltd., 1966), 1.

7. Kenneth N. Waltz, "Political Structures," in *Neorealism and Its Critics*, ed. Robert O. Keohane (New York: Columbia University Press, 1986), 90.

8. Hinsley, *Sovereignty*, 131–140, 156.

9. Lea Brilmayer, *American Hegemony: Political Morality in a One-Superpower World* (New Haven, CT: Yale University Press, 1994), 218–220.

10. Gidon Gottlieb cites the 1990 document of the Copenhagen meeting of the Conference on Security and Cooperation in Europe, stating that "the will of the people, freely and fairly expressed through periodic and genuine elections, is the basis of the authority and the legitimacy of all government," in Gidon Gottlieb, *Nation Against State: A New Approach to Ethnic Conflicts and the Decline of Sovereignty* (New York: Council on Foreign Relations Press, 1993), 20–21.

11. Brilmayer, *American Hegemony*, 218–220.

12. Gearoid O Tuathail, "Thinking Critically about Geopolitics," in *The Geopolitics Reader*, ed. Gearoid O Tuathail, Simon Dalby, and Paul Routledge (New York: Routledge, 1998), 2.

13. Ellen L. Frost, "Globalization and National Security: A Strategic Agenda," in *The Global Century: Globalization and National Security, Vol. I*, ed. Richard L. Kugler and Ellen L. Frost (Washington, DC: National Defense University Press, 2001), 46.

14. Benjamin R. Barber, "Jihad vs. McWorld," in *Globalization and the Challenges of a New Century*, ed. Patrick O'Meara, Howard D. Mehlinger, and Matthew Krain (Bloomington: Indiana University Press, 2000), 27.

15. Frost, "Globalization and National Security: A Strategic Agenda," 35.

16. Frost, "Globalization and National Security: A Strategic Agenda," 45.

17. Samuel P. Huntington, "Culture, Power, and Democracy," in *Globalization, Power, and Democracy*, ed. Marc F. Plattner and Aleksander Smolar (Baltimore, MD: The Johns Hopkins University Press, 2000), 7–8.

18. Scholar (Interview #18).

19. Military Official, Foreign Ministry Official (Interviews #12 and #41).

20. Communist Party Official (Interview #5).

21. Foreign Ministry Official (Interview #7).

22. Stated by more than half of the Chinese respondents.

23. Scholar (Interview #15).

24. Scholar (Interview #20).

25. Communist Party Official (Interview #1).

26. Military Official (Interview #11).

27. Foreign Ministry Official (Interview #42).

28. Military Official (Interview #12).

29. Scholar (Interview #20).

30. Scholar (Interview #26).

31. Communist Party Official (Interview #5).

32. Military Official (Interview #11).

33. Scholar (Interview #15).

34. Scholar (Interview #20).

35. Scholar (Interview #30).

36. Foreign Ministry Official (Interview #7).

37. Foreign Ministry Official (Interview #8).

38. Scholar (Interview #19).

39. Military Official (Interview #9).

40. Scholar (Interview #22).

41. Communist Party Official (Interview #5).

42. Foreign Ministry Official (Interview #8).

43. Scholar (Interview #15).

44. Foreign Ministry Official (Interview #4).

45. Military Official (Interview #9).

46. Military Official (Interview #12).

47. Scholar (Interview #14).

48. Scholar (Interview #17).

49. Scholar (Interview #18).

50. Foreign Ministry Official (Interview #4).

51. Scholar (Interview #15).

52. Scholar (Interview #17).

53. Scholar (Interview # 19).

54. Scholar (Interview #17).

55. Communist Party Official (Interview #1).

56. Foreign Ministry Official (Interview #2).

57. Scholar (Interview #16).

58. Ministry of Finance Official (Interview #3).

59. Scholar (Interview #15).

60. Foreign Ministry Official (Interview #8).

61. Military Official (Interview #9).

62. Scholar (Interview #15).

63. Scholar (Interview #22).

64. Military Official (Interview #12).

65. Government Official (Interview #13).

66. Scholar (Interview #21).

67. Ministry of Finance Official (Interview #3).

68. Jochen Hippler, *Pax Americana?: Hegemony or Decline* (Boulder, CO: Pluto Press, 1994), 187.

69. Senior Navy Official, in an interview with the author, New Delhi, India.

70. Ajit Kumar, Finance Secretary, in an interview with the author, New Delhi, India, 7 March 2001.

71. Kanti Bajpai, Professor of International Relations and Strategy, Jawaharlal Nehru University, in an interview with the author, New Delhi, India, 3 March 2001.

72. I. K. Gujral, Former Prime Minister of India, in an interview with the author, New Delhi, India, 26 February 2001.

73. Senior Military Official, in an interview with the author, New Delhi, India.

74. Ajit Kumar, Finance Secretary, in an interview with the author, New Delhi, India, 7 March 2001.

75. Senior Navy Official, in an interview with the author, New Delhi, India.

76. Senior Navy Official, in an interview with the author, New Delhi, India.

77. Brajesh Mishra, National Security Adviser and Secretary to Prime Minister Vajpayee, in an interview with the author, New Delhi, India, 22 February 2001.

78. General V. P. Malik, Former Chief of Army Staff, in an interview with the author, New Delhi, India, 2 March 2001.

79. Ajit Kumar, Finance Secretary, in an interview with the author, New Delhi, India, 7 March 2001.

80. General V. P. Malik, Former Chief of Army Staff, in an interview with the author, New Delhi, India, 2 March 2001.

81. Senior Official, Ministry of External Affairs, in an interview with the author, New Delhi, India.

82. M. V. Rappai, Visiting Fellow, Institute for Chinese Studies, in interviews with the author, New Delhi, India, 2001 and 2004.

83. Lt. Gen. V. R. Raghavan, President of the Delhi Policy Group, in interviews with the author, New Delhi, India, February 2001 and April 2004.

84. General V. P. Malik, Former Chief of Army Staff, in an interview with the author, New Delhi, India, 2 March 2001.

85. K. Subramanyam, Defense Editor, *Times of India,* in interviews with the author, New Delhi, India, February 2001 and April 2004.

86. Manmohan Singh [Prime Minister (2004–)], leader of the Opposition in the Rajya Sabha, in an interview with the author, New Delhi, India, 6 February 2001.

87. Ajit Kumar, Finance Secretary, in an interview with the author, New Delhi, India, 7 March 2001.

88. Senior Military Official, in an interview with the author, New Delhi, India.

89. Bangaru Laxman, President of the Bharatiya Janata Party, in an interview with the author, New Delhi, India, 24 February 2001.

90. I. K. Gujral, Former Prime Minister of India, in an interview with the author, New Delhi, India, 26 February 2001.

91. Senior Navy Official, in an interview with the author, New Delhi, India.

92. Chintamani Mahapatra, Professor at Jawaharlal Nehru University, in an interview with the author, May 2005.

93. Senior Military Official, in an interview with the author, New Delhi, India.

94. Rahul Mukerjee, Political Analyst, Centre for Policy Research, in an interview with the author, New Delhi, India, 30 January 2001.

95. Senior Navy Official, in an interview with the author, New Delhi, India.

96. Ajit Kumar, Finance Secretary, in an interview with the author, New Delhi, India, 7 March 2001.

97. Ajit Kumar, Finance Secretary, in an interview with the author, New Delhi, India, 7 March 2001.

98. G. V. C. Naidu, Defense Analyst, Indian Defense Studies and Analyses, in an interview with the author, New Delhi, India, 8 February 2001.

99. Manmohan Singh [Prime Minister (2004–)], Leader of the Opposition in the Rajya Sabha, in an interview with the author, New Delhi, India, 6 February 2001.

100. Lt. Gen. V. R. Raghavan, President of the Delhi Policy Group, in interviews with the author, New Delhi, India, February 2001 and April 2004.

101. Kanti Bajpai, Professor of International Relations and Strategy, Jawaharlal Nehru University, in an interview with the author, New Delhi, India, 3 March 2001.

102. Senior Official, Ministry of External Affairs, in an interview with the author, New Delhi, India.

103. The view of the majority of Chinese respondents.

104. The view of the majority of Indian respondents.

CHAPTER 5

Political Institutions and the Hierarchy of Interests

Introduction

Political institutions play a central role in determining the hierarchy of national interests in a country. The criteria for state legitimacy lead to prioritization of national objectives according to (1) what is critical for maintaining the state as a viable entity and (2) what are the main interests articulated by decision makers. States that depend upon performance criteria for sustaining political legitimacy face difficulty in maintaining political stability under crisis conditions, whereas states that have established political and legal institutions and processes for systematic decision making are more likely to have a durable political system to face crises.

According to the respondents, the political system has a critical effect on the ranking of different variables and the priority of national interests in countries. Although both China and India face many similar threats, because of the different political system adopted by each country, their national interest prioritization has been affected. Thus, democratic institutions make a difference in India, as do the institutional frailties of one-party rule in China.

In China, the respondents placed protection of state unity as the highest priority, and protection of economic sovereignty and growth the second priority. In both of these cases, respondents noted that failure could mean the end of Chinese Communist Party (CCP) leadership. Respondents felt that for the CCP, legitimacy was based upon the ability of the Party to perform the security and economic functions well. In addition, the integrated nature of the Party and state in the People's Republic of China (PRC) implied that Party and state legitimacy were intertwined. Thus failure of one could lead to failure of the other. Performance as a basis for legitimacy posed an inherent problem for the CCP in that internal and external divisive forces concurrently threatened Party and state legitimacy.

In India, the political system of parliamentary democracy with multiple parties provided the state, but not a particular party, with popular legitimacy. Separation of authority and accountability into the state and the political party protects the state from suffering the fate of the party. Although a political party could suffer from poor performance and be defeated by electoral processes, the democratic state could retain legitimacy under the rule of a different party or coalition of parties. Indian respondents did not mention national unity as a priority issue; similarly territorial integrity remained of low concern. In the presence of separatist movements analogous to those in the PRC, respondents did not find the possibility of secession threatening to state legitimacy. The respondents, reflective of a spectrum of political parties, felt that the vacuum created by the failure of any other particular party translated into success for their own and did not represent a setback to the state. Rather than threats to territorial sovereignty, Indian respondents found protecting economic sovereignty to be the highest priority national interest. The ability for the Indian respondents to agree on economic and political sovereignty as the prime interest was the result of a confluence of interests at the decision-making levels of society, across the multiple political party distinctions.

State Legitimacy

Before proceeding, a discussion of the bases for legitimacy in the state can provide a framework for understanding the political process in both China and India. The state wields authority over its populace based upon the assumption that its authority is legitimate. However, locating the source of legitimacy for the modern state can be complex. Max Weber provided the foundation for modern discussion on political legitimacy in outlining three types of authority that provide the basis for legitimacy[1]:

1. Rational grounds—resting on a belief in the legality of enacted rules and the right of those elevated to authority under such rules to issue commands (legal authority).
2. Traditional grounds—resting on an established belief in the sanctity of immemorial traditions and the legitimacy of those exercising authority under them (traditional authority); or finally,
3. Charismatic grounds—resting on devotion to the exceptional sanctity, heroism or exemplary character of an individual person, and of the normative patterns or order revealed or ordained by him (charismatic authority).

Weber notes that these are the "pure" forms; in reality it is some combination or permutation of the three that usually exists. Seymour Martin Lipset posits that legitimacy is simply based upon perceptions of legitimacy: "Legitimacy involves the capacity of the system to engender and maintain the belief that the existing political institutions are the most appropriate ones for the society."[2] According to Lipset, legitimacy is not tied to the form or effectiveness of a regime but is rather a reflection that the political system reflects the values of the people it represents. Thus, with societal change and the concomitant shift in values, a legitimacy crisis may occur "if 1) the status of major conservative institutions is threatened during the period of structural change; 2) all the major groups in the society do not have access to the political system in the transitional period, or at least as soon as they develop political demands."[3] The system's stability depends upon its capability to prove effectiveness to the major groups in the new social structure, thereby building new legitimacy. Lucian W. Pye also contends that a legitimacy crisis can stem from societal change: "Thus all advances in the developmental syndrome, with any concomitant changes in the relationships among equality, capacity, and differentiation, are likely to produce reactions that affect legitimacy and can bring on a major crisis."[4] Structural change or other causes of the erosion of state legitimacy require the institution of new bases for authority to preclude a crisis from occurring.

In the cases of China and India, the grounds for legitimation that have developed since the revolution and independence are not the same. The Indian state relies largely upon legal authority instituted by the revolutionary Congress Party in the state constitution and sustained by subsequent political parties. In addition, the reliance upon popular elections for determining the representation and leadership adds the element of what can be called popular legitimacy, a legitimacy emanating from the widespread feeling that the government has popular support for its actions and policies. For China, the Communist Revolution brought Mao as a revolutionary and charismatic leader to the fore, and an ideological basis for CCP legitimacy as well. After Mao's death, Deng Xiaoping inherited the role as charismatic leader, albeit with the charismatic part somewhat diminished. Weber describes this transition process from the charismatic leader to his successors as "routinized charisma":

> [P]recisely this quality of charisma as an extraordinary, supernatural, divine power transforms it, after its routinization, into a suitable source for the legitimate acquisition of sovereign power by the successors of the charismatic hero. Routinized charisma thus continues to work in favour of all those whose power and possession is guaranteed by that sovereign power, and who thus depend upon the continued existence of such power.[5]

The Party endured a transition from ideological bases of legitimacy to performance-based criteria, elucidated in the four modernizations. Deng Xiaoping began an attempt to transform the grounds for Party and his personal leadership legitimacy to the legal sphere during the reform era, but he was unable to complete the task. Instead, he instituted an authority system that was almost purely based on the ability of the Party and the state to perform the tasks of the state well, what can be referred to here as performance legitimacy.

This chapter outlines for both China and India the current political systems and decision-making processes and the implications of these institutions and processes for national-interest formation in each country.

China
The Political Process

The political system of the PRC is divided into the organs of the Party, the state, and the military, which overlap in organization and function. A small number of individuals from these organizations are responsible for decision making for the entire country, and policy direction is determined by the CCP.[6]

The Chinese Communist Party

The Party is organized at the center into the Party Congress, the Central Committee, the Politburo, and the Standing Committee of the Politburo. According to the Constitution of the CCP, the Party "must conduct its activities within the limits permitted by the Constitution and the law."[7] However, the CCP alone also has the power to adjust the Constitution through its oversight of the legislative and judicial process: "It must see to it that the legislative, judicial, and administrative organs of the state and the economic, cultural, and people's organizations work actively and with initiative, independently, responsibly, and in harmony."[8] The CCP is hierarchical and centralized in structure. The National Party Congress is the largest political body representing the Party and is nominally the head of the CCP.[9] Its size does not reflect its influence, however, and it is considered more "a vehicle for announcing and legitimating some major decisions rather than for initiating and deciding important policies."[10] According to Kenneth Lieberthal, the Central Committee members are chosen primarily by the Politburo, although the official mechanism for their election is through the Party Congress. In addition, their role is largely formal: "[W]ith few exceptions the Central Committee meetings (called plenums) discuss and announce policies rather than decide them."[11] The more significant bodies for decision making are the Politburo and the Standing Committee of the Politburo. The Politburo members are the "top leaders of the Party, the state, the civilian and military bureaucracies, and a few important localities."[12] Although the Politburo is "the command headquarters of the Party,"[13] the most powerful group within the Party is actually the Standing Committee of the Polit-buro, a small group of select members of the Politburo who actually direct decisions for the Party. The General Secretary presides over the Politburo, the CCP, and the Secretariat (the Party staff). The general structure of the Party at the center is replicated in each of the geographic divisions, the province, the county, and the township.

The State

The State Council is responsible for running the daily administration of the government through the various ministries and councils. Its organization includes the Premier, Vice Premiers, state councilors, and the heads of the ministries and commissions.[14] The Premier is in name chosen by the National People's Congress but, in fact, is chosen by the Standing Committee of the Politburo. Whereas the CCP outlines policy directions for the government, the State Council implements these policies in coordination with the Party. The ministries have some latitude in determining the appropriate policies for their specialized area (i.e., foreign affairs, foreign trade, etc.). However, ultimate authority lies with the Party: "[I]f the government does not agree with the preferences of the Party, then the Party should use its authority over Party members in the bureaucracy to impose these preferences on the government."[15] The structure of most of the ministries, like that of the Party, is replicated at the province, county, and township levels.

The Military

The Central Military Commission of the CCP, led by the General Secretary, controls the People's Liberation Army and national security affairs.[16] The Central Military Commission has the same rank as the State Council in the Chinese government hierarchy.[17] Although a Military Affairs Commission and a Defense Ministry exist in the state arm of the government, these organizations are considered powerless.[18] In addition, a select group at the top controls most decisions: "The closer to the acme of the system, the less command derives from specified rules and norms."[19] Thus, the Central Military Commission holds considerable authority and is subordinate only to the CCP. The CCP Constitution defines the relationship between the CCP and the PLA as follows: "The CPC upholds its leadership over the People's Liberation Army and the other people's armed forces; strives to strengthen the building of the PLA; and fully gives play to the PLA's role in consolidating national defense, in defending the motherland, and in taking part in socialist modernization construction."[20] The ability of the CCP to command the military reflects a critical difference between the role of political parties in China and India. Whereas the military of India exists to defend the state, the PLA exists to defend the Chinese Communist Party: "[I]t is a measure of party dominance of the system that the PLA is sworn to defend the Communist Party rather than the state."[21] In addition, the responsibility of the PLA to attend to "socialist construction" validates its involvement in a wide area of domestic affairs, as well as in defense against foreign threats.

Democratic Centralism and Fragmented Authoritarianism

The governmental organizations of the PRC listed above follow the method of "democratic centralism" in decision making. This process involves free discussion and consultation within the group until a decision has been made (the democratic aspect) and then a unified implementation of the decision without allowing dissent or criticism (centralism).[22] Democratic centralism entails a prolonged process of consultation and processing of large amounts of information before decisions can be reached. However, once the policy has been determined, opposition is no longer allowed. Consequently, the process has been described as more authoritarian than democratic: "Among organizations, democratic centralism implies the hegemony of the party. The function of mass organizations and even the state and the people's congress system is on the consultative side of the process. To oppose party leadership on an issue would be quite risky, and to organize opposition could be condemned as factionalism."[23]

Below the highest levels of policy making, a similar mechanism is at work. Consultation and bargaining is necessary at all levels of the bureaucracy to determine and implement the specific decisions. Although the CCP retains ultimate authority in policy making, the State Council and its ministries, as well as the PLA, provide policy alternatives at the operational levels of the bureaucracy. The existence of multiple bureaucratic actors vying for limited resources has led to a situation where bargaining becomes necessary to push forward policies. David M. Lampton has described some of the circumstances that can lead to the need for bargaining: "collective leadership, disagreement among authoritative elites, parties of about equal bureaucratic rank, decisions of high complexity with multiple trade-offs, and decisions in which interdependencies are complex and extensive."[24] In addition, the existence of vertical and horizontal organizational lines of authority (*tiao* and *kuai*)[25] further complicate the decision-making process. Vertical lines of authority refer to the hierarchical bureaucratic levels, and horizontal lines refer to the various territorial divisions where bureaucracies are replicated. Kenneth Lieberthal explains these divisions as the "numerous reporting lines throughout the system— through the party, through the government, to the territorial organs, and so forth."[26] The existence of these plural sources of authority within the government creates dilemmas for decision making and bargaining. Individuals in the bureaucracy must determine which boss has precedence, and often a consensus must be reached before action is taken. Lieberthal has described this decision-making process as one of "fragmented authoritarianism."[27]

An unintended consequence of the use of bargaining as a standard practice for governance is the erosion of the legitimacy of governing institutions in China. Lampton has noted the risk to state legitimacy of continued reliance on bargaining as a decision-making process:

> Because bargaining is extensive, the legal framework is poorly developed, and social norms and system legitimacy suffered egregious harm in the Cultural Revolution era, it is exceedingly difficult to separate legitimate and necessary bargaining activity from corruption. It is essential that the system create a legal framework and affirm widely shared values, procedures, and norms to govern this activity. The race is between the process of establishing these norms and the loss of system legitimacy.[28]

The State-Party Nexus and Implications for Legitimacy

At the heart of the legitimacy problem for the PRC is the fact that the Party is the basis for the state. Party control over the State Council, the bureaucracy, and the PLA ties the success of the Party to the success of each of the arms of the government. In addition, the integrated political system depends upon the continued legitimacy of the Party for ensuring system legitimation. Consequently, the failure of the Party could translate into the downfall of the state. The dangers inherent for a state in which the role of leader and administrator was combined evaded the Party but were noted by the Shah of Persia early in the twentieth century.

> The attempt to abolish and replace the office of the Grand Vizier by bureaucratic departments under ministers with the Shah's personal chairmanship failed in Persia during the last generation. This change would have placed the Shah in the role of a leader of the administration, personally responsible for all its abuses and for all the sufferings of the people. This role not only would have continuously jeopardized him, but would have shaken the belief of his very "charismatic" legitimacy.[29]

In the post-Mao era, however, the concept of reforming the political system to increase the legality of the system was attempted. Premier Zhao Ziyang addressed some of these issues tentatively in his proposals for political reform in 1987, prior to his purge from government:

> Separating the functions of Party and government is a major reform in the system of Party leadership. It must be pointed out that when there is no distinction between Party and government, the Party's position is in fact

lowered and its leadership weakened; only when the two are separated is it possible for the Party to ensure its leadership and improve its methods.[30]

Clearly, fostering legitimation of the Party has been a concern for the leadership in China for some time. Although the reforms suggested by Premier Zhao were not undertaken, the goal of bolstering Party legitimacy through other means has remained a primary objective. In the absence of a valid political opposition capable of taking over leadership of the state, the CCP must maintain in any way possible its leadership over the polity in order to avoid state disintegration. Conversely, in a democratic state, the political party in power can lose legitimacy and be thrown out of power without endangering the stability of the political system. As one party is defeated, another comes to take its place within the agreed upon norms and structures of the existent political system. The ability for opposition parties to participate in the political process and vie for leadership even when out of power provides a political consensus on the existence of the democratic system and is the foundation of state legitimacy. In the case of the CCP and the PRC, it is impossible under current norms for the state to permit an alternate party to inherit authority. A political consensus to preserve the authority of the CCP-state exists because a collapse of the CCP's authority, and thereby a collapse of the state bureaucracy, implies a loss for all political participants in the system. Thus, the lack of political alternatives in the event that the CCP loses support encourages the Party to place a premium on preserving authority and legitimacy through continuous positive performance.

Performance Legitimacy

The intertwined nature of the Party and the state in the Chinese political system presents a problem for maintenance of state stability in China. Whereas in a democratic polity, legitimacy is derived from the popular vote and is therefore popular legitimacy, the authoritarian state faces the dilemma of locating a durable source of legitimacy in place of the popular vote. In the Maoist era, the Communist Party derived legitimacy from being the party of revolution and from the personal legitimacy Mao carried as the revolutionary leader. According to Yan Jiaqi, "CCP rule is a kind of modern 'divine politics,' requiring self-legitimation from above in the absence of electoral legitimation from below."[31] The Socialist ideology served as the philosophical basis for state legitimacy: "No matter who gains power, he needs to legitimize himself by proving the coherence of his policies with Marxist-Leninist-Maoist ideology."[32] The combination of the CCP's effective revolutionary performance, Mao's leadership, and the Socialist ideology combined to bolster the legitimacy of the Party. In the post-Mao era, however, leaders have not held the same charisma as Mao for the people, and ideology has declined as a credible legitimizing force. With the advent of the Chinese market economy and privatization, the incompatibility of a Socialist political ideology became increasingly clear. Chinese respondents questioned the logic of retaining the Communist Party when the ideological basis for its rule had disappeared.[33]

To accommodate for the loss of personal charismatic and ideological legitimacy, the CCP has emphasized performance legitimacy as the primary logic for its exclusive hold on political power. Its ability to maintain high levels of performance on issue areas of concern to the citizenry is critical to retaining political legitimacy. Chinese respondents repeatedly noted that, in particular, the CCP must continue economic growth in order to maintain its legitimacy as the sole representative of the state. Respondents said improvement in living standards, low unemployment, and maintaining national dignity were all necessary for the CCP to maintain legitimacy.[34] In addition, the state's ability to prevent the separation of Taiwan also acted as an indicator of regime legitimacy.

Respondent A: The Communist Party and the Chinese government see that only by adopting free markets to develop the economy can it help its legitimacy. The last 20 years of experience has shown that economic development is the most important source of political legitimacy.[35]

Respondent B: (Regarding joining the WTO) If you make mistakes, it means large unemployment and a large number of companies go bankrupt. It means a threat to their power. In the 1990s, of the governments that failed, many were because of economic failure.[36]

Respondent C: The main challenge is not from the economy but from politics. China has utilized its full potential within the constraints of the current political regime. So, if you want to upgrade more, you have to break the current political regime.[37]

Respondent D: In China, people say the road to the White House is very expensive. Yes, expensive, but in a non-democratic system, it is easy to get your power—it is a cheap road to Zhongnanhai. But afterwards, you have to pay more to guarantee your power, even ten years later you have costs to guarantee authority. They have to protect themselves with the idea of morality. This is for the guarantee of their power.[38]

Respondent E: If Taiwan did declare independence, China would declare war. Because of the nationalism in China, no leader can survive without responding.[39]

Respondent F: If Taiwan claims independence and the government does not do anything, the government is done for. That is the only way to keep stability here. This also explains why China does not want external intervention and pressure. This pressure may cause disruption of institutions. It is a question of the political legitimacy of the PRC.[40]

Other scholars of Chinese politics have also noted the challenges faced by the PRC in maintaining legitimacy. Lieberthal notes that economic growth has had the unintended consequence of weakening national unity through increasing disparities of income among the different regions of China[41] and eroding state legitimacy through rampant corruption.[42] In order to meet these challenges, he underscores the necessity for the political regime to prove its legitimacy through continued performance: "The resulting situation provides very strong incentives for the top leaders to continue to do all they can to keep the economy growing at a very rapid pace to try to buy off political upheaval."[43] Merle Goldman and Roderick Macfarquhar reiterate the paradox that successful economic reforms have created serious problems for the Party: "Although the economic growth and rising incomes generated by the reforms were meant to enhance the authority of the party-state, they have actually undermined it."[44] Richard Baum and Alexei Shevchenko warn of the possible calamity that awaits a rigid state in China: "Given the probability of high societal stress, an institutionalized capacity for flexible response may be essential to prevent centrifugal forces from overtaxing the system's adaptive capacity"[45]; in other words, the state could collapse. Joseph Fewsmith concurs with this view but places the focus on fissures within the Party: "Given the tensions within the Party and the passing of the generation that made the revolution, it is certainly possible that a repetition of the sort of social movement that took place in 1989 could irrevocably divide the Party and bring about its collapse."[46]

Ominously, some respondents for this research concluded that the Chinese political system had already lost all legitimacy; thus the Party should undertake the responsibility to transform the regime before it collapses: "If the current authority is wise, it will allow a change of political regime. Otherwise, there will be a revolution, in maybe five or ten years."[47] In marked contrast with the Chinese responses, Indian respondents did not mention regime legitimacy as a problem at all. The possible effect of poor performance on system stability in China underscores that the Party must pursue policies that foremost sustain the legitimacy of the Party and the state.

Legitimacy and the National Interest

The premium on high performance to support Party and state legitimacy is a critical factor in the CCP's determination of the ranking of the PRC national interests. Chinese respondents stated that protecting national unity and territorial sovereignty were the primary reasons for pursuing a defense modernization and economic reforms program. Thus in the hierarchy of national interests, national unity and territorial sovereignty were the highest priority, and economic sovereignty was second.

According to respondents, the importance of national unity and territorial sovereignty as the national interest stems from their centrality in assuring Party and state legitimacy. Concurrently, the Party's weak hold on political legitimacy exacerbates the problems of national unity and territorial integration already existing in the PRC. Lucian Pye has addressed this predicament:

> With respect to the sequence of crises, the questions of the creation and maintenance of the basic institutions of government are directly affected by the outcome or the onset of the other crises. On the other hand, well established and firmly institutionalized structures and processes of government can greatly reduce and even completely overcome the strains that might arise from situations of potential crisis in the other areas of nation building.[48]

Thus, weak state legitimacy in China can lead to problems of state unity, which in turn further weakens state legitimacy, thereby creating a circular dilemma that can best be resolved by changing the basis for political legitimacy.

India

The Political Process

The Constitution of India determines the basis for the government of India. It has established a parliamentary democracy with power vested in the Executive Branch, the Parliament, and the Supreme Court. The Executive Branch includes the President, the Council of Ministers, and the bureaucracy. However, the Prime Minister retains the actual responsibility to govern the country, as head of the Council of Ministers.

The Executive Branch

Although the President[49] is formally the head of state in the Indian Constitution, in practice it is the Prime Minister who holds the power of the Executive Branch. The Prime Minister is the leader of the majority party in the popularly elected Lok Sabha (the lower house) or the member who has the confidence of a majority coalition. A Council of Ministers is selected by the Prime Minister to administer the various responsibilities of the government. Additionally, the Prime Minister is head of the Cabinet, creating an overlap between the legislative and executive branches of government. The Cabinet, composed of the principal members of the Council of Ministers, heads the bureaucracy and oversees the government's activities. The Executive Branch holds the highest level of authority to make policy decisions on behalf of the state,[50] although its existence is largely dependent on the governing party maintaining confidence of the majority in Parliament.

The Parliament

The Parliament is comprised of the President, the Lok Sabha (the lower house), and the Rajya Sabha (the upper house). The primary responsibility of the Indian Parliament is to create legislation; however, the Parliament's actions are ultimately bound by the Constitution. The Lok Sabha members are elected to five-year terms, although the Lok Sabha may be dissolved prior to that time, leading to fresh elections. The allocation of seats to each state is based upon population, and elections are on the basis of universal suffrage.[51] The Rajya Sabha has both nominated and elected members. Twelve members are nominated by the President "from among persons having special knowledge or practical experience in respect of such matters as literature, science, art, and social service."[52] The elected members are actually indirectly elected by members of the state legislative assemblies for six-year terms. One-third of the Rajya Sabha is retired every two years. Of the two houses of Parliament, the Lok Sabha has greater authority. The Prime Minister is selected as the leader of the majority in the Lok Sabha, and the Cabinet thus depends upon the Lok Sabha for its support. The Lok Sabha also solely controls bills for taxing and spending.[53] Also, because the Rajya Sabha is indirectly elected whereas the Lok Sabha is directly elected, the Lok Sabha is considered to be more representative of the people, and more responsible.[54]

The Judiciary

The Indian Supreme Court interprets the Constitution and ensures that all legislation conforms to the Constitution.[55] The Indian Constitution also gives the Supreme Court the power to supersede the authority of Parliament in deciding the constitutionality of legislation: "As in the United States, so in the Indian Republic, all questions arising under the Constitution or involving its interpretation fall within the jurisdiction of the ordinary courts of law, subject, however, to the final authority of the Supreme Court."[56] However, a two-thirds majority in Parliament can constitutionally supersede the Supreme Court through emergency powers, which are discussed in the next section of this chapter. The purpose of instituting a Supreme Court for interpreting laws for both the federal government and the states was to promote Indian national unity. In founding the judiciary, a member of the Constituent Assembly noted that "the unconscious process of consolidation which a uniformity of laws and interpretation involves makes the unifying unconscious and therefore more stable."[57]

Fundamental Rights and Emergency Powers

In addition, the Constitution provides for Fundamental Rights and Directive Principles designed to protect the citizenry from the state and each other. The rights (Articles 13–32) include "the Right of Equality, the Right of Freedom, the Right Against Exploitation, the Right to Freedom of Religion, Cultural and Educational Rights, the Right to Property, and the Right to Constitutional Remedies."[58] These rights protect the ability of minorities to continue usage of their language and culture, which proved to be central to maintaining state unity. The Constitution also abolished the practice of untouchability and public discrimination based upon religion, race, caste, sex, or place of birth.[59] The Directive Principles set forth a general direction for state policy, which is to promote social welfare through social, economic, and political justice.[60] "The Fundamental Rights reflect both India's assimilation of Western liberal tradition and its desire for the political freedoms it was denied under colonial rule."[61]

However, the Constitution also provides for the use of special emergency powers through which civil liberties can be curtailed. Through the Emergency Provisions described in Part XVIII of the Constitution, the President can declare a state of emergency if he believes that national security is threatened by external or internal forces (Article 352) or if the financial stability of India is similarly threatened (Article 360).[62] During an Emergency, the Parliament is not restricted by the freedoms of the Fundamental Rights listed above in making laws (Articles 353 and 354).[63] The President may also decide to declare an Emergency in a given state or states, taking over the powers of the state legislature (Article 356).[64] Proclamation of Emergency must be approved by Parliament within six months. Historically, the Indian government made declarations of national emergency in 1962, in response to the war with China; in 1971, in response to the war with Pakistan over Bangladesh; and most radically from 1975–1977 by Indira Gandhi "in response to an alleged threat to internal security by the political opposition."[65] During the Emergency, the Indian government engaged in preventive detention, detention without trial, and arresting persons without specifying charges.[66] By allowing the Executive Branch to suspend fundamental rights for two years, the Supreme Court's credibility suffered.[67] Raju G. C. Thomas addresses the central problem that arose from the use of Emergency powers by Indira Gandhi: "the constant suspicion of whether governmental actions to restrict individual freedoms are really motivated by the need to protect the integrity of the state or are merely an excuse to protect and preserve the government in power."[68] Nonetheless, Thomas notes that with regard to the use of Emergency powers, the situation in India since independence has been generally satisfactory: "So far no prime minister has grossly misused the privilege although Mrs. Gandhi came close to doing so between

1975 and 1977. In the end, even she restored democracy after 22 months of Emergency rule that was declared in the interests of national security."[69]

The Fundamental Rights detailed in the Constitution and the outcry over the misuse of Emergency powers reflect a deep interest by the Indian people in preserving their rights vis-à-vis the state. According to Indian respondents, there exists a tradition of a less intrusive state in India that allows greater authority to rest in the hands of the people.

> Respondent A: The reason that [economic reform] was absorbed by such a large percentage of the population is because of India's psyche, which is anarchic. At the root of the mind is a suspicion of the state. Any move that lessens the interaction of the state, people welcome it.[70]

> Respondent B: There is awareness. The domestic politics are a gross reality for India. It is democratic, there is no heavy hand anywhere. No single leader can have so much power. Forces are unleashed. Some say even that there shouldn't be a central government. In the West, soft government is despised. In India it has been imposed.[71]

Political Parties

India has had a multiparty system since independence, although the Congress Party was by far the dominant party for the first 40 years. In the 1957 election, the Congress Party had 365 seats in the Lok Sabha, the Communists as the next largest party had 30, and the Socialists, regional, communal parties, and Independents altogether held 135 seats.[72] The Congress Party's unrivaled dominance of Parliament for decades led many observers to believe that India's political system was a one-party democracy. Since then, the balance has shifted significantly. After the Emergency, the 1977 elections revealed the growing influence of opposition parties. The resentment of the Indian electorate to Indira Gandhi and the Congress Party's abuse of power during the Emergency helped to fragment the Congress Party's support base and empower the various parties in opposition. In the 1977 elections, the Janata Party took 298 out of 542 Parliamentary seats, becoming the first political party to defeat the Congress Party since independence.[73] Significantly, the Janata Party included as a major element in its alliance the Jana Sangh, later renamed the Bharatiya Janata Party (BJP). The BJP as the leader of a broad coalition then won the national elections in 1998. Although the Congress Party was able to return to power under Indira Gandhi (1980–1984), Rajiv Gandhi (1985–1989), and Narasimha Rao (1991–1996), opposition parties such as the BJP had gained enough strength to provide viable political resistance, as seen by the long tenure of A. B. Vajpayee (1998–2004). The Congress Party under Manmohan Singh was able to regain the helm, but only with the help of a wide coalition of parties in the 2004 elections. The dynamics of modern Indian politics have placed a premium on forming coalitions.

According to Maya Chadda, the decline of the Congress Party as the sole dominant party and the rise of a new and more varied political map represent "the increasing differentiation and complexity of India's expanding economy and society because of advances in industrial and technological capabilities."[74] The flux of political parties largely reflects changing interests and interest groups in society that have resulted from globalization. The broadened political base of different parties also reflects the gradual rising participation of social groups through the existence of successive national and local elections.[75]

Popular Legitimacy

The multiparty parliamentary democracy system of governance allows a progressively large section of the Indian population to be involved in the political process. In joining a particular political party, the various interests in India are able to articulate their political preferences and have influence on political processes through their representatives. Opposition parties carry significant weight in that any given party can maintain a majority in Parliament only with the accordance of other parties with different platforms. This serves to moderate and broaden the platforms of the winning coalition and ensures that the Prime Minister must accommodate a wide variety of interests. In addition, the inclusion of the opposition parties in the political process ensures that the national interest policies of the state reflect the interests of a broader portion of the political spectrum rather than the interests of an individual party. As a consequence, the political process has shown a remarkable level of consistency in terms of support for major policy agendas, such as the economic reforms and defense modernization programs.

> Respondent A: During the 1990s while reforms were begun by the Congress government, now there are a number of politicians in combinations across the country of different political parties all following the same path. All the major political parties have taken a turn at the center. No matter what they said in opposition, when they came to power they did the same thing. This has created that kind of consensus for movement in the direction of [economic] reforms. I think there is no question about consensus having built up.[76]

> Respondent B: Governments fight elections and come to power, but they can't do it if the people don't want it. In India, we muddle through. When we do it right or wrong, we don't overdo it.[77]

> Respondent C: Domestic social forces are evolving. Democratic rights have become much more important to the people than they were under Nehru. After 50 years of democracy, people are more conscious of their rights. Independence groups were more tolerant because they saw the British. After that, people became more critical of their government.[78]

Respondent D: In India for 40 years you had Congress in power. The opposition was in opposition. Then, there was the United Front in 1989, then the coalition partners in 1996, the BJP in 1998. You have a series of opposition parties dealing with power for the first time. The BJP has had a telescoped time period of learning. They learned that you need to continue with liberalization, privatization, encourage investment, even if it means inequality. They are realizing that there are limits to the government's ability to set the agenda.[79]

Respondent E: In the last 10 years India has moved from a monolithic system to coalition politics. This is not a new trend, it reflects India. There are regional forces and other divisions, so coalitions fit best. We can't have a single agenda, like Congress. Many people broke away for this reason. Now there are many forces. Congress was a national movement, not really a party. As soon as it became a party, factionalism set in. In a country like this, you can't have a national party. Coalition politics will streamline itself. It may not be 24 partners, not so varied an agenda. There will be a coalition of partners that represents the country well. A stable coalition vs. coalition, which is a new experiment.[80]

The political mechanism allows the people and various parties to influence policy objectives, arriving at popular support for policies. This is reinforced by the internal workings of the bureaucracy, where individuals of differing party loyalties handle the various policy issues. Thus the ruling party does not carry absolute authority over all levels of decision making, and the members of the bureaucracy do not carry a personal interest in supporting a certain party's hold on political power. The transfer of power from one party to another does not imply any great changes for the bureaucracy at the subministerial levels. Last, the independent judiciary allows for a separation of the legal process from party inclinations and preferences. The result of these facets of the Indian political system is a regime that displays a remarkable amount of legitimacy with the population.

The fact that system legitimacy does not pose a problem in India is reflected in that Indian respondents did not mention regime legitimacy as a problem during the interviews. In comparison with their Chinese counterparts for whom the legitimacy problem loomed large, the Indian respondents felt that failure to perform on the part of the party in power did not have implications for political legitimacy, regime collapse, disruption of institutions, or revolutionary behavior. Rather, some Indian respondents said that the political party in power pursued certain policies to improve its standing in the next elections. However, the party's failure to do so would have implications for that particular party's continued leadership of the government, but not on the legitimacy of the system or the stability of the state. Thus, political legitimacy did not enter as a significant factor in Indian respondents' ranking of national interests. For

Indian respondents, the primary national interest was protecting economic and political sovereignty through defense modernization and economic reforms. This determination was based upon a set of economic ideals for the country that were progressively agreed upon through successive governments in the 1990s. Political legitimacy, national unity, and territorial sovereignty were not significant factors in their calculation of national interests.

Conclusion

The nature of the political system and institutions plays an integral role in deciding which threats are most critical to the state. Elements perceived as risking the existence of the state itself must be addressed most immediately, as the primary purpose of the state is to survive. After political and territorial consolidation of the state has been accomplished, other state objectives can be pursued.

According to respondents, the survival of the Indian state is not an issue. The multiparty system of governance is one in which the functions of the bureaucracy are not tied to any particular party, and the liability for failure lies with the parties and not the state. Failure to meet the demands of the public on policy areas such as national unity, territorial integrity, economic sovereignty, or political sovereignty lead to declining support for the administration currently in power and does not translate into erosion of state legitimacy. For Indian respondents, the greatest threat to the country is in the form of globalization, which erodes state sovereignty in economic and political issues of importance. The essential national interest that is in need of state protection is economic and political sovereignty, and the policies for protecting the national interests are the economic reforms and defense modernization programs.

Conversely, according to respondents, for China the survival of the state remains a central question. Integration of the Party and state into mutually reinforcing structures of decision making, with military forces in the service of the Party rather than the state lends the political system to heightened risk. Failure of the Party in policy areas of importance and loss of legitimacy of the Party lead to loss of state legitimacy as well. Thus, Chinese respondents find that the survival of the state structure is the state priority. Territorial sovereignty and national unity are the greatest threats, but only in that they pose a certain risk to the legitimacy and stability of the Party and the state. If national unity and state legitimacy is secured, then the next national interest is preservation of economic and political sovereignty.

Although the political institution is not necessarily the main determinant of the national interest, the stability and legitimacy of the political system can exert a powerful influence on the formation of national interests. The absence of established processes for decision making in the state can erode state legitimacy, creating a situation in which the state must act to preserve its authority. In addition, institutions provide a prism through which existing strains and pressures existing in the state are filtered. Ultimately, the hierarchy of national interests will be determined by the exigencies of the state, incorporating the various pressures exerted on the political system by factors such as national unity, territorial integrity, economic sovereignty, and political sovereignty.

Notes

1. Max Weber, *Economy and Society,* ed. Guenther Roth and Claus Wittich (New York: Bedminster Press, 1968), 215.

2. Seymour Martin Lipset, "Social Conflict, Legitimacy, and Democracy," in *Legitimacy and the State,* ed. William Connolly (New York: New York University Press, 1984), 88.

3. Lipset, "Social Conflict, Legitimacy, and Democracy," 89.

4. Lucian W. Pye, "The Legitimacy Crisis," in *Crises and Sequences in Political Development,* ed. Leonard Binder et al. (Princeton, NJ: Princeton University Press, 1971), 136.

5. Max Weber, "Legitimacy, Politics and the State," in *Legitimacy and the State,* ed. William Connolly (New York: New York University Press, 1984), 60.

6. A. Doak Barnett, *The Making of Foreign Policy in China: Structure and Process* (Boulder, CO: Westview Press, 1985), 7–9.

7. "Constitution of the Communist Party of China," adopted by the 14th National People's Congress, 18 October 1992, in *Governing China: From Revolution Through Reform,* ed. Kenneth Lieberthal (New York: W. W. Norton & Co., 1995), 387.

8. "Constitution of the Communist Party of China," 387.

9. James C. F. Wang, *Contemporary Chinese Politics* (Englewood Cliffs, NJ: Prentice-Hall, 1992), 74.

10. Kenneth Lieberthal, *Governing China: From Revolution Through Reform* (New York: W. W. Norton & Co., 1995), 160.

11. Lieberthal, *Governing China,* 160.

12. Yan Jiaqi, "The Nature of Chinese Authoritarianism," in *Decision Making in Deng's China: Perspectives from Insiders,* ed. Carol Lee Hamrin and Suisheng Zhao (New York: M. E. Sharpe, 1995), 3.

13. Lieberthal, *Governing China,* 161.

14. Barnett, *The Making of Foreign Policy in China: Structure and Process,* 52.

15. Susan L. Shirk, "The Chinese Political System and the Political Strategy of Economic Reform," in *Bureaucracy, Politics, and Decision Making in Post-Mao China,* ed. Kenneth G. Lieberthal and David M. Lampton (Berkeley: University of California Press, 1992), 67.

16. Carol Lee Hamrin, "The Party Leadership System," in *Bureaucracy, Politics, and Decision Making in Post-Mao China,* ed. Kenneth G. Lieberthal and David M.

Lampton (Berkeley: University of California Press, 1992), 112.

17. Lieberthal, *Governing China*, 205.

18. Lieberthal, *Governing China*, 205.

19. Jonathan D. Pollack, "Structure and Process in the Chinese Military System," in *Bureaucracy, Politics, and Decision Making in Post-Mao China*, ed. Kenneth G. Lieberthal and David M. Lampton (Berkeley: University of California Press, 1992), 169.

20. "Constitution of the Communist Party of China," 387.

21. Lieberthal, *Governing China*, 205.

22. James R. Townsend and Brantly Womack, *Politics in China* (Boston: Little, Brown & Co., 1986), 86–87; see also Lieberthal, *Governing China*, 176.

23. Townsend and Womack, *Politics in China*, 86–87.

24. David M. Lampton, "A Plum for a Peach: Bargaining, Interest, and Bureaucratic Politics in China," in *Bureaucracy, Politics, and Decision Making in Post-Mao China*, ed. Kenneth G. Lieberthal and David M. Lampton (Berkeley: University of California Press, 1992), 34–35.

25. Lieberthal, *Governing China*, 169.

26. Lieberthal, *Governing China*, 169.

27. Kenneth Lieberthal, " 'The Fragmented Authoritarianism' Model and Its Limitations," in *Bureaucracy, Politics, and Decision Making in Post-Mao China*, ed. Kenneth G. Lieberthal and David M. Lampton (Berkeley: University of California Press, 1992), 8.

28. Lampton, "A Plum for a Peach: Bargaining, Interest, and Bureaucratic Politics in China," 58.

29. Max Weber, "Legitimacy, Politics and the State," 61.

30. Zhao Ziyang, "Advance Along the Road of Socialism with Chinese Characteristics," in *The China Reader: The Reform Era*, ed. Orville Schell and David Shambaugh (New York: Random House, 1999), 60.

31. Yan Jiaqi, "The Nature of Chinese Authoritarianism," in *Decision Making in Deng's China: Perspectives from Insiders*, ed. Carol Lee Hamrin and Suisheng Zhao (New York: M. E. Sharpe, 1995), 12.

32. Yan Jiaqi, "The Nature of Chinese Authoritarianism," 12.

33. Foreign Ministry Official (Interview #7).

34. Scholars (Interviews #16, #18, and #19).

35. Professor (Interview #37).

36. Journalist (Interview #39).

37. Economist (Interview #31).

38. Professor (Interview # 38).

39. Journalist (Interview #40).

40. Professor (Interview #35).

41. Lieberthal, *Governing China*, 267.

42. Lieberthal, *Governing China*, 267–269.

43. Lieberthal, *Governing China*, 269.

44. Merle Goldman and Roderick Macfarquhar, *The Paradox of China's Post-Mao Reforms* (Cambridge, MA: Harvard University Press, 1999), 4.

45. Richard Baum and Alexei Shevchenko, "The State of the State," in *The Paradox of China's Post-Mao Reforms*, ed. Merle Goldman and Roderick Macfarquhar (Cambridge, MA: Harvard University Press, 1999), 360.

46. Joseph Fewsmith, "Reaction, Resurgence, and Succession: Chinese Politics Since Tiananmen," in *The Politics of China: The Eras of Mao and Deng*, ed. Roderick Macfarquhar (Cambridge: Cambridge University Press, 1997), 527.

47. Economist (Interview #31).

48. Lucian W. Pye, "The Legitimacy Crisis," 137–138.

49. A College of Electors comprised of the elected members of Parliament and the elected members of the Legislative Assemblies of the states elects the President of India to a five-year term. The President is not necessarily a member of the majority party in Parliament. See Mohan Lal, "The President and Parliament," in *The Indian Parliament*, ed. A. B. Lal (Allahabad, India: Chaitanya Publishing House, 1956), 207.

50. C. V. H. Rao, "Parliament and Cabinet," in *The Indian Parliament*, ed. A. B. Lal (Allahabad, India: Chaitanya Publishing House, 1956), 184–191.

51. A. D. Pant, "Parliament: Its Organisation and Functions," in *The Indian Parliament*, ed. A. B. Lal (Allahabad, India: Chaitanya Publishing House, 1956), 18.

52. A. D. Pant, "Parliament: Its Organisation and Functions," 16.

53. Robert L. Hardgrave, Jr. and Stanley A. Kochanek, *India: Government and Politics in a Developing Nation* (Washington, DC: Harcourt Brace Jovanovich, Inc., 1986), 75.

54. A. D. Pant, "Parliament: Its Organisation and Functions," 28–29.

55. Hardgrave and Kochanek, *India: Government and Politics in a Developing Nation*, 92.

56. Sirdar D. K. Sen, *A Comparative Study of the Indian Constitution* (New Delhi: Orient Longmans Ltd., 1967), 269.

57. K. M. Munshi, quoted in Granville Austin, *The Indian Constitution: Cornerstone of a Nation* (London: Oxford University Press, 1966), 184.

58. Granville Austin, *The Indian Constitution: Cornerstone of a Nation* (London: Oxford University Press, 1966), 51.

59. Austin, *Indian Constitution*, 51.

60. Austin, *Indian Constitution*, 52.

61. Hardgrave and Kochanek, *India: Government and Politics in a Developing Nation*, 63.

62. Austin, *Indian Constitution*, 207–208; also see Raju G. C. Thomas, *Democracy, Security, and Development in India* (New York: St. Martin's Press, 1996), 74–75.

63. Raju G. C. Thomas, *Democracy, Security, and Development in India*, 74–75.

64. Austin, *Indian Constitution*, 209.

65. Hardgrave and Kochanek, *India: Government and Politics in a Developing Nation*, 64.

66. Hardgrave and Kochanek, *India: Government and Politics in a Developing Nation*, 65.

67. Hardgrave and Kochanek, *India: Government and Politics in a Developing Nation*, 94.

68. Thomas, *Democracy, Security, and Development in India*, 74.

69. Thomas, *Democracy, Security, and Development in India*, 77.

70. Manwender Singh, Defense Analyst and Freelance Journalist, in an interview with the author, New Delhi, India, 7 March 2001.

71. Senior Official, Ministry of External Affairs, in an interview with the author, New Delhi, India.

72. Norman D. Palmer, "India's Political Parties," in *Studies in Indian Democracy,* ed. S. P. Aiyar and R. Srinivasan (Bombay: Allied Publishers Private Ltd., 1965), 578.

73. Walter K. Andersen and Shridhar D. Damle, *The Brotherhood in Saffron: The Rashtriya Swayamsevak Sangh and Hindu Revivalism* (New Delhi: Westview Press, 1987), 214.

74. Maya Chadda, *Building Democracy in South Asia: India, Nepal, Pakistan* (Boulder, CO: Lynne Rienner Publishers, Inc., 2000), 48–49.

75. Chadda, *Building Democracy in South Asia: India, Nepal, Pakistan,* 49.

76. Isher Judge Ahluwalia, Director and Chief Executive of Indian Council for Research on International Economic Relations, in an interview with the author, New Delhi, India, 5 February 2001.

77. Rahul Mukerjee, Political Analyst for the Centre for Policy Research, in an interview with the author, New Delhi, India, 30 January 2001.

78. Senior Official, Ministry of External Affairs, in an interview with the author, New Delhi, India.

79. Sanjaya Baru, Journalist, *Financial Express,* in an interview with the author, New Delhi, India, 17 February 2001.

80. Swaran Singh, Professor of the School of International Studies, Jawaharlal Nehru University, in interviews with the author, New Delhi, India, February 2001 and April 2004.

CHAPTER 6

China-India Relations

Interests Drawing the Two Countries Together

In the last several years, China and India have slowly come to the conclusion that their national interests can be compatible. When asked, many leading officials and scholars in both countries say that remaining disputes on borders and Tibet are not worth a war. As neighbors with huge populations, high poverty rates, and developing economies, China and India face many common problems. Increasingly, working together appeals to the leaders of the two nations as the best way to tackle these problems and resolve their disputes.

Both countries have entered a higher level of development, and progress from here requires a strict focus on economic policies. As a result, they are currently addressing their challenges with very similar programs. Both countries are pursuing national policies that are meant to propel their economies and simultaneously strengthen their militaries. Both face the threat of growing income disparity, ethnic unrest, and separatism, and each is focused on modernizing and developing its economy. These interests place a premium for each country upon improving security relations with its neighbor, and increasing economic ties.

They also share several similar interests and goals vis-à-vis the international system, including territorial sovereignty, military development, environmental standards, human rights standards, and access to energy. The interest in territorial sovereignty holds with regard to Taiwan, Tibet, and Xinjiang in the case of China, and to Kashmir in the case of India. Paradoxically, agreement over the principle of territorial sovereignty brings both together, but differences over specific territorial questions still represent points of contention. Military development and modernization remain key objectives for both countries in their pursuits of becoming stronger players on the world stage. China and India share a critical interest in ensuring that environmental and human rights standards for their own development remain at the levels that the developed countries faced.

In addition, for China, high tensions with Taiwan provide a good reason to resolve old quarrels with India. China's concerns with internal security have a similar effect. Separatist movements in Xinjiang and Tibet continue to absorb much of its attention and reflect problems that China is facing regarding its ethnic composition. Rising unrest from unemployment and gaping inequalities in income distribution between regions are exacerbating these ethnic divides. Securing its external borders and improving relations with India and other neighboring countries allow China to focus on these growing internal problems.

A critical difference is Indian policy makers are more confident than their Chinese counterparts regarding their ability to deal effectively with domestic ethnic and economic forces. They overwhelmingly state in interviews that the unity of the Indian state does not hinge upon keeping Kashmir, whereas in the view of most Chinese policy makers, a separation from Taiwan could mean the end of China as we know it.[1] Rather than concern itself with national unity, India is trying to refocus its national efforts on economic growth in order to match China's success. Though Indian growth rates have averaged 6 percent to 7 percent in the past decade, growth needs to be even faster to eradicate poverty and raise living standards. Conflict and tensions with neighboring China and Pakistan have posed a large economic hurdle for India in the past, impeding foreign investment by increasing risk and absorbing critical budgetary resources. Recent diplomatic overtures may alleviate this problem and allow China and India, in particular, to focus on their rapidly expanding economic relationship. For India, the desire to maintain stability and achieve rapid and robust economic growth provides a strong impetus for ameliorating relations with China. For China, growing trade with India is yet another reason to pursue ties.

The Evolution of China-India Relations

China has a long history of relations with India, beginning with cultural and religious contact between the two by 100 c.e. Buddhism traveled from India through the Silk Route in Central Asia to China, mixing with the existing Daoist and Confucian philosophies there. However, the massive Himalayan mountain range formed a natural barrier, limiting extensive communication between the two civilizations. On the positive side, the absence of regular contact limited conflicts between these neighbors. As travel and communication became easier, disagreements surfaced.

During the twentieth century, contact became far more frequent, and the emergence of independent India and Pakistan added complexity to these interactions, as did the Cold War and the interests of the great powers. After a short period of warm relations during the early 1950s, frictions over borders and geopolitical alignments strained the relationship. China developed close relations with Pakistan after 1971, providing political support and military assistance to India's foe. The growing ties between China and Pakistan led India to view both as collaborators against India's interests. A war between China and India in 1962 left both countries deeply suspicious of the other's intentions. And disagreements on Tibet and borders provide tangible cause for wariness.

After decades of tensions, India and China are now moving closer and resolving some of their differences, a paradigm shift that could change the strategic realities of Asia. At the same time, Pakistan and India are making efforts to ameliorate relations with each other. Former Indian Prime Minister Vajpayee's visit to Beijing in 2003 produced a promising set of agreements to help settle the long-standing border dispute, increase trade, and decrease mutual distrust. This diplomatic initiative was received warmly, as both countries are moving toward a more interest-oriented approach to bilateral relations. Premier Wen Jiabao's visit to New Delhi in 2005 had a similar positive effect. Jiabao and Indian Prime Minister Manmohan Singh established a "Strategic and Cooperative Partnership for Peace and Prosperity" between China and India during their meeting, and they marked 2006 as the "India-China Friendship Year." A critical factor in drawing the two countries together has been their growing economies. However, while the probability of military conflict is declining, bilateral economic competition and geopolitics could be the source of possible friction in the relationship.

In addition, China's relations with Pakistan, while still warm, now face a multitude of new challenges. September 11 and the war in Afghanistan have increased the salience of terrorism for the United States and China. Pakistan's neighbors are increasingly concerned about the role of Pakistani radical groups as a destabilizing force in Afghanistan and China's western province of Xinjiang. Pakistan's lack of economic competitiveness relative to India makes it less attractive in a new Asia where economic realities determine geopolitical relations.

Security Relations

Relations following revolution in China and independence in India were warm. A prevalent phrase reflecting the Indian view of China in the 1950s was "Hindi-Chini bhai-bhai," meaning that Indians and Chinese are brothers. Then-Prime Minister of India Jawaharlal Nehru viewed Asia as a type of family of nations working together against imperialism. Revealing a worldview similar to that of contemporary Chinese leaders, he wrote, "[W]e stand for the freedom of Asian countries and for the elimination of imperialistic control over them."[2] Nonalignment would ensure the ability of each nation to pursue its interests without imperialist or superpower intervention. Peace as a strategy was made explicit in the concept of *panchsheel*, or the Five Principles of Peaceful Coexistence, which both China and India adopted during the 1955 Bandung conference.

By the late 1950s, however, relations began to sour. Although China had assured India in earlier correspondence that the Tibet issue would be resolved by peaceful negotiations, China employed military force in 1950 to subjugate Tibet.[3] These actions alarmed the Indian government and set the stage for future Indian support of the Dalai Lama and the cause of the Tibetan people. In 1954, India recognized Chinese authority over Tibet in a bid to improve relations with China. However, the relations between the two countries began to deteriorate, and many Indians felt deceived by China.[4] In 1959, the Dalai Lama escaped an attack by the Chinese government and fled to India along with a following of Tibetans. The Indian government provided the Dalai Lama immediately with political asylum as well as residence. From his base in Dharamsala in India, he worked for Tibetan freedom from China and protection of Tibetan human rights, an agenda looked upon with some anxiety by Beijing.

A poorly demarcated border between China and India caused further frictions. The McMahon Line, drawn by the British in 1914, was rejected by China, leading to prolonged territorial disputes. Existing tensions over Tibet and the dispute over the shared border finally led to a war between the neighbors in 1962. China's victory in the war did not resolve the territorial argument and instead produced a legacy of mutual suspicion.

China's first nuclear test in 1964 also had an impact on Indian strategic thought. New Delhi saw those nuclear tests, closely following India's military defeat by China, as a strong argument for pursuing a nuclear capability. Under Indira Gandhi, India performed its first nuclear test in 1974. Although described as a "peaceful" nuclear explosion, the tests were also a strategic response to rising tensions in the region. Deep-rooted suspicions that had grown between China and India over Tibet and boundaries were compounded by the realities of Cold War alignments.

During 1962–1963, China and Pakistan had reached agreements on border delimitations that indicated growing security collaboration against Indian interests.[5] Pakistan also played a critical role as the intermediary for President Nixon's détente with China. Prior to Nixon's presidency, close relations between China and Pakistan had posed a problem for the U.S.–Pakistan relationship. In contrast, President Nixon viewed the ties as an opportunity. In 1969, Nixon arranged for the establishment of secret communication with China with Pakistan as intermediary, an association that led to the 1971 breakthrough in relations between the United States and China.[6] As China entered a triangular relationship with the United States and Pakistan, India developed warm relations and strong defense ties with the Soviet Union. In the following years, Islamabad strengthened defense relations with Beijing and benefited diplomatically from the partnership.

Despite these problems, both Zhou Enlai and Indira Gandhi moved to begin normalizing relations. Diplomatic relations were finally reinstated in 1976, breaking the tense impasse, and bilateral border talks were begun in the 1980s. In 1986, Indian military exercises in the border areas of Sumdorong Chu led to more turmoil. After Rajiv Gandhi's visit to China in 1988, a China-India Joint Working Group was established to expand the scope of confidence-building measures then in place. After 1996, more measures were introduced: border military meetings were held twice a year, hotlines were established between the two countries' militaries, each side notified the other in advance of exercises and movements, and a higher level of defense interaction and transparency in general was adopted.[7] Nonetheless, both sides have retained thousands of troops along their disputed borders for years. The end of the 1980s marked the beginning of renewed efforts on both sides to improve the bilateral relationship. Li Peng visited India in 1991, followed by Indian Prime Minister Narasimha Rao's visit to China in 1993. Rao's visit produced significant progress with the signing of the "Agreement to Maintain Peace and Tranquility along the Line of Actual Control." In 1996, Jiang Zemin visited India and both countries signed an agreement on additional military confidence-building measures, consolidating the trend of bonhomie.[8]

The Nuclear Tests

India's nuclear tests of May 1998 created a new set of tensions. Following the first round of tests, the Chinese response was muted, with the foreign ministry expressing only serious concern.[9] However, after India's second round, China condemned the Indian tests and criticized Pakistan's ensuing nuclear tests. China stressed that both India and Pakistan had undermined the international nonproliferation regime and thus should now sign the Comprehensive Test Ban Treaty (CTBT) and Non-Proliferation Treaty (NPT) unconditionally. In May 1998, Indian Defense Minister George Fernandes said, "China is potential threat number one," leading Beijing to interpret India's nuclear tests as a hostile maneuver aimed at China and exacerbating an already tense situation. Within a few days of the tests, the Chinese response turned sharply critical.

> The Chinese government is deeply shocked by this and hereby expresses its strong condemnation ... . The Indian government, which itself has undermined the international effort in banning nuclear tests so as to obtain the hegemony in South Asia in defiance of the world opinion, has even maliciously accused China as posing a nuclear threat to India. This is utterly groundless ... this gratuitous accusation by India against China is solely

for [the] purpose of finding excuses for the development of its nuclear weapons.[10]

Chinese leaders insisted that China was not a threat to India, and therefore Indian nuclear disarmament was a necessity. Various scholars in China argued that the Indian claim of a China threat was an excuse to garner sympathy from the West for its nuclear tests.[11] However, some Chinese scholars argue that the mixed reaction from China directly following India's tests reflected a lack of consensus among Chinese political and military leaders.[12] China states that its strategy toward South Asia is one of cooperation and that its military modernization is defensive and not directed at any particular country. Furthermore, the leadership notes that economic development is China's main priority; thus conflict is inimical to this national objective. Over time, the fact that neither India nor Pakistan is willing to forgo its nuclear capabilities became clear to the international community. China appears to have largely accepted the situation. The close military relationship between China and Pakistan complicates its dealings on this issue. China's assistance to Pakistan's nuclear and missile programs have undermined its credibility on nuclear nonproliferation. The close military relationship has also fueled Indian suspicions of a Chinese strategy of encirclement, creating further incentive for maintaining and expanding India's nuclear capabilities.

Recent Evolution of the Relationship

China and India have slowly come to an understanding that their national interests can be compatible. Both countries have committed themselves to the use of confidence-building measures and cooperative dispute resolution. China claims that India still occupies Chinese territory in Arunachal Pradesh, and India accuses China of occupying its territory. However, discussions begun in 2003 and finalized in 2005 have helped to ameliorate relations. During Prime Minister Vajpayee's visit to China in 2003 India moved to formally accept the Tibet Autonomous Region as a part of China, a long-standing sore spot. Then during Premier Wen Jiabao's 2005 visit to India, China accepted India's stance on the issue of Sikkim. Whereas in the past Chinese maps denoted Sikkim as a separate country, the new discussions between India and China concluded that Sikkim is officially a state of the Republic of India.[13] During the 2005 visit, China presented Indian officials with the new map denoting Sikkim as an Indian territory. Leading officials and scholars in both countries state that the remaining border disputes are not worth war. As the populations of these two countries comprise a total of a third of the world, this is no small achievement.

In India, widespread support exists for the Tibetan people, their right to autonomy, and their right to their culture. However, the Indian government's position on Tibet, a largely accommodating one, is influenced heavily by national security and economic concerns. India can benefit from a reduction in China's military presence in Tibet, and from increased bilateral economic interaction. Despite official statements that India has accepted China's sovereignty over the Tibet Autonomous Region, the Tibetan issue remains contentious. The Dalai Lama continues to reside in Dharamsala, India, along with thousands of supporters. He remains spiritually influential and widely popular in India, creating a disparity between official actions and public sentiment. Many Indians disagree with the Indian government's stance on Tibet and support an independent or at least autonomous Tibet. In addition, strong popular opposition exists to China's policy of resettling ethnic Han in Tibet. The massive Han migration is rapidly changing the ethnic composition of the region and will soon make Tibetans a minority in their own land.[14] Indians have also watched the destruction of various Tibetan Buddhist religious sites with dismay.

The U.S. role in Asia is also undoubtedly a significant factor in China's strategic calculus with regard to India. Soon after India's nuclear tests, China banded together with the United States to condemn India's nuclear program, creating apprehension in India that the United States and China might combine to restrain India. Conversely, calls within the United States to work with India to contain China have caused anxiety in China, providing Chinese strategists with incentives to warm relations with India. A closer relationship with India benefits China by precluding the United States from incorporating India into a containment strategy, whereas tensions between China and India would provide an opportunity for Washington and New Delhi to work together against China. Tensions between China and the United States over Taiwan give China even more incentive to resolve its disputes with India. China's primary geopolitical objective in Asia remains the favorable resolution of the Taiwan issue; thus the Chinese leadership is reluctant to expend military resources on territorial disputes to its south.[15]

China and India's growing economic and trade ties have contributed to an improving security relationship. Both countries have come to the understanding that economic cooperation is the key to the future, and closer diplomatic and security relations must follow. A senior military official in China noted, "I am not worried about relations between China and India because I think these two countries will come together to deal with the very similar challenges they will face in the future."[16]

The shift in relations was manifested in the recent bilateral military exercises between India and China.[17] The first exercises, held in November 2003, involved a joint naval search and rescue exercise off the coast of Shanghai and were symbolically important if limited in military signif-icance. Then in August 2004, the troops of both countries held joint moun-taineering training in Tibet. Military cooperation will undoubtedly decrease the possibility of miscommunication and misunderstanding, making conflict less probable. Joint exercises also serve to build confi-dence between the two countries' militaries. However, China and India will take time to deepen their security ties, and the exercises do not signal the imminent start of a military alliance. In the short term, economic coop-eration will serve to bring Beijing and New Delhi closer together, even as it adds some new competitive elements into the mix.

Evolving Economic Relations with India

Economics has been the main driving force in the new Sino-Indian bilateral relationship. China's economic success since it began "reform and opening" in 1978 set a positive example for India. However, New Delhi responded only a decade later, after an economic crisis forced India to reform its bureaucratic and largely socialized economic system. Liber-alization and growth has decreased the incentives for both China and India to engage in conflict with each other and increased the initiatives to reconcile differences.

Despite progress, India's gross domestic product (GDP) is approxi-mately $692 billion (U.S.), less than half of China's ($1.6 trillion). India's incoming foreign direct investment ($4.3 billion in 2003) also remains low compared with China's ($53.5 billion).[18] As India implemented reforms a decade after China, it will take time and effort for India to match China's success. However, India does maintain certain advantages. The banking sector is considerably healthier than China's. Insolvency is approximately 15 percent, whereas China's insolvency is estimated to be between 25 percent and 40 percent.[19] India's growth has been largely internally driven, with exports comprising only 15.3 percent of GDP (40 percent for China). This low export dependence makes the economy less vulnerable to fluctuations in international demand or other external shocks. The service sector also comprises a larger part of India's economy. Currently, 52.2 percent of India's GDP is derived from services, while 34.5 percent of China's economy is service driven.[20] Services are the present engine of growth for the Indian economy in the absence of a robust manufacturing sector and provide a stable engine for India's growth. And as the manufacturing sector grows, India has the capability of further increasing economic growth.

There is likely to be tremendous growth in trade between the two coun-tries in coming years. Trade volume increased from a paltry $260 million per year in 1990 to $13.6 billion for 2004, according to Chinese Customs

Statistics.[21] In addition, India's Petroleum Minister in January 2006 met with Chinese energy officials to put in place agreements for future energy cooperation. China's CNPC and India's ONGC already combined forces in mounting a joint bid for oil and gas fields in Syria in 2005. Trade provides a boost to both economies and increases interdependence. Of course, economics also provides a new field for competition. India eyes with envy China's rapid growth rates and competitiveness in the consumer-goods sector. For years, Indians were worried that cheap Chinese goods were flooding the Indian market and threatening domestic manufacturing. In the past few years, however, businesses are looking to China more as a model for attracting foreign investment. Indian businesses realize that much effort is needed to match China's performance in this arena, including added attention to education, infrastructure, and less bureaucracy.

China, for its part, is hoping to emulate India's success in the information-technology arena. In China, recent media reports indicate rising concern regarding India's increasing competitiveness in microchip manufacturing. Chinese analysts argue that because India's salaries are lower, costs are cheaper, thereby making Indian products more competitive. Language is also a factor. Chinese businessmen fear that U.S. businesses will prefer Indian products because of the Indian facility with English. In a strange turn of events, the Chinese population is now asking whether their market is likely to be flooded with cheap Indian goods. With common strengths and export markets, trade competition is inevitable. But competition on economic terms is certainly preferable to competition in the security arena, and beneficial to both.

China's View of a Rising India

Chinese leaders and scholars have for decades not considered India a peer competitor, but that may now be changing. China's reforms in the 1980s and the ensuing rapid growth in the 1990s allowed it to surge ahead of India as an economic powerhouse in Asia. The military capabilities of China were rapidly advancing, as China acquired nuclear weapons as well as the ability to deliver them to all parts of India.

China's membership in the U.N. Security Council also accorded it a status that India could not attain. At the same time, Chinese leaders were cognizant of the fact that India could eventually become a competitor, an eventuality that made the leadership uncomfortable. Officially and in general terms, China has supported the causes of the developing world in international forums. Premier Wen Jiabao has hinted at support of India's bid for a seat on the United Nations Security Council (UNSC).[22] During his April 2005 visit to India and discussions with Prime Minister

Manmohan Singh, he stated, "China understands and supports India's aspirations to play an active role in the UN and international affairs." However, China in the past has not supported an expansion of the U.N. Security Council to include new developing members such as India, Brazil, or Japan.[23]

India's development of a long-range, nuclear-capable ballistic missile has the potential to bring all of China into range. The Indian Navy's acquisition of an aircraft carrier creates concerns among Chinese defense strategists, as does the increasing effectiveness of India's Air Force.[24] In addition, India's rapid economic growth since the mid-1990s and its competitiveness in the information and service sectors have drawn the attention of Chinese leaders. Amelioration of ties has been the primary policy, which could deter India from aligning with the United States to contain China while providing a mutually beneficial economic relationship. Nonetheless, as India continues to grow, China's reluctance to accord the country status as a peer in the international arena could cause friction and could lead to renewed tensions.

China-India-Pakistan Trilateral Relations

While China's relationship with India has generally been growing closer over the last several years, its relationship with Pakistan has been growing more distant. During the Cold War and the 1990s, China maintained a close relationship with Pakistan, to India's dismay. During the 1960s, China emerged as the major weapons supplier to Pakistan, and the defense relationship was cemented over the following decades. Pakistan's dispute with India over Kashmir had its benefits for China. A critical military route from Xinjiang through Tibet in Kashmir was ceded by Pakistan to China, though the region remained under dispute with India.[25] The route provides logistical and military access for China into Tibet.

China's military assistance, including the transfer of nuclear and missile technology, to Pakistan has been a persistent irritant in Sino-Indian relations. In the 1980s and 1990s, China supplied F-5A and F-7 fighters to Pakistan, as well as several hundred tanks, antitank missiles, and other conventional weapons.[26] China provided the short-range, nuclear capable DF-11, or M-11 missile to Pakistan. Recently declassified documents indicate that Chinese nuclear transfers to Pakistan spurred consternation in the U.S. government for decades. In 1983, State Department analysts concluded that China was helping Pakistan with fissile material production, and 1992 papers revealed concern regarding China's "continuing activities with Pakistan's nuclear weapons programs."[27] In 1995, Pakistan procured approximately 5,000 ring magnets for uranium enrichment centrifuges from China.[28] Despite this, China continued to deny reports of these sales, stating after the 1998 tests that it had not transferred any technology to Pakistan that could be used for the manufacture of nuclear weapons.[29] Revelations of Pakistani nuclear and missile sales to Libya, North Korea, and Iran indicate that Pakistan's nuclear programs, made possible only with Chinese help, have now taken on a life of their own. Chinese sales of nuclear technology to Pakistan might have ended years ago, but they have enabled Pakistan to provide Chinese nuclear technology to other countries. And despite official denials of nuclear proliferation, it is possible that China had advance knowledge of the international transfers. This is a particular concern given numerous past statements that China would not allow retransfers of nuclear technology to a third country without China's prior consent.[30] In the 2004 investigations following the revelation of Pakistani nuclear transfers to Libya, Libyan scientists provided early Chinese nuclear weapons designs wrapped in bags and tagged with a Pakistani address to the International Atomic Energy Agency.[31]

China has assisted Pakistan heavily in the civilian nuclear arena as well. The first nuclear plant built in Chashma, Pakistan, by China became operational in 1999. Currently China is engaged in building a second nuclear power plant for Pakistan in Chashma, known as C-2. The plant is expected to be complete in six years.[32] China is also assisting Pakistan in the development of Gwadar Deep Sea Port in the province of Baluchistan, funding approximately 80 percent of the project. When completed next year, Gwadar is expected to be Pakistan's third largest port, providing Arabian Sea access to Central Asia, Afghanistan, and Xinjiang and shortening the distance from Xinjiang to the sea by approximately 2,500 kilometers.[33] Hundreds of Chinese workers are engaged in building the port. In May 2004, a terrorist bombing in Gwadar killed three of the Chinese workers, the first attack on Chinese nationals in Pakistan.[34] The incident drew international attention to the project and speculation about China's intentions in the Indian Ocean. Indian analysts fear Chinese entry into the Indian Ocean, whereas the United States is apprehensive of the proximity to Diego Garcia. Most recently, both countries have increased the level of military interaction through joint exercises. In August 2004, China and Pakistan embarked upon the first joint antiterrorism exercises between the two countries. Border troops from each country met in the Pamir Mountains of Xinjiang to engage in exercises simulating attacks upon terrorists.

However, China has in recent years emphasized its intent to pursue a balanced foreign policy toward India and Pakistan, effectively downgrading its Pakistan relationship. During the 1999 Kargil conflict between India and Pakistan, China notably did not support the Pakistani incursion, emphasizing the necessity to resolve the Kashmir dispute through negotiations rather than military means. This shift is likely a result of India's growing significance as an economic and military power in Asia.

Other issues are also increasingly affecting China's relations with Pakistan. Revelations of Pakistan's transfer of nuclear technology to North Korea placed China in a difficult position vis-à-vis the international community and North Korea. Initially, China found that it must scramble to defuse the situation in Northeast Asia created by North Korea's nuclearization. However, ultimately, China refused to implicate Pakistan, questioning the U.S. sources of information regarding Pakistani nuclear proliferation and the origin of North Korea's nuclear program.[35]

In addition, whereas Pakistan's support for fundamentalist groups was previously not a priority to China, reports now indicate that the numbers of Uighur separatists trained by Pakistan have created problems for China in Xinjiang. As a result, the issue has become a liability for Pakistan in the bilateral relationship.[36] Nonetheless, the strong historical relationship between the two countries is unlikely to disappear. Military cooperation continues, and China may want to maintain close ties with Pakistan as a hedge against being surrounded by a hostile United States, Japan, and India in an unknown future.

Security remains the focus of the China-Pakistan relationship and accounts for the majority of interactions. Despite efforts to foster broader ties, economic interests are a small component of bilateral relations. Trade has increased rapidly, but total volume remains at only about $3.4 billion, compared to $13.6 billion with India. Agricultural products form the bulk of Pakistan's exports to China, whereas manufactured products are generally imported by Pakistan.[37] Pakistan's weak manufacturing base is an impediment to growth in export trade of higher value-added goods to China, as Chinese products compete favorably against Pakistani goods. Both countries emphasize the need to expand economic relations, but financial constraints in Pakistan pose a hurdle to rapid growth in this arena.

Conclusions

India's relations with China appear to be moving in an increasingly positive direction, although disagreements remain. Growing economic ties are providing Cold Warriors on both sides of the border incentives to work past old differences. After a long period of tensions, even joint military exercises have become possible.

While the apparent warming of ties between India and China does not necessitate a cooling between China and Pakistan, the trilateral dynamic has changed. China's economic ties with Pakistan have grown rapidly in recent years, but they remain a fraction of the booming trade between

China and India. China has also undertaken a more balanced policy toward India and Pakistan, shifting away from its former policies of siding with Pakistan on the Kashmir dispute. In doing so, China has indicated that positive relations with India may increasingly be more critical to its interests than maintaining the status quo with a smaller and weaker Pakistan. At the same time, India has moved forward to improve the relationship with both China and Pakistan.

Recent diplomatic initiatives with India are likely to push forward this trend in Chinese foreign policy. At the same time, U.S. interests in Asia also create conditions for China to move closer toward India. Chinese leaders are apprehensive that a U.S.–Indian alignment could form to contain China. India's growth as an economic power in Asia and a military competitor make the scenario of containment even more formidable. In an effort to preempt any such possibility, Chinese leaders are fostering closer diplomatic relations with India.

Nonetheless, critical issues such as Tibet, border disputes, and Chinese military assistance to Pakistan still require attention. These issues will not be resolved swiftly or with ease. China's close military ties with Pakistan are a component of a broader security relationship between the two countries meant to protect each country's geopolitical interests in the region. Furthermore, as China and India grow as peer competitors in Asia, both countries will increasingly compete for leverage in the international arena. India may demand equal footing with China, whereas China may attempt to contain India. Casting new roles in the international system for these massive countries will be a challenge for the international community and will be critical to creating long-term stability in Asia.

Notes

1. Data from interviews with Indian and Chinese policy makers and scholars, 2001–2006.

2. Jawaharlal Nehru, *India's Foreign Policy: Selected Speeches, September 1946-April 1961* (Bombay: The Publications Division, Ministry of Information and Broadcasting, Government of India, 1961), 24.

3. Chih H. Lu, *The Sino-Indian Border Dispute: A Legal Study* (Westport, CT: Greenwood Press, 1986), 49–53.

4. John W. Garver, *Protracted Contest: Sino-Indian Rivalry in the Twentieth Century* (Seattle: University of Washington Press, 2001), 52.

5. Dennis Kux, *India and the United States: Estranged Democracies* (Washington, DC: National Defense University Press, 1992), 210.

6. Kux, *India and the United States: Estranged Democracies*, 279–281.

7. These measures were adopted in the "Agreement on Establishment of Confidence-Building Measures in Military Field along the Line of Actual Control in the India-China Border Area"; see Xia Liping, "China-India Security Relationship: Retrospects and Prospects," Shanghai Institute for International Studies, at

http://www.siis.org.cn/english/collection/xialiping.htm (accessed February 22, 2005).

8. See Garver, *Protracted Contest*, 7.

9. "China Seriously Concerned about Indian Nuclear Test," *Xinhua News Agency*, May 12, 1998.

10. "Chinese Government Strongly Condemns Indian Nuclear Tests," *Xinhua News Agency*, May 14, 1998.

11. Zou Yunhua, "Chinese Perspectives on the South Asian Nuclear Tests," Working Paper for the Center for International Security and Cooperation (CISAC), Stanford University, January 1999.

12. Ming Zhang, *China's Changing Nuclear Posture: Reactions to the South Asian Nuclear Tests* (Washington, DC: Carnegie Endowment for International Peace, 1999), 30.

13. "China Puts Sikkim in India Map as India Forgets Tibet," *The Economic Times*, April 12, 2005.

14. "Tibet: Chinese Pouring into Lhasa," *The New York Times*, August 8, 2002; "China Revives Controversial Tibetan Migration Project," *Agence France Presse*, January 23, 2002.

15. Chinese military officials and scholars, in interviews with the author 2001–2005.

16. Chinese military official, in a conversation with the author, Beijing, China.

17. "Naval Exercises Indicate Sea Change in Relations," *South China Morning Post*, November 15, 2003; "First India-China Naval Exercise Opens New Chapter in Ties," *The Press Trust of India*, November 15, 2003.

18. The World Bank, *World Development Indicators database*, August 2005, http://www.worldbank.org/data/countrydata/countrydata.html.

19. James Kynge, "China's 'Big Four' Banks Set for New Loan Plan," *The Financial Times*, February 5, 2004; "China Economic Review: China Mulls Multi-Bln-Dlr Bailout Plan on State Bank," *Xinhua News Agency*, January 17, 2005; Sonia Kolesnikov-Jessop, "China Soft Landing Has Cost," *United Press International*, July 19, 2004; Khozem Merchant, "India Set To Launch Bank Recovery Vehicle: A Plan to Restructure Distressed Public Sector Debt Could Face Legal and Political Hurdles," *The Financial Times*, April 10, 2002.

20. The World Bank, *World Development Indicators database*, August 2005, http://www.worldbank.org/data/countrydata/countrydata.html.

21. "India-China Bilateral Trade Touches USD 13.6 billion," *The Press Trust of India*, February 6, 2005; "Sino-Indian Trade Tops US $10 billion," *People's Daily Online*, December 28, 2004, http://english1.people.com.cn/200412/28/eng20041228_168942.html.

22. John Lancaster, "India, China Hoping to 'Reshape the World Order' Together; Once Hostile Giants Sign Accord on Border Talks, Economic Ties, Trade and Technology," *The Washington Post*, April 12, 2005.

23. Samuel S. Kim, "China and the Third World in the Changing World Order," in *China and the World*, ed. Samuel S. Kim (Boulder, CO: Westview Press, 1994), 136.

24. Interviews with Chinese policy makers and scholars, 2001–2005.

25. John W. Garver, *Protracted Contest: Sino-Indian Rivalry in the Twentieth Century* (Seattle: University of Washington Press, 2001), 205.

26. Garver, *Protracted Contest: Sino-Indian Rivalry in the Twentieth Century*, 235.

27. Siobhan McDonough, "Documents Show U.S. Unease Over Pakistan-China Security Cooperation," *The Associated Press,* March 5, 2004.

28. Daniel L. Byman and Roger Cliff, *China's Arms Sales: Motivations and Implications* (Santa Monic, CA: RAND, MR-1119-AF, 1999).

29. Garver, *Protracted Contest: Sino-Indian Rivalry in the Twentieth Century,* 222–223.

30. "China's Nuclear Exports and Assistance," *China Profiles* Database, Center for Nonproliferation Studies, Monterey Institute of International Studies, www.nti.org/db/china/nexport.htm.

31. "China's Nuclear Exports and Assistance to Pakistan," *China Profiles* Database, Center for Nonproliferation Studies, Monterey Institute of International Studies, http://www.nti.org/db/china/npakpos.htm.

32. "China Signs Deal to Build Second Nuclear Plant in Pakistan," AFX-Asia, May 5, 2004.

33. "China-Built Pakistan Port 'Draws Animosity' from India, U.S.," *The Straits Times Web site, BBC Worldwide Monitoring,* May 17, 2004.

34. "Bodies of Chinese Car Bomb Victims Flown to China from Pakistan," *Agence France Presse,* May 7, 2004.

35. Joseph Kahn and Susan Chira, "China Challenges U.S. on Pyongyang's Arms," *The International Herald Tribune,* June 10, 2004.

36. "Hong Kong Daily Cites Report on Uighur Muslim Leader Put to Death in China," *South China Morning Post* Web site, *BBC Monitoring International Reports,* October 24, 2004; Richard McGregor, "Uighur Training Angered Beijing," *The Financial Times,* October 18, 2001.

37. "Pakistan, China Pledge to Set up Free Trade Area," *Business Daily Update,* December 29, 2004.

CHAPTER 7

Implications

The oldest question in statecraft is how to discern what another state will do. One means is to study the objective circumstances of each state: geographic location, size, economic capacity, and involvement in particular markets. Such analysis can conceivably reflect areas of competition between states, but it cannot contribute insights into the effects of intangible factors, such as the national psyche. Another way of predicting state behavior is to study military capabilities. Although there is utility in ascertaining the capabilities of various states, the information drawn from these capabilities cannot provide a reliable analysis of national objectives. Conclusions based upon capabilities rely upon linear assumptions of historical trends. However, the future is not like the past. Situations and beliefs are dynamic, not enduring, facets of a nation. Additionally, states with comparable capabilities do not necessarily have the same objectives. A substantial analysis of national interests should incorporate national perceptions, as well as other factors of the state's domestic and international environment. Thus, a third method to discern national interests is to study perceived national objectives directly by asking elites why they follow particular policies. The advantages of this approach are that it factors in value questions directly rather than inferring them from size or geographic location and can provide the context for a more comprehensive and integrated understanding of national abilities and interests.

Domestic vs. Foreign Affairs in the National Interest

Another limitation of existing research is that scholars and decision makers in the United States commonly view domestic policies and objectives as sectoral interests and equate foreign policy with the national interest. This assumption does not appear to hold for all states. The Chinese and Indian positions that economic reforms are critical for the national interest belie that notion, as do the financial restructurings occurring on national levels in East and Southeast Asia after the 1997 financial crisis. Political reforms are also examples of national policies. In creating political institutions and the legal framework for the state, the national interest of political consolidation is served. The purpose of these domestic yet national policy programs is to strengthen overall economic and political national strength.

The interpretation of domestic objectives as national interests appears with more frequency in countries that are faced with fundamental economic or political weakness, and also in countries that are in the initial phase of political consolidation. The ability for the United States to use foreign policy as a proxy for the national interest is an indication that the U.S. decision-making elites believe there are no more critical economic or political threats to the American state. The United States last faced political and territorial consolidation in the aftermath of the Civil War, more than a century ago. Since then, the relative absence of internal threats to the unity and stability of the homeland has reinforced the impression that the national interest can be safely consigned to the external sphere. The sudden events of September 11 strained part of the foundation of these assumptions, leading to a national consensus for the development of homeland security. Nonetheless, the dangers are still externally defined for the United States, and the assumption that national interests are indistinguishable from foreign policy creates the false impression that this syllogism holds true for other countries as well.

Perceptions

The role of perceptions in the formation of national interest remains a critical component of the decision-making process. Rather than reality, it is the perceptions of reality that affect the formation of national interest and decision making. In China and India, the elites' perceptions of national interests may or may not reflect the objective nature of the exigencies of their respective states, but the perceived necessities of securing the unity of the state and of protecting the sovereignty of the state in the international arena have resulted in actual policy paths. Robert Jervis notes that an understanding of perceptions is central to making conclusions regarding intentions, "Both to interpret others' behavior and to design one's own behavior so that others will draw the desired conclusions from it, the actor must try to see the world the way the other sees it."[1] Recognizing the perceptions of our neighbors, partners, and competitors in the international arena can reduce misconceptions and possibly deflect conflict. Although studies regarding the capabilities of countries abound, perceptions are often overlooked or, worse yet, assumed. Ascribing intentions to countries according to their capabilities leads to poor policy analysis and dangerous predictions. Perceptions are more than a residual variable; the analysis of perceived national interests remains vital to understanding state behavior.

Institutions

In developing countries, political institutions that rely upon performance criteria for sustaining legitimacy may find themselves in dire circumstances in times of crisis. Until the political integration of the state is complete, the developing country must prioritize state integration as the primary national interest or risk state failure. Weak political and legal institutions enhance the risks of failure and deter proper integration. Various cases in recent history reflect the centrality of political institutions. During the Asian financial crisis, Indonesia's weak institutions could not sustain the economic and political pressures, leading to system collapse. The authoritarian regime had relied upon positive performance as a legitimizing force for decades. President Suharto was unable to perform adequately during the crisis, and his overwhelming connection with the political system destined the Indonesian state to share his fate. As President Suharto was ousted, the system collapsed, to be replaced by democracy. Karl Jackson underlines this point, "President Suharto in the aftermath of the Crash of 1997, like Ferdinand Marcos in the Philippines in the wake of the commodities recession of the 1980s, fell rather quickly: performance regimes that lack other (noneconomic) sources of legitimacy tend to collapse during sharp economic downturns."[2] In the dramatic Argentine economic crisis, the democratic system survived financial collapse, even though individual presidents did not. President de la Rua resigned amid protests, as did his successor Rodriguez Saa. Notably, democratic processes were followed in the swift search for consecutive presidents. After Saa, the presidency passed on to the leader of the senate, and then to the head of the lower chamber of congress.[3] Although the rapid switching of presidents, five times in a matter of months, is hardly considered a paragon of political stability, it is preferable to the alternatives of military rule or state collapse.

Although democratic institutions do not in themselves provide the sufficient conditions for institutional stability, the norms and legal framework that they may foster can be the foundation for political stability and institutional durability. Newly democratized states face the challenge of protecting their institutions from power-hungry competitors willing to undermine legal avenues and systemic corruption. Pakistan, democratic during several periods of its history, has yet to develop the norms and institutional framework that purvey the sense of institutional legitimacy that is necessary to maintain a durable democratic structure. In the absence of institutional stability and legitimacy, national interests pursued by the state may be increasingly focused upon an internal power struggle for the reins of leadership.

National Interests and Sino-Indian Relations

National interests serve as guideposts for viewing another country's foreign policy. By noting others' perceptions of the world and of their neighbors, some conclusions can be drawn regarding their foreign policies. Respondents' perceptions of China's and India's national interests reflected little tension between the two countries. The Chinese view that state unity is the main national interest creates tension with India primarily over the Tibet issue, and the Indian refuge for the Dalai Lama and Tibetans. Nonetheless, none of the Chinese respondents felt that this issue warranted military conflict. The majority of respondents reiterated that Sino-Indian relations had been gradually improving, and none expressed great concern about the long-disputed border region. Indian respondents echoed this view, noting that bilateral relations were better than they had been for decades. Both countries' respondents expressed the belief that concentrating on domestic economic growth was more important to the national interest than squabbles with the other. In contrast to Indian Defense Minister George Fernandes's view that defending against China was the main purpose behind the nuclear tests of 1998, Indian respondents in this study felt that the likelihood of conflict with China was virtually nonexistent.

Alternatively, on the issue of globalization, Indian respondents noted with mixed competitiveness and admiration the rapid growth and the potential of the Chinese economy. Competition exists for the same export markets and in areas such as software production, though both sides admitted that there are also opportunities for increased trade. Despite the existence of frictions over Tibet and trade, China and India appear to have similar national interests with regard to the role of international organizations and state sovereignty of decision making in the economic and political spheres. Respondents of both countries remarked that improved comprehensive national strength is necessary to gain leverage in international negotiations and preserve sovereignty over domestic economic and political decisions. Overall, the absence of conflicts regarding primary national interests and generally positive perceptions of "the other side" augurs well for bilateral relations.

Implications for U.S. Foreign Policy

Recognizing the significance of protecting state sovereignty for developing countries is fundamental for formulating effective U.S.

foreign policy. For Sino–U.S. relations, it means U.S. policy makers should note that territorial sovereignty over Taiwan is more important to many Chinese than continued economic development and that internal political considerations are crucial to the Chinese leadership. With regard to India, finding cooperative solutions through international organizations that incorporate India's concerns may be the most effective U.S. policy toward India in the long run. In addition, the absence of fundamental differences between China and India implies that relations between the two are more likely to be positive in the future. Working with this eventuality will lead to more successful foreign policy toward Asia in the future.

A significant commonality between the respondents of both countries is the reaction to the U.S. role in the Iraq War, the Gulf War, and Kosovo. This issue was more important to the Chinese respondents, who drew analogies to the possibility of U.S. intervention over the Taiwan issue. However, respondents from both China and India believe the lessons of these military interventions are that a strong defensive capability with a credible nuclear component is critical to protecting state sovereignty against international infringements. The overwhelming superiority of the U.S. military in these conflicts proved that procuring weapons to deter such attacks is necessary. The pursuit of a defense modernization program by both China and India demonstrates their resolve on this issue. However, the conclusions drawn by elites in China and India are unlikely to have escaped the notice of other countries. The utility of developing and procuring advanced weapons for protecting state sovereignty exists for other states as well. As developing countries continue to consolidate politically and economically, an increasing number will be compelled by their domestic constituents to pursue advanced technology weaponry to protect their own pursuit of national interests, regardless of the ultimate national objectives. The effectiveness of international agreements banning the spread and the use of such weaponry can be expected to be low, given the perceived consequences to states with poor capabilities, exemplified by the Iraq War and the Gulf War.

Avoiding a scenario in which multiple countries are pursuing spiraling arms races simultaneously is not simple. Reconfiguring international security relations and mechanisms is necessary and will require innovative thinking. For the United States, considering possible alternatives to existing mechanisms is requisite. Future military and nuclear acquisitions by developing countries will be with an eye to deterring infringements on sovereignty by the United States and by other powerful states. If the United States fails to take the lead in creating more cooperative mechanisms for international security, a recipe for disaster may await.

Areas for Future Research

In this book, elite views of two expansive policy programs were explored. By analyzing perceptions of the economic reforms and defense modernization programs in each country, it is possible to cover perceptions of a wide cluster of policies that can elicit the broadest possible response of national interests. Economic reform refers to a wide band of policies including issue areas as diverse as agriculture, technology, public welfare, and education. Defense modernization, similarly, incorporates security policy, technology, and scientific advancement. The broad nature of the questions and policy programs reduces the probability of overlooking the "true" perceived national interest of each country's respondents.

Insufficient research has been conducted regarding the effects of perceptions and political institutions upon the formation of national interest. This research constitutes a beginning for empirical studies of national-interest formation in other countries. Further research regarding national interests should be pursued. Using larger data sets, the findings of this research can be tested. Application of this analysis to policy programs other than economic reforms and defense modernization would also lead to interesting results. Research comparing popular views of the national interest with those of elites and studies using time series data could lead to new avenues in understanding national-interest formation.

In addition, through understanding China's and India's national interests, we can make some inferences about the direction of other developing countries' policies as they enter similar stages of development. Analysis of the national-interest formation of other countries would provide additional comparative data and fascinating implications for international relations.

Although knowledge of the perceptions of national interests does not imply that we can change national policies in the direction we please, understanding why nations act in the way they do can limit misperceptions and unintended consequences in international relations.

Notes

1. Robert Jervis, *Perception and Misperception in International Politics* (Princeton, NJ: Princeton University Press, 1976), 409.

2. Karl D. Jackson, *Asian Contagion: The Causes and Consequences of a Financial Crisis* (Boulder, CO: Westview Press, 1999), 17.

3. Thomas Catan, "Divided They Fall," *The Financial Times,* January 2, 2002, 12.

Conclusion

Decidedly different conceptions of national interests have propelled China and India along similar policy paths to economic reform and defense modernization. Divergent long-term motivations are even more remarkable given that both countries face many similar threats, such as internal income disparities, ethnic unrest, separatism, and challenges from the forces of globalization.

Interviews with respondents revealed different hierarchies of importance attached to each set of problems by the decision-making elites of China and India. Chinese respondents felt that national unity, comprised of territorial sovereignty and economic growth, were the most important national interests, whereas Indian respondents believed that facing the challenges of globalization by protecting economic and political sovereignty in the international arena was the most immediate and compelling national priority. The establishment of this hierarchy of interests in each country results from the perceived challenges to each state, as well as from the exigencies of the political institutions of each state. See Table 1.

Different perceived national challenges and dissimilar political institutions create different sets of intentions for China and India even though the sets of policies surrounding economic reforms and defense modernization remain similar. In the past two decades, both China and India have embarked upon ambitious and revolutionary plans for pursuing their respective national interests. The four modernizations adopted by China in 1978 included economic reforms and defense modernization as two of

Table 1   The Hierarchy of National Interests in China and India

	China	India
Primary priority	Protecting national unity: territorial integrity + economic development[1]	Globalization: protecting economic growth and political sovereignty
Secondary priority[2]	Globalization: protecting economic growth and political sovereignty	Economic development

the priority areas. India also made these choices, pursuing defense modernization, particularly missile and nuclear capabilities, through the 1980s and 1990s. India's economic reforms, begun largely after 1991, followed China's example in transforming a socialized economic system to one that accepted the inexorable spread of globalization. Significant similarities in approaches to modernizing the state exist in China and India despite differences on any individual policy guideline.

As both countries continued their progress in attaining record economic growth during the reform period, and in developing respectable defensive capabilities, an understanding of the motivations underlying the programs has become essential. Although Western policy makers and analysts tend to believe either that all states have the same priority in pursuing power or that state capabilities are an accurate predictor of state intentions, neither of these hypotheses is helpful in understanding the national interests actually being pursued. China and India are pursuing similar capabilities, but for divergent ends.

China's national interest has focused mainly upon protecting state unity, the most basic national interest for a state. When the existence of the state is at risk, it is difficult to pursue national interests with wider concerns. Although both Chinese and Indian respondents noted ethnic problems, separatism, and economic disparities as highly fractious elements challenging state unity, only the Chinese respondents felt that these posed a serious threat to the state. Separatist sentiments in Taiwan and ethnic unrest in Tibet and Xinjiang signaled problems emanating from the ethnic composition of the state. Disparities in income distribution between regions and within regions exacerbated ethnic divides. Furthermore, following the decline of the Communist ideology, a political definition for the state that could unify the diverse groups was absent. In sharp contrast, Indian respondents believed that the Indian state was far stronger than the centrifugal elements embedded in society and thus did not choose national unity as a prime national interest. None of the Indian respondents mentioned Kashmir as a critical issue. The unity of the Indian state did not hinge upon retaining Kashmir in whole or part, whereas to the majority of Chinese respondents a separation from Taiwan could mean the destruction of the state and fragmentation of the country.

The forces of globalization created both problems and possibilities for China in this context. The ability of high-technology weaponry to affect state sovereignty was demonstrated in the Iraq War, the Gulf War, and Kosovo. Similarly, respondents noted that the transfer of military technology and weaponry to Taiwan created a problem for the Chinese state's capability to defend territorial sovereignty. However, the more positive aspects of globalization created economic opportunities for China. Economic integration with the international economy could help China expand economically, spreading prosperity at home. Rapid growth also meant more funding for the defense modernization and an improved comprehensive national strength.

Globalization posed a more proximate threat to India in its ability to erode state sovereignty in trade and environmental issues, issues perceived to be central in ensuring future economic growth. Integration with the globalized economy was also viewed as necessary, however, in that it would expand India's competitiveness and growth. Echoing the Chinese response, Indian respondents noted that higher standards for military technology globally meant that India must also pursue advanced weaponry, in the form of missiles and nuclear capabilities. The combination of a strong economy and a viable nuclear deterrent could create a comprehensive national strength, thereby improving India's negotiating leverage across a wide expanse of international political and economic issue areas.

The divergent hierarchies of national interests observed in China and India lead back to the political institutions, and to the underlying issue of legitimacy. In China, performance legitimacy as the basis for Communist Party rule led respondents to underscore the inherent instability of the political system. A Party-state structure in which the system must share the consequences of Party actions implies that failure of the Party in times of crisis, i.e., Taiwan separation or economic failure, could lead to the loss of state legitimacy and system collapse. The stark nature of this contingency emphasized that the Communist Party is obliged to preserve the unity of the country in order to protect the legitimacy of the Party, and vice versa. In comparison, separation of the state and party functions in the Indian democratic system created system flexibility, in that failure of the party did not have ramifications for state stability or legitimacy. The assurance of stable political institutions in India allows a shift of focus from the internal challenge of state unity to external issues such as state sovereignty in international decision making.

Notes

1. Economic development indicates responses where the respondent did not mention globalization.

2. In India, the hierarchy does not indicate a sharp distinction between primary and secondary interests, whereas in China, there is such delineation. Few Indian respondents distinguished between pursuing economic development and accommodating globalization through reforms; most respondents viewed globalization as a path to development. Of over 40 respondents from each country, only 7 respondents from India chose development as a separate priority. In contrast, almost half of the Chinese respondents perceived accommodating globalization to be the secondary national interest.

China Interview Questions

Following is a list of the primary questions asked of all Chinese interviewees. All respondents were asked the questions on economic reforms, defense modernization, the country's role in the world, and national identity. Questions on decision making and foreign affairs were asked if time permitted. Additional questions were also asked if time allowed. Interviews averaged one to one and a half hours in length. Most Chinese respondents requested that their names not be used. I have indicated the interviewees by their general titles where their opinions have been cited in the text.

Economic Reforms

1. What do you think is the most important reason for pursuing economic reforms, from 1978 onward, and even now?
2. Why do you think the government is pursuing reforms?
3. Do you agree with these reasons?
4. Among economic factors (such as the need to increase the welfare of the people, improve living standards, etc.), geopolitical factors (the competition or threat from other countries), national identity issues (the historical definition of China as a nation and Chinese as a people), and other factors, which do you feel is most relevant? The next important? The overall ranking?
5. Why?
6. What do you believe are the main economic challenges facing China now?
7. Why?

Defense Modernization

1. What do you think are the most important reasons for having a defense modernization from the 1980s onward?
2. Why do you think the government is pursuing modernization?

3. Do you agree?

4. Among economic factors (such as the need to increase the welfare of the people, improve living standards, etc.), geopolitical factors (the competition or threat from other countries), national identity issues (the historical definition of China as a nation and Chinese as a people), and other factors, which do you feel is most relevant? The next important? The overall ranking?

5. Why?

6. What do you believe are the main security challenges facing China now?

7. Why?

General

1. What do you see as China's role in the world in the next 10 years?

National Identity

1. How would you define China? What defines the Chinese people?

2. Do you think that the Chinese national identity has an effect on China's economic and defense policies?

Decision Making

1. Who do you think are the main decision makers in China?

2. How does the decision-making process work?

Foreign Policy

1. What do you think is the direction of China–U.S. relations in the next 10 years or so? Positive, negative, neutral? Why?

2. What do you think is the direction of China-India relations in the next 10 years or so? Positive, negative, neutral? Why?

3. What do you think is the direction of China-Japan relations in the next 10 years or so? Positive, negative, neutral? Why?

India Interview Questions

Following is a list of the primary questions asked of all Indian interviewees. All respondents were asked the questions on economic reforms, defense modernization, the country's role in the world, and national identity. Questions on decision making and foreign affairs were asked if time permitted. Additional questions were also asked if time allowed. Interviews averaged one to one-and-a-half hours in length. I have indicated the interviewees by their titles where their opinions have been cited in the text.

Economic Reforms

1. What do you think is the most important reason for pursuing economic reforms, from 1991 onward, and even now?
2. Why do you think the government is pursuing reforms?
3. Do you agree with these reasons?
4. Among economic factors (such as the need to increase the welfare of the people, improve living standards, etc.), geopolitical factors (the competition or threat from other countries), national identity issues (the historical definition of India as a nation and Indians as a people), and other factors, which do feel is most relevant? The next important? The overall ranking?
5. Why?
6. What do you believe are the main economic challenges facing India now?
7. Why?

Defense Modernization

1. What do you think are the most important reasons for having a defense modernization from the 1980s onward?
2. Why do you think the government is pursuing modernization?
3. Do you agree?

4. Among economic factors (such as the need to increase the welfare of the people, improve living standards, etc.), geopolitical factors (the competition or threat from other countries), national identity issues (the historical definition of India as a nation and Indians as a people), and other factors, which do feel is most relevant? The next important? The overall ranking?

5. Why?

6. What do you believe are the main security challenges facing India now?

7. Why?

8. Do you think it is necessary to have a nuclear capability?

9. Why?

General

1. What do you see as India's role in the world in the next 10 years?

National Identity

1. How would you define India? What defines the Indian people?

2. Do you think that the Indian national identity has an effect on India's economic and defense policies?

Decision Making

1. Who do you think are the main decision makers in India?

2. How does the decision-making process work?

Foreign Policy

1. What do you think is the direction of India–U.S. relations in the next 10 years or so? Positive, negative, neutral? Why?

2. What do you think is the direction of China-India relations in the next 10 years or so? Positive, negative, neutral? Why?

3. What do you think is the direction of India-Japan relations in the next 10 years or so? Positive, negative, neutral? Why?

Bibliography

Ahrari, Ehsan. "China's Naval Forces Look to Extend Their Blue-Water Reach." *Jane's Intelligence Review* 10, no. 4 (1 April 1998).

Aiyar, S. P., and R. Srinivasan. *Studies in Indian Democracy*. Bombay: Allied Publishers, 1965.

Andersen, Walter K., and Shridhar D. Damle. *The Brotherhood in Saffron: The Rashtriya Swayamsevak Sangh and Hindu Revivalism*. New Delhi: Westview Press, 1987.

Annual Report 1992–1993. New Delhi: Ministry of Defense, Government of India, 1993.

Austin, Granville. *The Indian Constitution: Cornerstone of a Nation*. London: Oxford University Press, 1966.

Ayoob, Mohammed. "Nuclear India and Indian-American Relations" *Orbis* 43, no. 1 (Winter 1999).

Azam, Kousar J. *India's Defense Policy for the 1990's*. New Delhi: Sterling, 1992.

Babbage, Ross, and Sandy Gordon, eds. *India's Strategic Future*. New York: St. Martin's Press, 1992.

Barnds, William J. *India, Pakistan, and the Great Powers*. New York: Praeger Publishers, 1972.

Barnett, A. Doak. *The Making of Foreign Policy in China: Structure and Process*. Boulder: Westview Press, 1985.

Barnett, Robert, ed. *Resistance and Reform in Tibet*. Bloomington: Indiana University Press, 1994.

Baruah, Sanjib. *India Against Itself: Assam and the Politics of Nationality*. Philadelphia: University of Pennsylvania Press, 1999.

Beard, Charles A. *The Idea of National Interest: An Analytical Study in American Foreign Policy*. New York: The Macmillan Company, 1934.

Bedi, Rahul, and Lewis, J. A. C. "India to Buy 10 Mirage 2000Hs." *Jane's Defense Weekly* 34, no. 11 (13 September 2000).

Bell, Michael W., Hoe Ee Khor, and Kalpana Kochhar. *Occasional Paper 107: China at the Threshold of a Market Economy*. Washington, DC: International Monetary Fund, 1993.

Bhola, P. L. *Pakistan-China Relations*. Jaipur, India: R.B.S.A. Publishers, 1986.

Bidwai, Praful, and Achin Vanaik. *New Nukes: India, Pakistan, and Global Nuclear Disarmament*. New York: Olive Branch Press, 2000.

Binder, Leonard, Lucian W. Pye, James S. Coleman, Sidney Verba, Joseph Lapalombara, and Myron Weiner. *Crises and Sequences in Political Development*. Princeton, NJ: Princeton University Press, 1971.

Binnendijk, Hans, and Ronald N. Montaperto, eds. *Strategic Trends in China*. Washington, DC: NDU Press, 1998.

Boone, Peter, Stanislaw Gomulka, and Richard Layard. *Emerging from Communism: Lessons from Russia, China, and Eastern Europe*. Cambridge, MA: The MIT Press, 1998.

Bowles, Paul, and Gordon White. *The Political Economy of China's Financial Reforms*. Boulder, CO: Westview Press, 1993.

Brands, H. W. "The Idea of the National Interest." *Diplomatic History* 23, no. 2 (1999).

Brass, Paul R. *The New Cambridge History of India: The Politics of India Since Independence*. Cambridge: Cambridge University Press, 1990.

Brilmayer, Lea. *American Hegemony: Political Morality in a One-Superpower World*. New Haven, CT: Yale University Press, 1994.

Brown, Michael E., and Sumit Ganguly, eds. *Government Policies and Ethnic Relations in Asia and the Pacific*. Cambridge, MA: MIT Press, 1997.

Brundenius, Claes, and John Weeks. *Globalization and Third World Socialism: Cuba and Vietnam*. New York: Palgrave, 2001.

Buzan, Barry, and Gowher Rizvi, eds. *South Asian Security and the Great Powers*. New York: St. Martin's, 1986.

Catan, Thomas. "Divided They Fall." *Financial Times*, 2 January 2002.

Chadda, Maya. *Building Democracy in South Asia: India, Nepal, Pakistan*. Boulder, CO: Lynne Rienner Publishers, 2000.

Chatterjee, Partha, ed. *Wages of Freedom: Fifty Years of the Indian Nation-State*. New Delhi: Oxford University Press, 1998.

Chen, Baizhu, J. Kimball Dietrich, and Yi Feng. *Financial Market Reform in China: Progress, Problems, and Prospects*. Boulder, CO: Westview Press, 2000.

Chen, Feng. *Economic Transition and Political Legitimacy in Post-Mao China: Ideology and Reform*. Albany: State University of New York, 1995.

Cheng, Ruisheng. "China and South Asia in the 21st Century." China Center for International Studies (April 1998).

Chopra, Ajai, Woosik Chu, and Oliver Fratzscher. "Structural Reforms and the Implications for Investment and Growth," in *India: Economic Reform and Growth*, Occasional Paper 134. Washington, DC: International Monetary Fund, December 1995.

Cirincione, Joseph, Jon B. Wolfsthal, and Miriam Rajkumar. *Tracking Proliferation: A Global Guide with Maps and Charts*. Washington, DC: Carnegie Endowment for International Peace, 2002.

Clinton, W. David. *The Two Faces of National Interest*. Baton Rouge: Louisiana State University Press, 1994.

Cohen, Stephen P. *The Indian Army, Its Contribution to the Development of a Nation*. Berkeley: University of California Press, 1971.

Cohen, Stephen P. *Security of South Asia*. Chicago: University of Illinois Press, 1987.

Commission on America's National Interests, *America's National Interests*. The Commission on America's National Interests, 2000.

Connolly, William E. *Identity/Difference: Democratic Negotiations of Political Paradox*. Ithaca, NY: Cornell University Press, 1991.

Connolly, William E., ed. *Legitimacy and the State*. New York: New York University Press, 1984.

Connor, Walker. *Ethnonationalism: The Quest for Understanding*. Princeton, NJ: Princeton University Press, 1994.

Connor, Walker. *The National Question in Marxist-Leninist Theory and Strategy*. Princeton, NJ: Princeton University Press, 1984.

Cottier, Thomas, and Petros C. Mavroidis, eds. *State Trading in the Twenty-First Century*, World Trade Forum, vol. 1. Ann Arbor: The University of Michigan Press, 1998.

Das, M. N. *The Political Philosophy of Nehru*. New York: George Allen & Unwin Ltd., 1961.

Deng, Xiaoping. *Selected Works of Deng Xiaoping*. Vols. 2–3. Beijing: Foreign Languages Press.

Downing, John. "Maritime Ambition China's Naval Modernisation." *Jane's Navy International* 103, no. 4 (1 May 1998).

Drysdale, Peter, and Ligang Song, eds. *China's Entry to the WTO*. New York: Routledge, 2000.

Earle, Walter B. "Drama and Rationality in Foreign Policy." *Journal for the Theory of Social Behaviour* 19, no. 2 (June 1989).

The Economist Intelligence Unit. "India Country Profile 2001." *The Economist* (2001).

The Economist Intelligence Unit. "India Country Report." *The Economist* (February 2002).

Embree, Ainslie T. *India's Search for National Identity*. New York: Alfred A. Knopf, 1972.

Erickson, Erik. *Gandhi's Truth*. New York: W. W. Norton & Co., 1969.

Erickson, Erik. *Identity: Youth and Crisis*. New York: W. W. Norton & Company, 1968.

Gandhi, M. K. *Gandhi's Autobiography: The Story of My Experiments with Truth*. Washington, DC: Public Affairs Press, 1948.

Ganguly, Sumit. "South Asia after the Cold War." *Washington Quarterly* 15 (Autumn 1992): 173–188.

Garver, John W. "The United States and the India China Relationship" Paper for the Project for the American Century, 28 September 1999.

Gellner, Ernest. *Nations and Nationalism*. Ithaca, NY: Cornell University Press, 1983.

George, Alexander. "The Operational Code: A Neglected Approach to the Study of Political Leaders and Decision Making," *International Studies Quarterly* 13, no. 2 (June 1969): 190–222.

Goldman, Merle, and Roderick Macfarquhar, eds. *The Paradox of China's Post-Mao Reforms*. Cambridge, MA: Harvard University Press, 1999.

Gottlieb, Gidon. *Nation Against State: A New Approach to Ethnic Conflicts and the Decline of Sovereignty*. New York: Council on Foreign Relations Press, 1993.

Gupta, Rakesh, ed. *India's Security Problems in the Nineties*. New Delhi: Patriot Publishers.

Hamrin, Carol Lee, and Suisheng Zhao, eds. *Decision Making in Deng's China: Perspectives from Insiders*. New York: M. E. Sharpe, 1995.

Hardgrave, Robert L., and Stanley A. Kochanek. *India: Government and Politics in a Developing Nation*. Washington, DC: Harcourt Brace Jovanovich, Inc., 1986.

Harris, Peter. "Chinese Nationalism: The State of the Nation," *The China Journal*, no. 38 (July 1997): 121–139.

Harris-White, Barbara, and Gordon White, eds. *Liberalization and the New Corruption*. IDS Bulletin 27 (April 1996): 6–87.

Hartland-Thunberg, Penelope. *A Decade of China's Economic Reform*. Washington, DC: CSIS, 1989.

The Hindu. "Finance and Development—Which Way Now?" *The Hindu*, 26 January 2000.

Hinsley, F. H. *Sovereignty*. London: C. A. Watts & Co., Ltd., 1996.

Hippler, Jochen. *Pax Americana?: Hegemony or Decline*. Boulder, CO: Pluto Press, 1994.

Hirschman, Albert O. *National Power and the Structure of Foreign Trade*. Berkeley: University of California Press, 1980.

Holsti, Ole R. "The Belief System and National Images: A Case Study." *Journal of Conflict Resolution* 6, no. 3 (September 1962).

Holsti, Ole R. *Public Opinion and American Foreign Policy*. Ann Arbor: University of Michigan Press, 1996.

Holsti, Ole R., Randolph M. Siverson, and Alexander L. George, eds. *Change in the International System*. Boulder, CO: Westview Press, 1980.

Hoogvelt, Ankie. *Globalization and the Postcolonial World: The New Political Economy of Development*. Baltimore, MD: The Johns Hopkins University Press, 1997.

Hughes, Christopher. *Taiwan and Chinese Nationalism: National Identity and Status in International Society*. New York: Routledge, 1997.

The International Institute for Strategic Studies. "India's Military Spending: Prospects for Modernisation." *IISS Strategic Comments* 6, no. 6 (July 2000).

The International Institute for Strategic Studies. *The Military Balance 2004–2005*. London: Oxford University Press, 2004–2005.

Isaacs, Harold R. *Images of Asia: American Views of China and India*. New York: Harper Torchbooks, 1958.

Jackson, Karl D. *Asian Contagion: The Causes and Consequences of a Financial Crisis*. Boulder, CO: Westview Press, 1999.

Jervis, Robert. *Perception and Misperception in International Politics*. Princeton, NJ: Princeton University Press, 1976.

Ji, You. *The Armed Forces of China*. London: I. B. Taurus & Co., 1999.

Joshi, Vijay, and I. M. D. Little. *India: Macroeconomics and Political Economy, 1964–1991*. Washington, DC: The World Bank, 1994.

Keohane, Robert O., ed. *Neorealism and Its Critics*. New York: Columbia University Press, 1986.

Khalilzadeh-Shirazi, Javad, and Roberto Zagha. "Economic Reforms in India: Achievements and the Agenda Ahead." *Columbia Journal of World Business* 29, no. 1, 22 March 1994.

Khare, R. S. *Culture and Democracy: Anthropological Reflections on Modern India*. Lanham, MD: University Press of America, 1985.

Kim, Samuel, and Lowell Dittmer, eds. *China's Quest for National Identity*. Ithaca, NY: Cornell University Press, 1993.

Koslowski, Rey, and Friedrich V. Kratochwil. "Understanding Change in International Politics: The Soviet Empire's Demise and the International System." *International Organization* 48, no. 2 (Spring 1994): 215–247.

Krasner, Stephen. *Defending the National Interest*. Princeton, NJ: Princeton University Press, 1978.

Kreisberg, Paul H. *South Asia and the Indian Ocean: The Strategic Environment, 1995–2010*. Alexandria, VA: Center for Naval Analyses, 1996.

Krugman, Paul. *The Return of Depression Economics*. New York: W. W. Norton & Co., 2000.

Kugler, Richard L., and Ellen L. Frost, eds. *The Global Century: Globalization and National Security, Vol. 1*. Washington, DC: National Defense University Press, 2001.

Kux, Dennis. *India and the United States: Estranged Democracies*. Washington, DC: National Defense University Press.

Kynge, James. "China's Liabilities." *Financial Times,* 22 January 2002.

Lal, A. B. *The Indian Parliament*. Allahabad, India: Chaitanya Publishing House, 1956.

Li, Nan. *From Revolutionary Internationalism to Conservative Nationalism, Peaceworks 39*. Washington, DC: United States Institute of Peace, 2001.

Lieberthal, Kenneth. *Governing China: From Revolution Through Reform*. New York: W. W. Norton & Co., 1995.

Lieberthal, Kenneth G., and David M. Lampton, eds. *Bureaucracy, Politics and Decision Making in Post-Mao China*. Berkeley: University of California Press, 1992.

Lieberthal, Kenneth G., and Michel Oksenberg, eds. *Policy Making in China: Leaders, Structures, and Processes*. Princeton, NJ: Princeton University Press, 1990.

Lilley, James R., and David Shambaugh, eds. *China's Military Faces the Future*. Washington, DC: American Enterprise Institute, 1999.

Macfarquhar, Roderick., ed. *The Politics of China*. Cambridge: Cambridge University Press, 1997.

Manning, Robert A., Ronald Montaperto, and Brad Roberts. *China, Nuclear Weapons, and Arms Control: A Preliminary Assessment*. New York: Council on Foreign Relations, 2000.

Mansingh, Surjit. *India's Search for Power: Indira Gandhi's Foreign Policy 1966–1982*. New Delhi: Sage Publications, 1984.

Mao, Tse-tung. *Long Live Mao Tse-tung Thought*. (http://marxists.org/reference/archive/mao/selected-works/volume-9/mswv9_57.htm).

Mao, Tse-tung. *Selected Works*. 5 vols. Bejing: Foreign Languages Press.

Mehta, Ved. *A Family Affair*. New York: Oxford University Press, 1982.

Mehta, Ved. *Rajiv Gandhi and Rama's Kingdom*. New Haven, CT: Yale University Press: 1996.

Military Official. "China's Defense Policy." Paper presented at the Foreign Affairs College, Beijing, 29 May 2001.

Milner, Helen. *Interests, Institutions, and Information: Domestic Politics and International Relations*. Princeton, NJ: Princeton University Press, 1997.

Morgenthau, Hans J. *In Defense of the National Interest: A Critical Examination of American Foreign Policy*. New York: Alfred A. Knopf, 1951.

Morgenthau, Hans J. *Politics Among Nations: The Struggle for Power and Peace*, 6th ed. New York: Alfred A. Knopf, 1985.

Morgenthau, Hans J. *The Purpose of American Politics*. New York: Alfred A. Knopf, 1960.

Nathan, Andrew J., Zhaohui Hong, and Steven R. Smith. *Dilemmas of Reform in Jiang Zemin's China*. Boulder, CO: Lynne Rienner Publishers, 1999.

Nehru, Jawaharlal. *India's Foreign Policy: Selected Speeches, September 1946–April 1961*. Bombay: The Publications Division, Ministry of Information and Broadcasting, Government of India, 1961.

Nehru, Jawaharlal. *Selected Works of Jawaharlal Nehru*. New Delhi: Jawaharlal Nehru Memorial Fund, 1984.

Nincic, Miroslav. "The National Interest and Its Interpretation" *The Review of Politics* 61 no. 1 (Winter 1999): 29–55.

O'Meara, Patrick, Howard D. Mehlinger, and Matthew Krain, eds. *Globalization and the Challenges of a New Century*. Bloomington: Indiana University Press, 2000.

Panikkar, K. M. *Problems of Indian Defense*. Bombay: Asia Publishing House, 1960.

Perkovich, George. *India's Nuclear Bomb: The Impact on Global Proliferation*. Berkeley: University of California Press, 1999.

Plattner, Marc F., and Aleksander Smolar. *Globalization, Power, and Democracy*. Baltimore, MD: The Johns Hopkins University Press, 2000.

Prizel, Ilya. *National Identity and Foreign Policy: Nationalism and Leadership in Poland, Russia and Ukraine*. Cambridge: Cambridge University Press, 1998.

Puri, Rashmi-Sudha. *Gandhi on War and Peace*. New York: Praeger Publishers, 1987.

Qian, Wenrong. "Humanitarian Intervention and National Sovereignty—Lessons of Kosovo War." *Peace and Development* (Beijing) no. 3 (2000).

Rejai, M., ed. *Mao Tse-tung: On Revolution and War*. Gloucester: Peter Smith, 1976.

Rizvi, Gowher. *South Asia in a Changing International Order*. New Delhi: Sage Publications, 1993.

Robinson, Thomas W., and David Shambaugh. *Chinese Foreign Policy: Theory and Practice* Oxford: Clarendon Press, 1997.

Rosen, Stephen Peter. *Societies and Military Power: India and Its Armies*. Ithaca, NY: Cornell University Press, 1996.

Rosenau, James N., Vincent Davis, and Maurice A. East, eds. *The Analysis of International Politics*. New York: The Free Press, 1972.

Ross, Robert S., "Beijing as a Conservative Power" *Foreign Affairs* 76 (March/April 1997): 33–44.

Roy, Subroto, and William E. James, eds. *Foundations of India's Political Economy*. New Delhi: Sage Publications, 1992.

Rudelson, Justin Jon. *Oasis Identities: Uyghur Nationalism Along China's Silk Road*. New York: Columbia University Press, 1997.

Sa, Benwang. "World Military Situation in Retrospect and Prospect." *Peace and Development* (Beijing) no. 1 (2001).

Sandler, Shmuel. "Ethnonationalism and Foreign Policy of Nation States." *Nationalism & Ethnic Politics* 1, no. 2 (Summer 1995).

Schell, Orville, and David Shambaugh, eds. *The China Reader: The Reform Era*. New York: Vintage Books, 1999.

Sen, Amartya. *Development as Freedom*. New York: Knopf Publishers, 1999.

Sen, Sirdar D. K. *A Comparative Study of the Indian Constitution*. New Delhi: Orient Longmans Ltd., 1967.

Sharma, Shalendra D. *Development and Democracy in India*. Boulder, CO: Lynne Rienner Publishers, 1999.

Sims, Holly. "The Unsheltering Sky: China, India and the Montreal Protocol." *Policy Studies Journal*. 24 (Summer 1996): 201–214.

Singh, Ravinder Pal. *Arms Procurement Decision Making*. Stockholm: SIPRI, Oxford University Press, 1998.

Singh, R. K. Jasbir, ed. *Indian Defense Yearbook 1999*. Dehra Dun, India: Natraj Publishers, 1999.

Singh, Tavleen. *Kashmir: A Tragedy of Errors*. New Delhi: Penguin Books, 1996.

SIPRI. *SIPRI Yearbook 2005: Armaments, Disarmament, and International Security*. London: Oxford University Press, 2005.

Smith, Anthony D. *National Identity*. Reno: University of Nevada Press, 1991.

Smith, Chris. *India's Ad Hoc Arsenal*. New York: Oxford University Press, 1997.

Snyder, Jack, and Robert Jervis. *Coping with Complexity in the International System*. Boulder, CO: Westview Press, 1993.

Sondhi, M. L., ed. *Democratic Peace*. New Delhi: Har Anand, 2000.

Swaine, Michael D. *China: Domestic Change and Foreign Policy*. With Donald P. Henry. Santa Monica, CA: RAND, 1995.

Swaine, Michael D. *The Role of the Chinese Military in National Security Policymaking*. Santa Monica, CA: RAND, 1998.

Tanham, George.*Indian Strategic Thought: An Interpretive Essay*. Santa Monica, CA: RAND, 1992.

Taylor, David, and Malcolm Yapp, eds. *Political Identity in South Asia*. London: Curzon Press, 1979.

Tellis, Ashley. Documented Briefing: *Stability in South Asia*. Santa Monica, CA: RAND.

Tharoor, Shashi. *India: From Midnight to the Millenium*. New York: HarperPerennial, 1997.

Thomas, Raju G. C. *Democracy, Security, and Development in India*. New York: St. Martin's Press, 1996.

Thomas, Raju G. C. *Indian Security Policy*. Princeton, NJ: Princeton University Press.

Tongqi, Lin. "A Search for China's Soul." *Daedalus* 122, no. 2 (Spring 1993): 171–188.

Townsend, James R., and Brantly Womack. *Politics in China*. Boston: Little, Brown & Co., 1986.

Trubowitz, Peter. *Defining the National Interest: Conflict and Change in American Foreign Policy*. Chicago: University of Chicago Press, 1998.

Tuathail, Gearoid O., Simon Dalby, and Paul Routledge, eds. *The Geopolitics Reader*. New York: Routledge, 1998.

Vanaik, Achin. *The Furies of Indian Communalism: Religion, Modernity and Secularization*. New York: Verso, 1997.

Vasquez, John A. *Classics of International Relations*. Upper Saddle River, NJ: Prentice-Hall, Inc., 1996.

Waltz, Kenneth N. *Man the State, and War: A Theoretical Analysis*. New York: Columbia University Press, 1959.

Waltz, Kenneth N. *Theory of International Politics*. Reading, MA: Addison-Wesley, 1979.

Wang, James C. F. *Contemporary Chinese Politics*. Englewood Cliffs, NJ: Prentice-Hall, Inc., 1992.

Weber, Max. *Economy and Society, Vol. 1*, eds. Guenther Roth and Claus Wittich. New York: Bedminster Press, 1968.

Weiner, Myron. *The Indian Paradox: Essays in Indian Politics*, ed. Ashutosh Varshney. New Delhi: Sage Publications, 1989.

White, Gordon, ed. *The Chinese State in the Era of Economic Reform*. Armonk, NY: M. E. Sharpe, 1991.

White, Gordon. *Riding the Tiger: The Politics of Economic Reform in Post Mao China.* Stanford, CA: Stanford University Press: 1993.

Whiting, Allen S. "Chinese Nationalism and Foreign Policy After Deng." *The China Quarterly* 142 (June 1995).

Wolf, Martin. "India: Slow Reforms Promise Better Times." *Financial Times*, 19 September 1997.

Wolf, Martin. "Will the Nation-State Survive Globalization?" *Foreign Affairs* (January/February 2001).

The World Bank. *India: Sustaining Rapid Economic Growth, A World Bank Country Study.* Washington, DC: The World Bank, 1997.

Wu Jie. *On Deng Xiaoping Thought.* Beijing: Foreign Languages Press, 1996.

Yan Xuetong. *Zhongguo Guojia Liyi Fenxi.* Tianjin: Tianjin Renmin Chubanshi Chuban, 1996.

Yifu Lin, Justin, Fang Cai, and Zhou Li. *State Owned Enterprise Reform in China.* Hong Kong: The Chinese University Press, 2001.

Yingyi, Qian. "The Institutional Foundations of China's Market Transition." Washington, DC: The World Bank, April 1999.

Zhang, Ming. *China's Changing Nuclear Posture: Reactions to the South Asian Nuclear Tests.* Washington, DC: Carnegie Endowment for International Peace, 1999.

Zhu, Feng. "US Domestic Politics and NMD Deployment." *Peace and Development* (Beijing) no. 4 (2000).

Index

About the Author

ROLLIE LAL is a Political Scientist at the RAND Corporation in Arlington, Virginia. She is an expert on Asian security, terrorism, and organized crime, and she has written on a wide variety of issues related to India, China, Iran, Central Asia, North Africa, and political Islam. Dr. Lal is a co-author of *The Muslim World after 9/11* (RAND, 2004) and *America's Role in Nation-Building: From Germany to Iraq* (RAND, 2003). She is also the author of *Central Asia and Its Neighbors: Security and Commerce at the Crossroads* (RAND, 2006) and articles in the *Atlantic Monthly, Financial Times, International Herald Tribune, Chicago Sun-Times, San Diego Sun Tribune,* and *Daily Yomiuri.*

She has been a visiting scholar at the Chinese Academy of Social Sciences in Beijing, Peking University, and at the Indian Council of Social Science Research in New Delhi. Dr. Lal has also served as a Washington Correspondent for the Japanese newspaper *Yomiuri Shimbun.* She holds a B.A. in economics from the University of Maryland at College Park, and an M.A. in Strategic Studies and a Ph.D. in International Relations from the Johns Hopkins School of Advanced International Studies (SAIS).